C000130054

ASPECTS OF BARNSLEY
III

Aspects of BARNSLEY

Discovering Local History — III

Edited by
Brian Elliott

Wharncliffe Publishing Limited

First published in 1995 by
Wharncliffe Publishing Limited

Copyright © Wharncliffe Publishing Limited 1995

*For up-to-date information on other titles produced under the
Wharncliffe imprint, please telephone or write to:*

> **Wharncliffe Publishing Limited**
> **FREEPOST**
> **47 Church Street**
> **Barnsley**
> **South Yorkshire S70 2BR**
> **Telephone (24 hours): 01226-734555**

ISBN: 1-871647-27-4

A CIP catalogue record of this book is available from the British
Library.

Cover photograph: 'Elsecar at Sea', kindly supplied by the
Barnsley Canal Group.

Printed in Great Britain by Redwood Books, Trowbridge,
Wiltshire

CONTENTS

INTRODUCTION

by Brian Elliott

Writing in 1769 Arthur Young described the countryside between Sheffield and Barnsley as 'fine, it abounds with the beauties of landscape'. William Cobbett was given an enthusiastic welcome when he paused at Barnsley in 1830 'merely to change horses' but the subsequent account of this part of his 'Northern Tour' was considerably different to Young's impression: 'All the way along from Leeds to Sheffield it is coal and iron, and iron and coal'. Cobbett was living at a time when the West Riding, despite his own scepticism of the new census statistics, had become the most populous part of Yorkshire. Yet scenes of industry often took place in rural settings as can be seen in Melvyn Jones's study of ironstone mining on Earl Fitzwilliam's estate at Tankersley. Ironstone was needed for the Earl's ironworks at Elsecar which opened in 1795. About the same time an atmospheric engine of the type invented by Thomas Newcomen was installed, pumping water out of Fitzwilliam's Elsecar New Colliery. The engine is the only example of its type still standing on its original site anywhere in the country. Arthur Clayton's detailed research, undertaken a generation ago, has been included so as to give his work a wider local readership in the year of the engine's bicentenary. By the late 1790s coal was being carried on the new Elsecar branch of the Dearne and Dove Canal and Roger Glister's article on this 'Vital Link' provides us with an overview of a waterway surely deserving full restoration.

Three local examples of water-powered sites, part of a systematic study of the Dearne Catchment undertaken by Tom Umpleby, remind us of the historic importance of local watercourses. Harold Taylor's interest in textile history is reflected in an excellent piece of research and writing on Taylor Row and Barnsley's handloom weavers. John Goodchild's tribute to E G Bayford may be the first of a series on local historians and literary figures; whilst in the curious story of the Mitchell Memorial Hall he focuses on the somewhat unusual circumstances following the death of one of our leading engineers and colliery owners.

A lost building and the visit of one of America's greatest Wild West characters are the subjects of features by Brian Elliott. Sam Sykes's interest in local agricultural history is reflected in his well-researched article about a Dodworth estate. Phyllis Crossland's articles have always been popular with *Aspects* readers, this time providing us with a most interesting study of Penistone Market. Dr Jim Walker's fascinating account of local medical cures and associated characters is a most welcome continuation of his popular 'medical history' theme introduced to us in *Aspects 2*.

Articles by Ian Harley, Edna Forrest and Annie Storey illustrate the value of contemporary accounts and personal recollection. Autobiography, reminiscence and research are combined in Margaret Holderness's and Brian Elliott's study of pawnbroking.

Local history opens up one of the most significant routes to understanding the present by reference to the past. This has been recognised by many Barnsley teachers with excellent support from the authority's advisory service. The resultant experiences and work of young children is ably demonstrated in Andy Atkinson's refreshing comments and case-studies.

Aspects 3 would not have been possible but for the continued support of Timothy Hewitt, Managing Director of Wharncliffe Publishing Limited. *Aspects of Barnsley 4* is in preparation and *Aspects of Rotherham* is also now available. The book design team of Roni Wilkinson and Caroline Cox have once again worked very hard in the production of the book. Thanks are also due to Alan Twiddle for promotion and marketing and to the entire Wharncliffe team. Barnsley Archives and Local Studies continue to provide an excellent service for many of our contributors; as also does John Goodchild's Local History Study Centre at Wakefield.

Anyone interested in making a contribution to *Aspects of Barnsley 4* should, in the first instance, contact Brian Elliott c/o **Wharncliffe Publishing (Book Division) Limited, 47 Church Street, Barnsley S70 2AS** enclosing a brief description of the proposed work. If suitable, guidelines will then be issued.

1. CURES AND CURIOSITIES: TALL TALES OF OLD BARNSLEY

by Dr James Walker

WONDERS WITHOUT PARALLEL ARE PRESENTED here for your Edification and Amazement! Marvel at astounding human oddities (the Giant at the White Bear 1800), at feats of human endurance (Ninety-Four Round Jemmy Green Fight 1819), of miracle powers (Walking on Water 1837), of harnessed energy (Electro-biological Display 1853), of daring agility (Balloon-borne Gymnastics 1870) and of athletic prowess (Hundred-Pound Foot-Race 1901)!

Newcomers to the Barnsley of yesteryear, perhaps attracted by notice of such crowd-pulling curiosities, may not have anticipated that the Barnsley brand of showmanship applied as much to its medicinal activities as to its publicised events.

Introduction

First port of call for the newcomer arriving along the Racecommon Road (a principal link to the town from an old East-West turnpike

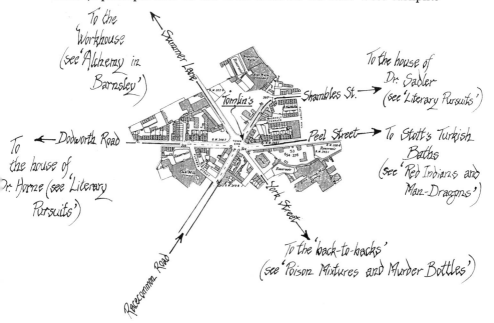

Choices for the traveller at Town End.

route) was the confluence of mills, shops, homes and streams forming Town End. Here was a choice of branching roads: to the heart of 'working-class Barnsley' or, for the destitute, to the Workhouse. The traveller with failing health could seek therapy with medicinal air-baths and herbs, or could go and consult one of the town's more eminent physicians. If the grandiose advertising claims confronting him were to be believed, however, he needed to look no further than Town End itself.

Liquid Refreshment at Town End

It was hailed as the 'Great Yorkshire Cure':- a prize-winning liquid medicine sold in four-and-a-half inch bottles with healing powers against a whole spectrum of ailments. Its inventor strived to establish its reputation in local folk-lore, a subject in which he had much expertise,[1] and Tomlin's Restorative Syrup joined a tradition of refreshing and re-vitalising liquids available at this busy corner of town...

The mineral waters from Shaw Well spring,[2] flowing to Town End, mingled there with the Whinney Nook spring-waters to form Sough Dyke, remarked upon in bygone days for its purity. Hand pumps at Town End were one source of supply for Barnsley wit Joseph Broadhead ('Watter Joe') who peddled this desirable commodity across town from about 1816. Whether he claimed it had particular health-giving properties is not known, but he did assert that it was used to make into medicines by at least one town doctor (Richard Crooks, 1777-1845).[3] Other water-vendors carried on the service even after the Barnsley Waterworks Company piped the plentiful waters of the Dearne into the town[4], and the tradition was personally supported by another physician, Dr Fred Jackson (1821-1892), who complained that the Company water was 'so very bad that he never used it, indeed he considered it was not good enough for his horse'.[5]

Opposite the town pumps stood a building on the Shambles Street corner at Town End, which Thomas Topham opened as a beerhouse in 1829. 'Tom Toppin' (his more usual name) was depicted in old almanacs as 'a well-known humourist' who (doubtless through drink) earned the title 'The Midnight Songster'. Capitalising on Watter Joe's fame, he hung a portrait of the water-vendor outside the premises to promote his own variety of liquid refreshment.

Broadhead retired from his watery trade in 1837, a year notable not only for the country's new Queen, but also for a watery Miracle that Never Was. Broadhead shared both lodgings and a wry sense of humour with Charles Rogers (alias 'Tom Treddlehoyle') who was launching his threepenny *Bairnsla Foaks Annual and Pogmoor Olmenack* and who

Turn-of-the-century view of Town End, showing Tomlin's Chemist (formerly the 'Watter Joe').

Probably the earliest photograph of Tomlins shop at Townend — taken in 1890s.

announced by poster that a distinguished Aquatic Gentleman, M.S. Von de Bughie, intended to walk on water along Barnsley Canal from the Old Mill Wharf to the Aqueduct and back again.[6] Billed as an 'Unparalleled Exhibition which has Excited the Wonder and Astonishment of Assembled Thousands, both in England and on the Continent', this demonstration for 'Admirers of Genuine Science' was said to have philosophical backing from De Bughie's native Germany.[7] In the manner of the astronomers of Gulliver's Laputa, the Laws of Gravity were to be suspended by the 'abstruse mathematical calculations' of applied philosophy, although the disbelief of the Barnsley public faced more certain suspension from the outset.[8] 'An immense concourse of spectators' fell victim to the elaborate hoax, lining the canal banks between Harborough Hill Bridge and the Aqueduct to witness what was ultimately a great non-event of the town's history.[9] Treddlehoyle,

AWARDED FIRST PRIZE

BY UNIVERSAL CONSENT.

Tomlin's Restorative Syrup.

THE GREAT YORKSHIRE CURE

FOR

Indigestion, Flatulence, Palpitation, Heartburn, Backache,
Constipation, Rheumatic Pains, &c., &c.

TOMLIN'S RESTORATIVE SYRUP, **1/-** & **2/6** per Bottle.

Post Free for **14** or **33** Stamps

Tomlin's mother Elizabeth lived on to be one of the Temperance Society's
oldest ever members: could it have been the Restorative Syrup?

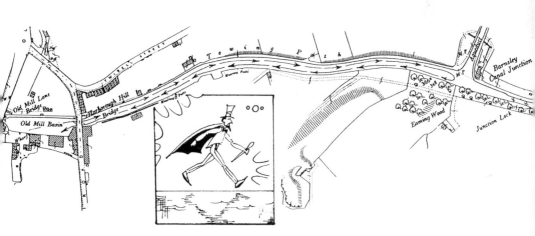

Van de Bughie's Amazing Journey, by a mode of transport even more unlikely
than riding a donkey backwards (a clue to the hoaxer).

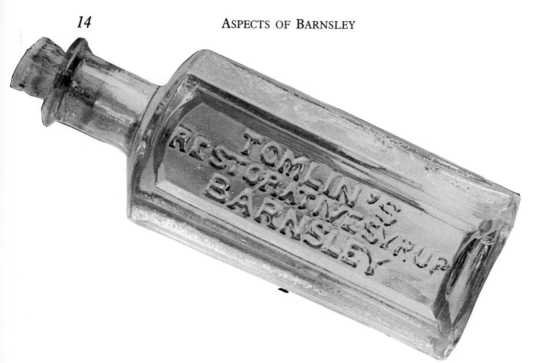

Tomlin, despite his family's devotion to Temperance, set up shop in a former beerhouse.

like his friend Watter Joe, was to be remembered in portrait form hanging outside a Barnsley beer establishment.

The Canal area acquired more miraculous connections years later when bottles embossed 'Eno's Fruit Salt' emerged from Wood Brothers' Glassworks for filling in London. This effervescent saline draught was also claimed to be a marvel, having refreshing and recuperative powers and establishing itself as a famous 'household remedy'. It was just the kind of patent medicine to be sold by provincial druggists like Albert Robert Tomlin, who in 1890 set up in the very same Town End premises from where Tom Toppin had finished trading in 1839; premises which, using paints and brushes, were given (fittingly) a new lease of life by restorative treatment. Watter Joe's portrait had been taken down, the building had been purchased by the Lingards (of *Chronicle* fame) and had operated as a herbal store for some years under tenant William Kelsey, who then moved on to Stairfoot (the Lingards were no strangers to patent medicines themselves: the *Chronicle* offices in Peel Square sold fifty-seven different varieties).[10] Tomlin, born in Pitt Street, Barnsley in 1850 (son of upholsterer and cabinet-maker Richard Tomlin, later of the *Temperance Hotel*, who progressed to the druggist business) was a mine of information on Barnsley folk-cures

1891 advertisement for Eno's Fruit Salt, bottled by Wood Brothers.

'Keep An Eye On' Town End Stores, for Percy's Fruit Saline.

and local 'lay' healers[11] and invented a number of his own nostrums including Tomlin's Botanic Extract and Tomlin's Nerve and Brain Tonic ('Restores Energy and Removes Nervous Prostration and Brain Fag').

While the painted gable-end of the building boasted of his Ointment for Skin Diseases, the name of his greatest liquid cure-all was emblazoned across the roof: Tomlin's Restorative Syrup, with its appeal to those still 'infatuated by the prospect of Universal Medicines'.[12]

Finally, that well-known one-armed purveyor of popular products, papers and postage stamps, Percy Wilson, sold a 'refreshing and purifying' liquid saline at Town End General Stores from 1935, openly intended to rival Eno's Fruit Salt, 'especially for the Spring and Summer'. In 1973 a vast collection of his pills, powders and potions was discovered by later occupiers of Town End Stores, Gerald and Gloria Alliott, packed in boxes hoarded in the eaves of the circa-1820s building.[13]

Alchemy in and around Barnsley

I had re-trod the steps of knowledge along the paths of time,
and exchanged the discoveries of recent enquirers for the dreams
of forgotten alchymists.

Mary Shelley's *Frankenstein*, 1818

Another hidden curiosity of medicinal history came to light in surroundings even older than Town End Stores when a hand-written recipe book of old 'cures' was unearthed during recent renovation work at Woolley Hall.[14] *Dr Headlam's Cough and Cold Mixture* contained antimony; a powder for *Incessant Sickness in the Stomach* consisted largely of mercury; while *Mrs Wentworth's Correcting Draught* was formulated from laudanum. All these ingredients were later classified as 'Poisons' by pharmacy laws, and the tale of their use locally takes us from the Wentworths of Woolley to the Wharncliffes of Wortley, wandering from the Watertons of Walton through Wakefield, Worsbrough, Wadsley and the West Riding Workhouses on the way...

The Celestial Bodies were held to influence illness (as the term 'Lunacy' suggests) and Alchemy permitted the earthly manifestations of the planets and stars to be put to use. A century before work commenced on the earliest parts of Woolley Hall, arcane metallic elements like mercury (the wondrous 'Living Metal' of the Ancients) and antimony (the starlike 'Key to Transmutation') were introduced into medical practice by the sixteenth century alchemist Paracelsus, along with opiates like Laudanum. These substances were in subsequent use by early apothecaries (for example at Worsbrough in the 1760s)[15] and from 1788 onwards were being administered to the ailing George III besides the customary bleeding, purging, starving and blistering.[16] With Royal involvement, the improved treatment of insanity became a national concern, and the Paracelsean medicines were to play a major role in reducing the need for physical restraint of those afflicted.

The relapsing madness of the King was marked by two great events in the West Riding: the baking of the first Denby Dale pie (1788) and the opening of the West Riding Pauper Lunatic Asylum, built to an inspired design[17] at Wakefield in 1818 (it was also the year that Mary Shelley's *Frankenstein* revived the name and ideas of Paracelsus, in a cautionary novel which was soon to strike a chord locally with the arrest of two Barnsley 'Resurrectionists' in 1829).[18]

In keeping with the *Poor Law Amendments Act* of 1834 it was expected that local Workhouses would provide wards for the insane poor, pending transfer to the Asylum where necessary. Barnsley patients, previously transported to York[19] (where concern over maltreatment had been a catalyst for national asylum reforms)[20] would have been among those admitted to the Wakefield premises, were numbers rapidly increased. Antimony and opium were the main sedatives used to calm patients, many of whom had already suffered the effects of mercurial compounds. Physical treatments included Spin Therapy in a revolving chair, Hydropathic water-packs and Electromagnetism (the latter method, evoking the magnetic healing of alchemy and the 'Animating Principle

Wakefield

Walton

Woolley

Worsbrough

Wortley

Wadsley

Some local 'Paths of Time' retrod.

Spin therapy: Revolutions in treatment in the West Riding.

of Life' theory of electricity,[21] was demonstrated in Barnsley Corn
Exchange in 1853 by mesmeric Electrobiologist Mr Zamoiski, who
exerted 'Extraordinary Power over his Patients' before enthralled
audiences).[22] Experiments were also afoot to test the effects of the new
nitrous oxide gas (first advertised in the local press in 1872 for 'Painless
Dentistry' at 'three shillings a Tooth without Pain, one shilling with
Pain') on Asylum inmates.[23]

   Intensive experimentation began in earnest during the 1860s when a
Dr James Crichton-Browne took charge of the Asylum, setting up the
first laboratory of brain research in the country. Crichton-Browne
(1840-1938) was a formidable-looking figure in Dundreary whiskers,
fervently opposed to teetotalism, insisting that 'no writer has done
much without alcohol'. His assistants developed a liking for elaborate
(or nonsensical) medical terms, describing cases of the 'Miasma Theory
of Noxius Effluvium' and telling patients that they had 'Catastrophe
of the Belorophon' or 'Evacuation of the Equatorial Provinces'. Starting
around 1867, his most macabre preoccupation lay in collecting human
brains for study, amassing a total of 400 from the Post-Mortem Theatre

Celestial influences at Walton Hall: Waterton's 1813 dodecahedronal world sundial.

of the Asylum (an easier source of salvaged organs than that used by Victor Frankenstein); each brain he carefully weighed and inspected, commenting 'The social failures who take refuge in the Workhouse are light of brain as well as of pocket'.[24]

His work led to a knighthood from Queen Victoria and he was proposed to the Royal Society by no less than Charles Darwin, receiving a mention (along with his theories) in Darwin's *The Descent of Man* (1871).[25] That other naturalist and intrepid traveller, Charles Waterton, remembered more for his eccentric adventures around the world than for contributions to science, provided a venue for excursions for the Asylum inmates in the grounds of his home, built on an island in a lake at Walton, between Barnsley and Wakefield.[26] Waterton also pioneered his own use of mercury as the preserving chemical in his 'taxidermy without stuffing' process, both for whole creatures and for his 'Creations' (parts of various animals attached together like zoological parodies of Frankenstein's efforts).[27]

As demand for Asylum places escalated, Lord Wharncliffe (of Wortley Hall ancestry) oversaw the building of a new South Yorkshire Asylum at Wadsley, which opened its doors amid great ceremony in 1872 with a large transfer of patients and to a catchment area which included parts of Barnsley. Some listed reasons for entry on the admissions register make interesting reading:-

Heredity	Family Affairs
Unjustly charged with carelessness	Prodigal Life
Disappointments in marriage	Women
Religious Doubt	Dog Bite
Oversensitiveness	Fright
Childbirth	Sunstroke

A visiting inspectorate with the title 'Commissioners in Lunacy' was suitably impressed in 1873, commenting favourably on the patients' dinner of 'Irish Stew, Bread and Beer' (the new Asylum had its own brewery).[28]

The potent alchemical compounds and their calming influences were, like beer, in demand outside such institutions as well as inside, despite the *'discoveries of recent enquirers'* into less toxic alternatives.[29] Barnsley infants were dosed with mercury (see next section) and a published history of the South Yorkshire Asylum relates how antimonial powders

> *were used by the general public, especially in the Northern manufacturing districts, where suffering wives regularly bought a supply of Antimony, known as 'quietness', to put in the tea of a drunken husband.[30]*

Poison Mixtures and Murder Bottles

In nineteenth century Barnsley the public houses were not only places of intoxication to the detriment of 'suffering wives'; they also offered public entertainments in various forms. That century started with a curious attraction at the White Bear Inn (soon to be renamed the Royal Hotel after Queen-to-be Victoria paid a visit) above Market Hill, when the skeleton of a world-celebrated giant named O'Brien, linked to an ancient myth, was exhibited at an entry charge of one shilling per spectator. The eight-feet-four-inches Irishman's bones had been procured by cabinet-maker-turned-surgeon John Hunter by bribing O'Brien's attendants to the tune of £500.[31]

A very tall tale of the White Bear: Charles O'Brien, a giant of mythical ancestry.

Market Hill itself was the scene of many public events and gatherings over the years, with everything from Royal Celebrations to the Wombwell Wild Beast Exhibitions. 'Almost the whole town' turned out there one August night in 1805 when the beating of the drums heralded news that the French had invaded (Barnsley's finest volunteers, undaunted by the reputation of Napoleon's armies, set off fearlessly down Old Mill Lane, taking the road through Cudworth. They had marched as far as Hemsworth before word arrived that there had been a false alarm: burning straw in a field had been mistaken for a signal beacon).[32]

Open-air amusements like bear-baiting entertained large crowds, but a Market Hill druggist called James Cocker was not amused. Ever a contrary character, having opened his shop in the year Tom Toppin and many other traders were opening beerhouses (1829: following the Beer Act), he put a halt to one bear-baiting event by drawing a gun, which could not have endeared him to many. Then, through a diverse run of career interests including Postmaster, chemist, constable and restaurant proprietor, he managed to upset his own workers and went on to introduce power-looms to Barnsley. His unpopularity thus sealed, especially among the large weaving community, he promptly left town.[33]

Inevitably though, machine-weaving overtook hand-weaving, and the rapid proliferation of linen-mills established the early nineteenth-century township as a foremost centre of textile manufacture. The booming population crowded into dense back-to-back terraces, working mothers relying on communal baby-minders so that they could return to the loom after childbirth. In such conditions, any short-cuts in infant care caught on quickly, such as 'Poison' mixtures containing opiates 'to make them sleep, and prone they lie in stupor all the day'[34] or containing the likes of calomel (a mercury compound) as a cooling agent in fevers. In addition, bottle-feeders which could be left unattended with the baby had obvious appeal, although the accompanying risks of infection and choking provided their nickname of 'Murder Bottles'. The infant

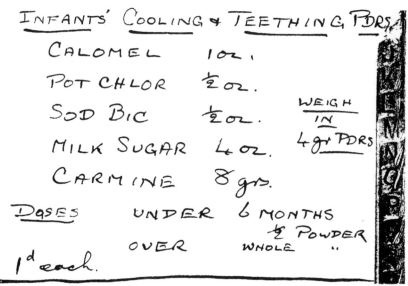

INFANTS' COOLING & TEETHING PDRS.

CALOMEL	1 oz.	
POT CHLOR	½ oz.	
SOD BIC	½ oz.	WEIGH IN
MILK SUGAR	4 oz.	4 gr. PDRS
CARMINE	8 grs.	

DOSES   UNDER 6 MONTHS ½ POWDER

OVER   WHOLE   ,,

1ᵈ each.

A 'Poison Mixture' (from an old Worsbrough Dale chemist recipe book).

fed from a padded leather teat at the end of a flexible tube leading from the neck of the bottle, which therefore did not need to be supported, and following introduction in the 1850s local glassmakers like Beatson Clark and Wood Brothers soon entered into mass 'Murder Bottle' production to meet a growing demand.

Despite mounting condemnation from health professions, manufacture continued right until the 1930s, covering a similar time-span to a medicinal movement which forms the next subject of our story.

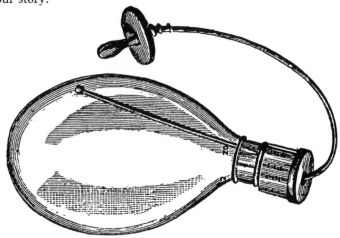

A 'Murder Bottle'.

Red Indians, Man-Dragons...or just Hot Air?

Around 500 people gathered excitedly in the Queen's Ground on an
October day in 1901 to see the £100 Foot-Race prize money claimed.
Harry Hartley put in a determined effort, but in the end was beaten 'by
a clear yard and a half' by his fleet-footed rival, S. Bedford of
Castleford.[35] According to one Barnsley source, however, Bedford
owed his winning performance to an unusual therapy which even
modern dope-testing would be unable to detect...

In direct opposition to the ways of chemical medicine were the
Medical Botanists, promoting more gentle cures of herbs, roots and
barks, with a do-it-yourself emphasis. The locally-produced *Working
Man's Model Family Botanic Guide* poured scorn on the esoteric legacy
of Paracelsus ('mercury had destroyed more lives than the sword, fire
or pestilence') and on the man himself ('he professed to have found out
the Elixir of Life... but died aged forty-eight').[36] Encouraged by the
spirit of 'Self Help' prevalent at the time,[37] the movement gained ground
rapidly in the region: even John Wesley's influence contributed (he had
been a keen proponent of plant remedies)[38] and a 'heal yourself' message
was preached that did not rely on professional mystique, just as the
pursuit of botany did not rely solely on the travels of Victorian gentlemen
explorers. While such explorers enhanced the gardens of Wentworth
Castle with rare specimens and wisdom from the far East, local 'fringe'
medicine was enriched by botanical wisdom and samples from the

The Botanical Pharmacy.

ESTABLISHED 1840.

WILLIAM FOX & SONS,

MEDICAL BOTANIC PRACTITIONERS,

56, SNIG HILL, SHEFFIELD.

William Fox was author of the *Working Man's Model Family Botanic Guide*.

West. Dr Albert Isaiah Coffin spoke from experience gained first-hand from the Seneca tribe of North American Indians, when having abandoned a medical apprenticeship he had 'gleaned all I could regarding the herbs, barks etc., with which they were acquainted'.[39]

With commendable timing, the launch of Coffin's crusade here coincided with the People's Charter of 1838, and his West Riding assistant Dr John Skelton soon drew up *Six Propositions of Vegetable Medicine* as if to echo the six-point Chartist agenda. Drawing on the disaffected mood of working families, Botanical Medicine promised the people a taste of self-determination which the attempts at political reform failed to deliver: hence, as soon as the show was over for Chartism, the local stage was set for Dr Skelton's theatrical debut of 1849. Barnsley townsfolk flocked to see him expound the Botanical system and condemn the harsh medical practices of the day in a programme of weekly lectures at the old Theatre on Wellington Street,[40] memorably 'illustrated with diagrams, skeletons and diseased stomachs'.[41]

Even the use of plants with ancient necromantic links was revived, such as the magical Mandrake (Man-Dragon), once said to thrive in the ground below gallows and to scream when torn from the earth. In 1860, by which time coal was replacing linen as the leading industry in Barnsley, a local miner called John Staniforth wrote of the curative powers of a Mandrake mixture in his recovery from a paralysing illness, and his letter is quoted in the *Family Botanic Guide:-*

> *My occupation is that of a coal-miner, and, working in the wet,*
> *I caught a severe cold. I was under the treatment of several*
> *doctors round about where I was living. I had homeopathists,*
> *water casters, and several of the faculty, but to no use. I then*
> *had an eminent physician from Rotherham. I was under his treatment*
> *for six weeks, and blistered, leeched, and my feet put in hot water*
> *and salt.*

Despite such measures, the weakness in his legs progressed, and another doctor was summoned:

> *He wished me to go into Sheffield General Infirmary, but, having*
> *no desire for it, a friend of ours said that if there was any cure for me*
> *it was in Medical Botany.*

Just two weeks after taking his Mandrake mixture, at the recommended doses:

> *I could move my toes, the strength of my body gradually returned...*

and he was shortly able to resume his occupation:

> *...to the no small astonishment of my neighbours.*[42]

The 'regular' physicians remained sceptical, pointing to the dubious qualifications of Coffin, Skelton and others, and denouncing them as charlatans. However, as Barnsley's unashamed Quack-Doctor Samuel Wigfield (1766-1842) had found, the public acclaim of a few successful cures, authentic or otherwise, was of much greater influence than degrees or diplomas (Samuel Wigfield of Howbrook, Wortley graduated from the meagre rewards of nail-making to become 'Skilful in the Cure of Fevers' and built up an extensive practice).[43] The movement's anti-vaccination stance was particularly irksome to the physicians, who had already encountered much resistance to smallpox vaccination in spite of the local influence of Lady Mary Wortley Montagu's initiative in the previous century; ironically the Wortley Montagu family itself may not have provided the best advertisement for the vaccinator's cause as further twists in the tale developed. Towering above the rhododendron rarities at Wentworth Castle is the obelisk recording how Lady Mary had championed the cause by having her infant son Edward inoculated while staying in Turkey; Edward, on reaching adulthood, claimed that the inoculation had infused him irrevocably with Turkish blood, and in due course set out for the East where he acquired a long beard and a saffron turban, learned fluent Turkish, converted to Islam and posed as an Ottoman prince, so losing his claim (and failing to provide an heir) to the Wortley estates.[44]

How a popular botanical alternative to the 'Poison Mixtures' of old was invented in Barnsley has been dealt with elsewhere,[45] but another application of Coffin's teachings emerged in the town — the heated air-bath. The *Family Botanic Guide* recounts how this healing technique of the Indian tribes involved enclosing the sufferer in a construct of bent willows and animal skins, in the presence of heated stones and herbs. Once again, support was quoted from learned circles, dating back to the experiments of botanist Joseph Banks (of Captain Cook's

An example of Dr Coffin's local influence 'Composition Powders'.

Established in 1877, Stott's business typified the opportunism of the Medical Botanists.

voyages) who had conducted studies of the effects of hot air on the human body by sealing himself in a high temperature chamber.[46] An ethos which revered the role of Heat as a Vital Force inspired local Medical Botanists like Thomas Garbutt of 43 Castlereagh Street, Thomas Lowe of 8 Union Street and Joseph Cryer Stott of 122 Sheffield Road, offering hot-air immersion therapy backed by the usual media marketing. To accompany the treatment, patrons of these Botanical Establishments were recommended a dose of 'Composition Powders', from an original herbal recipe of Coffin himself, and sold at threepence per ounce.

Just before the 1901 Foot-Race, one hopeful contender left the premises of J.C. Stott (whose 'Turkish Bath' apparatus more than matched the Indian system with a wooden-clad room above his Sheffield Road shop supplied with '20,000 cubic feet per hour of filtered hot air') and feeling suitably invigorated, set out for the Queen's Grounds. The Grounds had opened in 1870 amid earlier hot air, when a promised display of aerial gymnastics by noted equilibrist Monsieur Mario had failed to get off the ground (literally) due to balloon problems.[47] This time, however, the crowd was not disappointed by the performance given — and neither was Stott, who lost no time in advertising Bedford's achievement to boost trade, declaring in the next *Lodge's Almanack* that his herbal heat-baths had empowered the victor, 'giving him Health, Strength, Activity and Endurance...to Win the Race'.[48]

The legend etched into the door-glass of the chemist shop across the road (125 Sheffield Road) read 'Teeth Carefully Extracted'[49] and Stott missed no opportunity to keep abreast of his contemporaries. Being no exception to the Barnsley versatility which must be familiar to the reader by now,[50] he provided dentistry and also artificial teeth, competing with Oscar de Miromonde of Sackville Street ('Sets of Teeth in Gold or Platinum') and Oglesby of Cheapside ('Constructed of Polished Ivory, each Tooth a Thing of Beauty'). Stott's repertoire of herbs, false teeth and heat baths has been described by one local writer as 'a bizarre combination of brewing, chewing and stewing'.[51] The premises today maintain this tradition of variety, with John Clayton dealing in meat products, football-programmes and deep-freezers.

Literary pursuits (and stranger diversions)

Whilst Treddlehoyle's Canal Hoax and the Hundred-pound Foot-Race marked the beginning and end of Victoria's reign, one over-inflated Barnsley event stood out in the year of her birth: the Green v. Whike 'big fight'. On 2 April 1819, in front of a gentleman's residence at Full Dews near Wombwell, two far-renowned pugilists (Jemmy Green of Worsbrough and Johnny Whike of Barnsley) fought 'a long and bitter battle' for sixty guineas a side, with an audience of thousands and with spectators even crowding the windows of the house to gain a better view.[52] Worsbrough's champion, son of James Green of the Edmunds Arms (which did 'a roaring trade' at the time) eventually prevailed with Whike conceding defeat after an extraordinary ninety-four rounds. Printed reports and ballads of the fight circulated the length of the country and 'caused a vast amount of sensation at the time'.[53]

Away from the hurly-burly of Barnsley's great crowd-drawing spectacles, gentler pastimes were proceeding. Just three days after Green's hard-won victory was born one of the town's literary luminaries: John Hugh Burland. In his *Annals of Barnsley* he recorded many noteworthy events, and gave some attention to a group of characters inhabiting Church Street in the early nineteenth century (he lodged in the area himself for a time, overlooking Star Lane in 'an upstairs garrett', which he was obliged to share with two human skeletons).

Johnny Whike was not the only Barnsley notable to see stars and feel for bumps on the head: Thomas Lister (1810-1888) numbered astronomy and phrenology among a diverse range of learned pursuits

Thomas Lister was Postmaster 1839-1870, a position previously held by the contrary James Cocker.

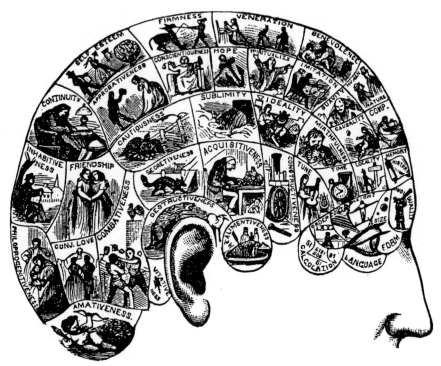

Phrenology, available at Church Street Post Office, alongside Botany, Ornithology and Astronomy.

followed in his Church Street Post-office (behind the classical columns which now adorn Locke Park). His phrenological abilities, displayed with other 'accomplishments' in his shop window, were of such repute that (in Burland's words) novices converged on the Post-office 'to have their heads examined', and his naturalist interests led to an acquaintance with Charles Waterton. With his celestial telescope, through which students would view the planet Venus, Lister might well have hoped to observe the skyward ascent of Waterton, who once invented a 'flying machine' and prepared to launch himself into the heavens from the roof of his outhouse.[54]

Lister's poetic leanings (*The Rustic Wreath, etc*) were called upon at such stately occasions as the Martin-Edmunds/Wortley wedding at Worsbrough Hall in 1855, where he delivered a suitable recitation while the Worsbrough Quadrille Band paused for breath.[55]

Opposite the Post-office was the shop of dialect writer Charles ('Treddlehoyle') Rogers, running a painting and decorating business adjoining the surgery of Dr Richard Crooks, with whom he shared notoriety for his use of language. Dr Michael Thomas Sadler had

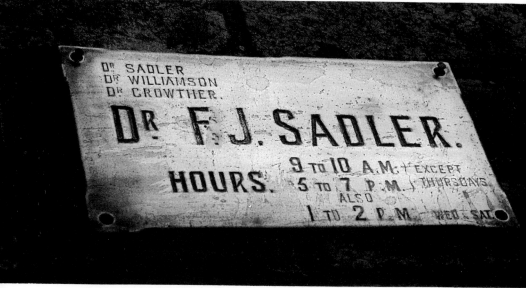

The last Dr Sadler of Church Street: in practice there from 1899.

interests ranging from the divine to the mundane, described by Burland as 'an enlightened philosopher' who had to 'fight year in, year out, for safer drains'. The threesome of Lister, Rogers and Sadler were together hailed as 'a literary triumvirate whose reign was long and commendable'.

Dr Robert Iberson joined Sadler's practice in 1848, probably relieved at the demise of Crooks (under whom he had been apprenticed) who had been 'a great swearer' with a reputation for inflicting punishment rivalling that of Jemmy Green, as his apprentices were regularly 'beaten with a walking stick'.

Succeeding his father as Barnsley's Officer of Health, the second Dr Michael Thomas Sadler followed on in medical practice in their imposing Church Street residence, and was also appointed Medical Officer for Worsbrough. He had six children; the eldest later distinguished as Sir Michael Ernest Sadler, with another son Francis Joseph becoming the third and last Dr Sadler of Church Street. Michael Ernest it was who married Mary Anne Harvey, daughter of the illustrious Charles Harvey, and their son in turn was Michael Sadleir the novelist and author of *Fanny by Gaslight* (1947).

Church Street was home to chemist A R Tomlin, secretary of Barnsley Literary Society, and here he wrote at length for the *Barnsley Independent* on *Local Folk Lore*. His work was compiled into a book in 1894, describing pagan rituals, omens and incantations, midnight burials and

headless apparitions, and relates how young men of the area (still as influenced by Venus as they were in the days of Lister's telescope) would consult him requesting 'ticing stuff' to charm a sweetheart.[56] Years later, since his 'Great Yorkshire Cure' somehow failed to rid the county of consumption, Tomlin's house (number 46) became the West Riding Tuberculosis Centre.[57]

Nearby was the birthplace of Dr John Fletcher Horne (1848-1941), mayor of Barnsley for the first two years of this century, who had a prolific literary output. Residing at *The Poplars*, Dodworth Road, having qualified at Apothecaries' Hall in the year Tom Treddlehoyle of Dodworth Road was buried at Tankersley (1874), his many published works included an account of the Lost Cities buried by Vesuvius[58] and a definitive history of drilling holes in the head (*Trephining in its Ancient and Modern Aspects*). He was born on Market Hill, son of linen-draper

Prolific writer and physician J.F. Horne, chronicler of Brain Surgery and fabled Lost Cities, who was Mayor of Barnsley 1900-1902.

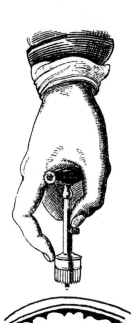

Trephining the Skull: an operation dating from Antiquity.

'No writer has done much without alcohol' claimed one contemporary of J.F. Horne (Stoneware ale bottle from the Coach and Horses, the Horne's family business for 94 years).

Travel in style from Market Hill, suggests Lingard's Illustrated Almanack of
1870 (William Horne succeeded George in 1875).

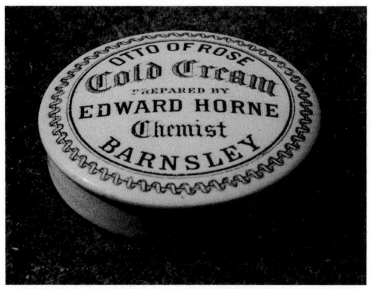

Edward Horne dealt in medicines in a shop across from the Coach and Horses, from 1860 to 1902.

William Horne, who held tenancy of the *Coach and Horses Hotel* between 1875 and 1895.[59] William was a brother of Edward Horne, chemist, who in 1860 had taken over the Market Hill druggist shop vacated by the London-bound James Cocker. Edward Horne devised his own tooth-cleanser and his own cold cream, dispensed in pots with ceramic lids bearing his name (now collectors' items) as well as his much-touted panacea for local afflictions: Horne's Bronchitis Mixture.

Conclusion

Our traveller, concluding his tour of curious marvels and marvellous cures, might well have learned to take the mixture of hyperbole with a suitable dose of caution. In doing so he follows the example of Alexander Pope, who no doubt called upon inherited Barnsley wit in his epitaph to a deceased purveyor of quack Worm Powder:

> *O learned friend of Abchurch Lane,*
> *Who sett'st our entrails free,*
> *Vain is thy art, thy Powder vain,*
> *Since worms shall eat e'en thee.*

Notes and References

1. Tomlin, A.R., *Local Folk Lore*, 1894 ('A compilation of folk-lore characteristic of the neighbourhood of Barnsley').
2. Currently receiving renewed attention.
3. Elliott, B. 'Owd Watter Joe', *Aspects of Barnsley*, 1993 p108.
4. After the Waterworks Act, 1837.
5. Ranger, W. *Report to the General Board of Health of the Town of Barnsley* 1852, p27.
6. See *Lodge's Almanack*, 1902.
7. Newton's concept of Gravity had been fiercely opposed by a German philosopher-mathematician, Liebniz; while Sir Walter Scott wrote of the 'mixture of hyperbolic Germanisms with which tales of wonder are usually told' (1818).
8. Swift, Jonathan, *Gulliver's Travels*, 1726. Grandville's surreal illustrations accompanied a popular new edition in the 1830s.
9. Burland, J.H. *The Annals of Barnsley and its Environs*. Despite an unconfirmed sighting of the improbable De Bughie at Chapeltown, he failed to materialise.
10. Advertisement, *Lingard's Illustrated Almanack*, 1870.
11. Tomlin, *op. cit.*
12. The words of Lady Mary Wortley Montagu, who denounced all such panaceas.
13. *Barnsley Chronicle*, 9th December 1994 p52.
14. *Barnsley Chronicle*, 25th November 1994 p68.
15. Sigsworth, E. and Brady, V. (Eds.) *The Ledger of William Elmhirst, Surgeon and Apothecary*, 1987.
16. Mary Queen of Scots, born a year after the early demise of Paracelsus, passed on the genetic legacy of Porphyria (through her son James I) down the Royal bloodline culminating in the madness of George III.
17. Design advice came from Samuel Tuke of the innovative York Retreat.
18. Burland, 'The Resurrection Men', *op. cit.*
19. For example, Joseph Mitchell was removed to York Asylum in 1816 by authorisation of Mr Wentworth of Woolley Hall (see Worsbrough Parish Records).
20. Samuel Tuke, joined by Godfrey Higgins of Doncaster, exposed the abuses at the York Asylum and the two were instrumental in the reforming legislation of 1815.
21. As expounded by Humphrey Davy (of miner's lamp fame) and Dr Erasmus Darwin (grandfather of Charles), both influences of Mary Shelley.
22. Burland, *op. cit.* Zamoiski was a travelling Polish showman, with an act no doubt inspired by Mesmer himself, i.e. combining electromagnetic stage-props with hypnotism.
23. Thorpe, F.T. *The Middlewood Hospital, Sheffield: One Hundred Years*, 1972.
24. Crichton-Browne, J. 'On the Weight of the Brain', *Brain*, April 1878, p504.
25. Darwin, C. *The Descent of Man*, 1871, p301. The work also quotes Charles Waterton's description of the extraordinary Bell-bird.
26. Smith, D. & T. *South and West Yorkshire Curiosities*, 1992, p47.
27. Mercury was subsequently used to embalm fallen soldiers of the American Civil War, returned at Lincoln's request.
28. Thorpe, *op. cit.* In 1914 Barnsley patients were re-directed again — to Storthes Hall at Huddersfield, built 1904.
29. The largest recorded dose of Laudanum in Barnsley was given to subdue a restless elephant in a Churchfield circus in the 1920s (see ref.49 below).
30. Thorpe, *op. cit.*
31. Gould, G. & Pyle, W. *Anomalies and Curiosities of Medicine*, 1896, p.313. Charles O'Brien was one of two 'Irish Giants' claiming descent from mythical tenth-century king Boru.
32. Wilkinson, J. *History of Worsbrough*, c.1880.
33. *Lodge's Almanack*, 1901.
34. Burland, J.H. 'To Michael Thomas Sadler' *Poems on Various Subjects*, 1865. Burland's words referred to 'Infants Cordial' a soporific of sugar and laudanum.
35. *Barnsley Chronicle*, 17 October 1901.
36. Fox, William, *Working Man's Model Family Botanic Guide to Health*, 1861, Sheffield.
37. Taylor, H. 'Village life in Mapplewell and Staincross' *Aspects of Barnsley*, 2, 1994, p118.
38. Wesley, J. *Primitive Physic, or an Easy and Natural Method of Curing Most Diseases*, 1781.
39. Bellamy, D. & Pfister, A. *World Medicine: Plants, Patients and People* 1992, p182. For more on Dr Coffin (1790-1866) see ref. 45 below.
40. Opened in 1815, the year that the second Denby Dale Pie celebrated Napoleon's defeat. Two Sheffield clergymen described the theatre as a 'Synagogue of Satan' (1819).
41. Burland, J.H., *The Annals of Barnsley and its Environs*. Skelton also founded a Botanic 'Sick and Burial Society' in Leeds.

42. Fox, *op. cit.* Fred Billington, chemist (see *Aspects of Barnsley*, 2) subsequently developed his Billington's Mandrake Bitters, dispensed in medicinal bottles.

43. Burland, *op. cit.*

44. *Beetons Dictionary of Universal Biography*, 1870, p726.

45. Walker, J A 'Quackery, Fiddling and Bloodsucking; Pills, Potions and Pork Pies', *Aspects of Barnsley*, 2, 1994, p73 (Nurse Harvey's Gripe Mixture).

46. Macauley, Dr *Thrilling Tales of Enterprise, Heroism and Adventure*, 1886. Banks sailed with Cook on his astronomical quest to the South Seas to observe the transit of Venus across the Sun (and found Venus in the form of the Tahitian Princess).

47. Taylor, H. 'The Day the Balloon Went Up', *Aspects of Barnsley*,   2, 1994, p35.

48. Stott, J.C. Advertisement, *Lodge's Almanack*, 1902.

49. Spooner, H.W. 'A Barnsley Chemist's Apprenticeship in the 1920s' *Barnsley Family History Society Journal* Vol.1 No.2, April 1993. Unqualified tooth-pulling was legal before 1921 (provided the word 'dentist' was not used).

50. One of the best examples being a Joe Wilkinson of Thurlstone, recorded as a 'Chemist and Druggist, Tooth Extractor, Gun and Pistol Maker, Watch, Clock and Musical Instrument Repairer' (1861).

51. Dickinson, G.C. 'Barnsley South-East, 1904' *Old Ordnance Survey Maps*, Alan Godfrey Maps, 1990.

52. Burland, *op. cit*

53. Wilkinson, *op. cit* p266. In Wilkinson's account there were ninety-two rounds, compared with Burland's ninety-four. On a previous occasion a 'dreadful combat' had been recorded in ballad form:-the defeat of the Dragon of Wortley by a local hero, in a centuries-old poem.

54. Concerned friends and servants persuaded him to abandon the venture, leaving another Yorkshire squire, George Cowley, to launch the first ever manned heavier-than-air flight in 1853.

55. *Barnsley Times*, 1 September 1855.

56. Tomlin, *op. cit.*

57. Headed by Dr Herbert Crowther, a keen astronomer in the Church Street tradition.

58. Horne, J F *The Mirage of Two Buried Cities*, 1900.

59. William, Thomas, George and Edward Horne were sons of George Horne (senior), a veterinary surgeon from Staincross.

Acknowledgements

Thanks to all the following for their assistance:-

Mrs Norah Wordsworth and family; Gerald Alliott; Sue Watts; Steve Manning; John Walker; Wendy Shepherd; Alan Stables of Woolley Hall; Mrs M. Tasker; David Dainty; John Sadler; Maurice Clayton; Archives and Local Studies Staff, Barnsley Library. Thanks also to Brian Elliott (editorial advice), Mavis Sadler (keyboard skills) and Tim Montgomery (photography).

2. TOWN END IN 1870

by Ian Harley

PICTURE TOWN END NOWADAYS and your mind will no doubt conjure up a large roundabout containing a few rocks and flowers, lines of queuing motor vehicles and the odd pedestrian.

Older Barnsley residents, however, will no doubt remember the busy six-lane end junction which, on one hand, seemed designed to present an old-fashioned image of the town to visitors but, on the other, was a fascinating collection of shops, businesses, houses, alleyways and yards.

Interestingly, one elderly Barnsley resident carried out a similar recollection exercise in the 1930s and remembered the Town End he knew in the 1870s.

The Chronicle of Saturday, July 21, 1933 published his recollections, printed under the initials J.W.R. and the title 'Old Barnsley'. I make no apology for the fact that this article is copied word for word:

Town End! how different! By how many lineal feet has the level of the wide space on which the six busy roads converge been raised since we first knew it in the [1860s] 'sixties'? It was no uncommon sight in those days immediately after a summer storm to see water to the depth of several feet for some hours covering this busy spot, making traffic, vehicular and pedestrian impossible.

At the corner of Peel Street and Shambles Street was a little shop, entrance to which was down three steps. This was occupied by Sammy Armitage for the sale of butchers' meat, and rarely escaped inundation during storms. William Exley, who kept similar premises as a grocery at the bottom of York Street, suffered similarly until his building was altered completely by putting in new windows and raising the floor considerably above the road level.

At the corner of Peel Street and York Street was a wheelwright's establishment, kept by old Bashforth and his sons. The original 'Wheat Sheaf' Inn, a somewhat sombre and insignificant structure, built of brick, faced Dodworth Road and adjoined a shop and house occupying the corner, tenanted by Robert Hough, hairdresser and umbrella maker, who later removed to Sheffield Road. This house was entered from Racecommon Road through ornamental wrought iron gates. More interesting and decidely picturesque were the ancient pumps and cattle troughs which stood opposite at the junction of Dodworth Road and Shambles Street. A circular pond, enclosed by a low stone wall with rounded copings, occupied a considerable space between Town

End, Summer Lane and Shambles Street, and when the wall came to be raised some three feet, great disappointment was felt by the juvenile community, who were thus deprived of the pleasure of seeing the goldfish with which some kindly person at some time enriched this water.

Before leaving Town End, let us — in imagination — assume a position near the weather-beaten and wrinkled wooden casing of one of the old pumps and note some of those who pass about the hour of noon, say, in the year 1870 or thereabouts.

It is half past twelve. Hark! Taylor's bell! How much that means to thousands of Barnsley's population as its welcome sound breaks on the air! See, from Peel Street, Shambles Street, York Street, and Racecommon Road stream hundreds of good-looking, be-shawled white-aproned women — the women who do the work at Taylor's, Pigott's, Carter's, Spencer's and Richardson's linen factories. The men seen in the crowd are the 'tuners', mechanics, warehousemen and clerks from these mills.

A few minutes and the streets are again clear. Vision is now attracted by a stately and almost statuesque elderly gentleman, clad in grey, mounted, riding from his mill at the top of Pinfold Hill to his beautifully situated house at Keresforth. Shortly, he is followed afoot by his tall, well-groomed and athletic son, a well-known and popular figure in Barnsley, a true sportsman, who, by his personal influence and financial aid, was for many years the principal support of the Barnsley Cricket Club.

Almost immediately there now comes into view, from Shambles Street, a fine old English gentleman, with features and head suggestive of a Viking. Mounted on a grey pony, attired in brown with grey tall hat with black band, he is now returning to Dodworth Hall after a morning spent at his office at the mills. Fond of a noon-day stroll along Sackville Street as a constitutional, it is characteristic of this man of a generous spirit to greet the passer-by with a remark, casual, but always witty, cheerful, and encouraging.

What is this which now strikes us as making halting and stilted progress towards York Street? The rear aspect consists of an ancient long coat reaching from neck to heels, a quite indescribable hat, arms extended sideways at an angle, and a walking stick protruding apparently from each rigid sleeve. Ah! a turn of the head. A countenance! We now recognise Tommy Wallacks on his way to St. George's to 'blow' the organ for a practising pupil. Woe to the boy who comes within reach of one of those sticks!

Now, emerging from Summer Lane is something quite unique. An equipage indeed! Is it from Lilliput? A phaeton, the step almost touching the ground, drawn by a pair of diminutive cream-coloured ponies, long manes, long tails, high harness — a turnout remarkable in appearance, and thrilling. But what of the sole occupant? Reins in hand, reclining comfortably, is observed an elderly gentleman of somewhat unusual appearance. Short in stature, very stout, rotund, fresh of countenance, wearing gold-rimmed spectacles and the inevitable silk hat — we have before us the pioneer of the eider-down quilt and clothing industry, the inventor or joint-inventor of that boon to mankind — 'warmth without weight.' [James McLintock] *He is on his way from the Utilitas Works to his home at Longcar Park.*

Coming from Racecommon Road, we now notice two bachelor brothers, [the Wilsons] *linen magnates, who take the Shambles Street route to Cockerham Road. Also from the same road, come father and son from the Shaw Mills. A tall and erect old gentleman, approaching 80 years of age, accompanied by a son destined to become one of Barnsley's most noted public men in the capacity of councillor, alderman, Mayor and magistrate.*

There now flits across from York Street, a plumber, speedy and competent. Tall, thin, wearing a peaked cap, sporting a very pronounced goatee — this silent tradesman bears the responsibility of a reputation for many virtues.

By the appearance, also from York Street, of one of the town's grand old men, one is led to feel that 'All's well with the World.' He saunters towards Town End, enjoying his after-lunch smoke from a long pipe,

Shambles Street, Old White Bear Yard, 1930. *Kenneth Graham*

wearing his white linen apron, over which he has put on loosley a broadcloth frock coat, the usual silk hat surmounting his silvering hair.

Standing as we are, in imagination, at the bottom of Dodworth Road, the association of this thoroughfare with the linen trade comes into one's mind; for a little later in the day, it is probable there would pass before us some of the exploiters of the remnant of the poor handloom weavers, some merchants, yarn agents, and at least one, of the finest type of the 'Knights of the road' — the men responsible for the sale of Barnsley's linen output.

The day advances and it is now some time since the Taylor bell rang the 'twenty-five past' one. The workpeople have returned, the children are at school and in the comparative quiet of a summer afternoon, the familiar sounds associated with the spot where we now stand greet our willing ear.

A thirsty horse drinks greedily from the trough near my feet, a tinkle from a piano comes across from the opposite side of Dodworth Road, the smitten anvils clang from the blacksmith's near, the constant hammering from the old foundry, the hissing of the circular saws from the Peggy Mill, and the usual street medley. A parting glance round, a struggle, for the present, against the allurements of old Shambles Street, and thankful for the blessing of memory, we, perhaps reluctantly, come back to the thoughts and duties of 1933.

3. TAYLOR ROW AND THE HANDLOOM WEAVERS OF BARNSLEY

by Harold Taylor

TODAY TAYLOR ROW IS NO MORE than a short, almost anonymous link, easing Barnsley traffic between Doncaster Road and Sheffield Road. For much of the nineteenth century, by contrast, the long rows of cottages which lined it, housing a busy and crowded community of handloom weavers, formed a street of great character.

In 1851 forty-five families were packed into its thirty-four cottages, and in addition more than thirty lodgers were living with them at some time. Although the majority of the tenants were Barnsley-born, there was a good-sized complement of people who hailed from other parts of the country, most noticeably the seventeen who had been born across the Irish Sea. There were a few representatives of Lancashire, Westmorland, Durham, Somerset and Scotland. A number had originated in local villages, Ardsley, Darton, Cudworth and Cawthorne. Others had been born a little further afield, at Clayton West, Skelmanthorpe and Kirkburton.

What a babel of dialects would have been heard in the Row, and what different backgrounds and traditions would feature among the various families! Nearly all, however, had two things in common — they earned a living in the loomshop and endured a high degree of poverty for most of the time.

All but nine of those whose occupations are stated in the Census of 1851 were linen workers. Barnsley had been a magnet for many of them, drawing them in with the prospect, or at least the hope, of work in the town's linen industry. Perhaps they had received promising news from relatives or friends already working there. Some had brought weaving skills with them from areas where the local textile industry was in difficulties but others brought no such relevant skills.

The diverse origins of the population in Taylor Row reflected an important feature of Barnsley as a whole in mid-century, for by this time its numbers had grown more than four-fold in fifty years, largely through in-migration.

An important feature of each dwelling in the Row was the provision of a loomshop, so that it was possible for a family both to live and work at home. The whole street could be called a 'Residential Factory'.

Taylor Row in mid-century stood on the very edge of town and on the fringe of an extensive and crowded area of weavers' cottages as will

MAP 1. Part of Barnsley, surveyed for the Local Board of Health 1856. The heavily outlined area was 'Wilson's Piece'.
The map shows a number of 'back-to-back' houses in and near that area.

be seen on Map One. The houses in the Row were certainly built before 1825,[1] and possibly only a year or two before that date. A large area of land had become available for building on this south side of the town as a result of the enclosure of Warren Common, following an Act of 1777. A number of linen manufacturers — owners of warehouses — acquired land on the former common, among them the Wilson family, members of which had pioneered the linen industry in Barnsley in the 1740s. The gridwork pattern of roads between New Street and Heelis Street, lined with weavers' cottages, came to be known as 'Wilson's Piece'. Plot 818, shown on Map Two, which had been in the ownership of Thomas Woodcock, 'yeoman', and the Rev. John Pickles, was subsequently acquired by Edward Taylor, a native of Cawthorne, or by his son, another Edward.[2] The father is said to have established a

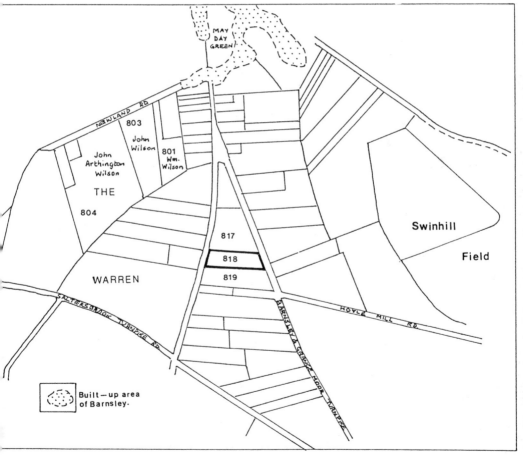

MAP 2. Part of the Fairbanks map of 1779 showing land enclosed through an Act of 1777. Plot 818 later became the site of Taylor Row. Note the Wilson family plots on the former Warren Common.

linen business in the town in 1775,[3] young Edward taking over after his father's death in 1806. Taylors had a linen warehouse in Shambles Street from which yarn was taken out by cottage handloom weavers and returned there in due course as woven cloth. The cottages in Taylor Row were available for occupation by weavers, most of whom may have worked for Taylors. This would certainly have been convenient and time-saving for them, as another warehouse had been established at the western end of the street. There was, however no obligation for tenants to work as weavers, certainly not by 1841, for the census of that year records a miner among them.

By the 1840s Taylors had opened a linen mill on a site between Shambles Street and Peel Street but, like some other mill owners in the town, continued to employ cottage weavers long after power looms for weaving linen had been introduced in Barnsley in 1837.

Evidence derived from the Rate Valuation Lists of 1848 make it possible to build up a picture of handloom weaving in Barnsley in mid-century, by which time the role of cottage weavers here had virtually reached its peak, and to place Taylor Row in context. The Lists record the 'loom capacity' of each dwelling, street by street. Since some of the looms were rented from the landlord, and could be called back to the owner's warehouse yard, and indeed **were** during some of the labour disputes,[4] the Valuation Lists may not show the actual number of looms in operation at the time but, at least, they reveal in a most impressive way how intensively concentrated was the weaving industry on this side of the town, and how numerous the cottages involved in it.

Map Three, based on the 1848 data, shows how the 'loom capacity' varied from one to six, but that three or four-loom shops were most numerous. Taylor Row was fairly typical in that eighteen or nineteen of its thirty-four cottages could accommodate four looms, whilst there were twelve two-loom shops, two with three looms and one with six. It stood in marked contrast, however, to nearby Union Street, where twenty of the fifty-nine cottages had six-loom shops.

Clearly there could be no standard size for a Barnsley loomshop, but contemporary accounts indicate that in the case of cellar or basement loomshops they were six feet high with floors about four feet below street level.[5] A cellar created favourable conditions for weaving linen in that the air tended to be damp, thus reducing the likelihood of the brittle threads snapping on the loom. Even so an occasional sprinkling of the yarn with water and an application of a flour and water sizing agent was necessary in order to minimise the problem. For the speculative builder and the landlord a loomshop beneath the living accommodation, rather than at street level, offered a further advantage in that more cottages could be packed into a given site.

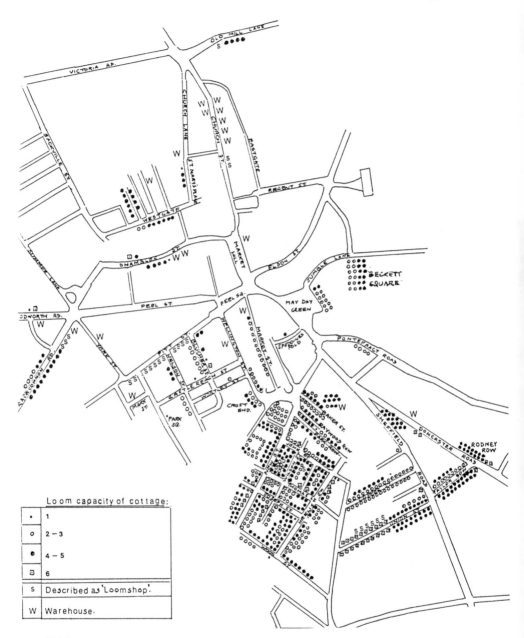

MAP 3. Loom capacity of cottages in Barnsley, based on the Rate Valuation Lists of 1848. Note the concentration of weavers' cottages in the south east area of the town. Symbols represent the correct number of loomshops on each street but not the precise location of each one in a street.

PLATE 1. South side (rear) of Taylor Row in the 1960's. (*Barnsley Archives*)

Since the weaving cellars needed a window space to admit light, ceilings needed to be above street level. As a result, a distinguishing feature of the dwelling was the short flight of steps leading from the street to the door of the living room. Plates One and Two, of the south side of Taylor Row and of Heelis Street (in 'Wilson's Piece'), illustrate this well. We are fortunate to have available an illustration in the 1852 Report to the Barnsley General Board of Health to show us the arrangement of an 'Underground Weaving Shop'. Although this engraving does not feature it, many cellars had barrel-vaulted roofs, giving added strength to the whole building.

The diagrams A and B show the interior layout of cottages on each side of Taylor Row as they were in the 1960s, shortly before demolition.

On the south side of the street a staircase led from the single living room to two bedrooms. There is oral evidence that access to the cellar loomshop was originally gained directly from the street, the internal staircase being a later modification.

On the opposite side of the street, however, the cottages had no cellars and therefore no steps leading up to the front doors, the steps at the rear of some of them being provided simply because the slope of the site made them necessary. On this side of the street there were two downstairs rooms, the smaller being used as a kitchen by the later tenants. Since a Deed of 1831 describes twelve of these dwellings as having two-loom shops, it would appear that the smaller room housed the looms. The very first purpose-built weavers' cottages in Barnsley, in Park Row, had loomshops at street level,[6] but the cellar loomshop was soon adopted thereafter. The ground level shops in Taylor Row would appear therefore to have been unusual in the town. However, there were a few street level loomshops in Ardsley and there were numerous examples in other linen weaving areas, such as Knaresborough and the Northallerton district.

There were other variations among the weavers' cottages on this south side of the town. Some of the dwellings in Heelis Street had but one

Weavers' cottages in Heelis Street in the 1960's. (*Barnsley Archives*)

Taylor Row from Sheffield Road. The cottages on the left (the north side of the street) had no cellars, therefore no steps to the front doors. (*Tasker Trust*)

bedroom. There were rows of 'back-to-back' houses too in 'Wilson's Piece', where living space would be very restricted. Some of the cottages in Heelis Street had access to the cellar or basement loomshops by means of a backdoor at ground level because the ground sloped away considerably behind these houses. Some of the dwellings in Beckett Square — formerly on the site of present-day Barnsley's covered market — were different again, having been adapted to serve as weavers' cottages from existing buildings.

As mentioned earlier, there was a warehouse at the Sheffield Road end of the northern side of Taylor Row, but by 1831 it had been converted into two, three-loom cottages. By the 1870s, when handloom weaving in Barnsley was in decline, these two units had been modified again to serve as a police station. It is perhaps surprising that this conversion had not been carried out earlier in view of the rough behaviour which occured in the vicinity from time to time. An incident which took place in 1837 serves to illustrate this. The top of Taylor Row 'was notorious for the assembly of children and young men, who congregated there for the purpose of abusing nearly everyone who passed by'.

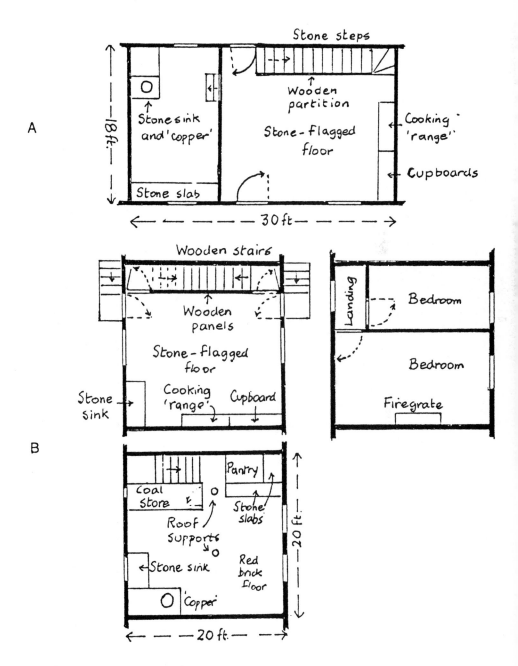

Samuel Cooper's linen warehouse of about 1820 in St Mary's Place, with adjacent stable block and coach-house. (*Barnsley Chronicle*)

Old dwelling in the former Beckett Square, sub-divided and probably adapted for occupation by handloom weavers. Beyond are what appear to be purpose-built weavers' cottages. Chimney stack is of the former Union Foundry. (*Tasker Trust*)

Late one afternoon in the March of that year, a day when snow was lying on the ground, a William Rawdon was driving pigs along Sheffield Road when he was pelted with snowballs by a gang of youths. The resulting quarrel deteriorated into a fight, during which Rawdon drew a knife and stabbed two of of the youths. William Cherry, who lived in the Row, was wounded in the side, and another young man stabbed in the back. Rawdon made off but was apprehended at Worsbrough Common by a constable Kershaw.[7]

The Enumerators' notebooks of the 1841 Census for Taylor Row show very well how whole families could be involved in the loomshop.

The Cherry household, which included William, already mentioned, provides a good example:

Thomas Cherry	(50)	'Linen Weaver'
Hannah Cherry	(50)	" "
William Cherry	(25)	" "
Thomas Cherry	(24)	" "
John Cherry	(24)	" "
Joseph Cherry	(20)	" "
George Cherry	(15)	" "
Emmanuel Cherry	(12)	" "
Richard Cherry	(8)	No occupation stated

(Census Enumerators were instructed to round down all ages over fifteen to the nearest five. In this case the officer did not apply the rule consistently.)

Although all the workers here are described as 'weavers', some members of the family, probably Hannah and young Richard, would work as 'winders', winding yarn onto the loom beam. Others would help in sizing the yarn.

Elsewhere in the Row Hannah French, aged 72 and Hannah Thompson, aged 70, being elderly, worked as 'winders'. In the household of George Shirt in 1851 George (72) and his son John (37) were 'weavers', whereas the youngsters Charles (13) and George (8), his grandsons, were 'winders'. The role of the wife as winder for her husband's loom could be of critical importance, since her illness or confinement for child-bearing could seriously hinder his work.

The 'master weaver', generally the head of household, was directly responsible to the 'manufacturer' at the warehouse, in many cases paying rent to him for the cottage and the looms. Looms would be operated by the master himself, by members of his family and by others — 'journeymen weavers', and perhaps apprentices. Journeymen paid the master for use of the loom, for sizing materials, for yarn-dressing brushes and for candles.[8] Few would be encouraged to serve apprenticeships, however, on account of the periodic influx of new, unskilled workers into the town who, it is said, could learn to weave, after a fashion, in about three weeks!

It is clear that some boys worked for masters in cottages other than their own, though there were 'never more than four children working together.'[9] An 1842 report on the Employment of Children on the Yorkshire Coalfield records an interview (not in Taylor Row) with a Thomas Dunk, aged 14, which illustrates the point.[10]

Thomas explained:

> *I am a weaver. I have been weaving between three and four years.*
> *I began to wind when I was nine years old. I weave about fourteen*
> *hours a day and stop about half an hour for dinner. It tires me a good*
> *deal in my arms. I get about five shillings a week, which the man I*
> *weave for takes, and he clothes and feeds me. I am well used generally.*
> *Some boys are well used and some ill; they beat some a good deal.*

Poverty spurred the masters to keep youngsters working for such formidably long hours. Thomas Dunk's brother John, who was two years younger, told the Commissioner:

> *I am a winder to a weaver. I begin to wind at seven in the morning*
> *and leave off at ten at night. I stop half an hour at dinner and half*
> *an hour at tea.*

There were many days, however, when no work was available. Tom Hillingley, a master weaver, told the Commissioner:

> *Lads work fifteen hours a day when there is work to do but there is*
> *no regularity. One half or one third of the weavers in the town would*
> *do all the work there is to do, the work is so irregular.*

Lodgers would provide welcome labour in the good times. Seasonal changes in the demand for particular types of fabric would be reflected in the movement of lodgers into and out of the town. There were thirty-four lodgers living in Taylor Row on Census night, 1851, all but three of them staying in weavers' households. In both 1851 and 1861 the lodgers in the Row were predominantly weavers, thirty-three out of thirty-four in the first year and sixteen out of eighteen in the latter.

Although about half of those who were there in 1851 were natives of Barnsley, about a third were of Irish origin. The Censuses of 1851 and 1861 for Taylor Row also record lodgers who had been born in Westmorland, Lancashire and Scotland. In Heelis Street in 1851 over a third of the homes were shared with lodgers, about three quarters of them working in the loomshops.

As already suggested, the lodgers formed a transitory population — 'birds of passage'. Of the thirty-four lodgers living in Taylor Row in 1851, only one was still there ten years later, and of those living there in 1861, all but one had moved on by 1871. How many other moves took place between the census years we cannot know!

It was not only the lodgers who were mobile. A comparison of successive Census records reveals that about 40% of the heads of family in Taylor Row in 1851 had moved in during the last nine years. As a large proportion were Barnsley-born, it may be, however, that they simply 'flitted' short distances from one part of the town to another, from time to time. It is not surprising that 'the town's middle classes looked on the weavers as a nomadic race!'

'A weaver is a degraded being'. (Parliamentary Report of 1840).

It is clear from contemporary accounts that for the most part Barnsley's handloom weavers lived in great poverty and in considerable discomfort and that some worked in conditions which were very injurious to health. The 1852 Report to the Barnsley Board of Health takes us inside a number of dwellings to see some of the worst examples of bad housing conditions in the town. The fact that Taylor Row does not feature in the Report may suggest that conditions there were not of the worst.

Flooding of cellar loomshops was a serious problem. In one six-loom shop in Top Fold, May Day Green, a man was seen working in water nearly two feet deep! He had already baled out more than forty-seven gallons of water that day, and expected to bale out the cellar again two or three times more before nightfall.

Polluted water made the problem still more serious, and the 1852

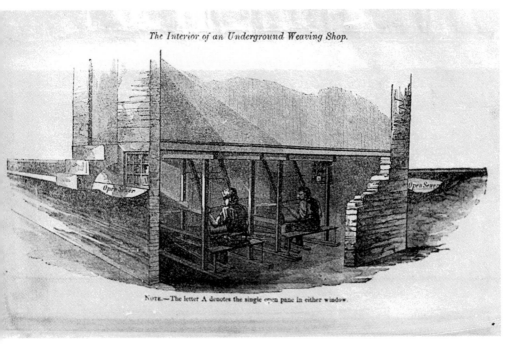

The Interior of an Underground Weaving Shop.

NOTE.—The letter A denotes the single open pane in either window.

'The interior of an underground weaving shop'. From the 1852 Report to the Barnsley Board of Health.

Report provides a graphic account of this to accompany its illustration of an 'Underground Weaving Cellar':

> *The chief evil arises from the surface drainage of the streets in which they are situated. The ceiling of the weaving shop is generally about two feet above the surface of the ground, and is provided with a window which does not open, the sill being on a level with the street outside. In the window there is generally a small aperture for the admission of air. Immediately under this window and aperture runs an open channel to carry off the liquid refuse of the neighbouring houses, so that every breath of air that comes into the weaving shop is poisoned in its passage over the filthy and half stagnant gutter. Add to this the fact that the permeable nature of the drains allows much of the liquid sewerage to saturate the ground, as well as the walls of many of the underground weaving shops, so that in wet weather the surface water runs into them from the streets. In some instances the overflowing contents of the adjoining soil pits are discharged into the shops, the occupants of which are obliged to bale them out two or three times a day. A large proportion of the weaving population who work in their own shops are living in and breathing the atmosphere of a cesspool.*

One of the town's linen manufacturers added his own comment, that

> *the work brought in by handloom weavers had the most offensive and unhealthy odour. The smell,* he said, *was peculiar and quite indescribable.*

Living conditions, no less than working conditions left a great deal to be desired in many of the cottages. In mid-century some cottages needed to use cellars as bedrooms, so crowded was the accommodation. In one of the cottages in Heelis Street a cellar bedroom was reached by way of a passage in which standing water was such a problem that stepping stones were placed there to cross it. In Mason's Yard a family of weavers occupied one of two rooms in a building, the other being in use by another tenant for the stabling of a horse and mule and the rearing of pigs. Liquid from this chamber sometimes ran down into the loomshop below, 'getting among the coals and creating a stench so overpowering that the workers were frequently obliged to go out of doors.'

Dr. Sadler, medical officer of the east division of Barnsley, giving evidence for the Report, remarked that

> *the interior of weavers' houses are far from distinguished by cleanliness. A cheap and liberal supply of water would be an inducement to greater cleanliness, and tend to promote the health and comfort of the labouring population.*

Some of the streets outside the weavers' doors presented a discouraging scene of squalor too. Heelis Street, Copper Street and Wood Street, among others, were 'entirely unprovided with drainage, so that house refuse of every kind had to be thrown on the surface of the street.' The 'Barebones district', to the south of Wilson's Piece, was 'without a proper supply of water, and neither drained, scavenged or lighted.'

Such accounts would perhaps be thought to exaggerate the problem in the weaving area, yet the Board of Health's Superintendant Inspector, William Ranger, prefaces the descriptions with the remark that these examples were given lest he should be considered to overstate the case. Even so, the Keyser Report of 1840 had given a much more favourable picture:

> [The weavers'] *dwellings present an appearance of comfort much superior to that of weavers in other places. The cottages are ......built of stone for the most part, in the airy and dry situations for which the town and neighbourhood afford abundant space, the situation being remarkably healthy. The cellars in which they work are not more damp than is desirable for carrying on their trade. Well ventilated, and even where the inhabitants are suffering from extreme poverty, their houses have a look of cleanliness and order. There are exceptions to this rule, but they are not very numerous.*

William Ranger, however, provides a long list of 'exceptions', particularly in the matter of overcrowding. In some cases the problem was temporary, as at the house in Wilkinson's Alley — not specifically identified as a weaver's cottage, though in Wilson's Piece — where, in a room approximately ten feet square and open to the roof slates, a family of four (a woman and her daughter, son-in-law, and their child) had taken in six other persons to stay a few nights with them, an Irishman, his wife, and four children. The woman, who was ill, lay on the floorboards, covered with a piece of harding, there being no bedding in the room. In 1841 the cottage of John Rushforth in Taylor Row housed John and his wife, daughters Ann and Martha (22 and 12), sons George and Robert (20 and 10), and two younger children six and two, in addition to Fanny Brook (20) and her four year old child.

Some of the cottages on the north side of Taylor Row featured cramped accommodation too. Seven or eight of them were occupied by different families upstairs and downstairs. In a Deed of 1831 the upper floors are described as 'chambers or tenements over cottages', and the Rate valuation list of 1839 records the low rateable value of fifteen shillings for each of them, compared with £3 for the downstairs accommodation. The valuation lists of 1861 and 1875 identify the 'chambers' as 'Back

Taylor Row', suggesting that access to them was by way of the back doors.

The sense that the Barnsley weaver was looked down upon as a 'degraded being'[11] by some sections of the community is suggested by a comment in the Symons report on the Mines of the Yorkshire Coalfield in 1842:

> *Barnsley is a capital place for comparison between weavers and colliers. The weaver sits pottering over his work for fifteen hours, and spends a third of his time wishing it done. The collier generally strips and sets to work as if he thought a coal-pit the very last place to loiter in — and that the hardest work while there was the shortest way out.*

Weaver James Hitchen offered a more objective view of the condition of weavers' children:

> *Take 100 collier-boys and 100 weaver-boys, and the collier boys will be the strongest and healthiest.*[12]

Weavers were paid on a piecework basis, and the rates of pay were low. Periodic downturns in the linen trade, as well as pressure from rival manufacturers in the town, and competition from producers elsewhere, particularly in Scotland, had prompted employers to revise the rates downwards during the earlier decades of the century. An equivalent length of 'plain drill', which had earned a weaver £2-10-0 (£2.50) in the years 1811 to 1814, brought in no more than £1-4-0 (£1.20) by 1838. The Barnsley weavers' union insisted that no-one should work for lower pay, yet there were some who were driven by sheer poverty to do so during strike periods, despite the abuse to which they were subjected as 'blacklegs' by the other weavers.

From time to time an influx of men, or indeed of whole families into the town to seek work had the effect of keeping rates of pay down by creating a surplus of labour. The 1840 Keyser report details the experience of a weaver who, having moved back to Knaresborough, described how five years previously fifty Irishmen had come into Barnsley one morning, 'each proposing to become a weaver'. They had never worked as weavers before, but 'they got friends and got work, which they did very badly.' The facility with which a man could become a weaver was, he complained, 'a special evil of the town.' It is likely that such inexperienced workers were set to weave fabrics belonging to the lower end of the quality range, as they certainly were in Leeds.

The problem of poverty was made seriously worse by the withdrawal in 1823 of the traditional right of 'fent'. This valuable perquisite had given each weaver the right to keep for himself the last yard of each 'half piece'. The linen could be made into clothing such as shirts, shifts and aprons, and 'had always assured weavers of a good supply of warm clothing'.[13] Alternatively the linen could be bartered for food, or even for ale. However, manufacturers were complaining that the material was competing on the market with their own wares, and that 'fents were getting longer!'

The noisy clamour of the weavers who gathered on May Day Green on the 5th May in angry protest at the loss of fent could well have been heard in Taylor Row, only a few hundred yards away. The inhabitants would certainly have known that the meeting was called when they heard the beating of frying pans in the street, the usual signal for bringing the workers together.

The disturbances which followed, and especially the bitter resentment at the activities of 'blacklegs', prepared to 'work without fent', led to the arrest of three of the leading participants and their sentencing to terms of imprisonment in Wakefield Gaol, two of them to serve two months hard labour on the treadmill.[14] It has been claimed that the weavers never recovered from the loss of fent, but 'sank to the lowest depth of degradation and misery.'[15]

A dispute of even bigger proportions followed the employers' decision to cut piece-work rates in 1829, following two poor years in the linen trade, due in part at least, to cheaper imports from abroad. Resentment among the weavers came to a head in May, when a noisy crowd which had assembled in an open space in the 'Barebones', attacked the house of Samuel Cooper in Church Street. (His warehouse still stands in St. Mary's Place.) Disturbances broke out from time to time through the following summer, causing the authorities to call out the Yeoman Cavalry and to summon the 14th Lancers from Sheffield Barracks. A particulary serious incident took place in the evening of August 27th, when a crowd moved off from the Barebones into the countryside west of the town to attack and severely damage Keresforth House, the home of linen manufacturer Jackson. The garden was wrecked, windows and furniture smashed, and a bonfire made of his books.[16]

The rioting and the protests of the summer and autumn months brought no gains. By November the weavers were returning to work, at reduced rates of pay. However, the periodic disputes between weaver and manufacturer, the 'pugnacious and refractory conduct of weavers towards their superiors',[17] and the 'radical' politics associated with the weavers over many years make a compelling story in their own right.

Trade recessions continued to cause severe problems from time to time. 1840 was a particularly bad year, with hundreds unemployed. Several manufacturers became bankrupt, and some weavers left the town. A relief fund of £300 ran out after five or six weeks. Fortunately fifty or sixty of the unemployed men were able to find temporary work,

The layout of cottages in Taylor Row:
A — the north side of the street — ground plan
B — the south side — weaving cellar, living room and bedrooms.

for three large engineering schemes were in progress at the time, the excavation of the cutting to make way for Eldon Street North, the construction of Peel Street, and the laying of water mains by the recently formed Barnsley Water Company.[18]

Even in the better times, when order books were full, there were circumstances which were against the weavers. Some manufacturers paid their workers in tokens, rather than in coin of the realm, tokens which could only be converted into goods at the employer's own 'tommy shop', where prices might sometimes be set at levels slightly above those in ordinary shops.

Yet another cause of complaint was the amount of time the weavers had to spend either in setting up looms for new work or in walking to and from the warehouse. They reckoned that 'at the very lowest average' this amounted to the equivalent of one in week eight, time for which there was no remuneration.

Overcrowding, poor sanitation, damp workplaces, long hours and poor diet all conspired to cause illnesses which cut into working hours and doubtless shortened the life of some. A Reverend Cook, 'who showed himself thoroughly acquainted with the condition of the working population', told the Board of Health inspectors in 1852 that 'the general health of the weavers was extremely bad, and that a weaver at fifty years of age was an old, broken down man, and indeed, completely emaciated.' Another witness remarked that 'work was often put into the hands of a weaver apparently in good health, and a few days afterwards he would hear that the man was dead and the rest of the family laid up in illness.'

Against the almost unmitigated gloom of the descriptions given thus far, some of the comments found in the Keyser Report of 1840 shine with surprising brightness, especially when set beside passages from the Ranger Report of 1852.

The moral condition of the Barnsley weavers, writes Keyser, is highly spoken of by their employers and others with whom I have conversed on the subject, and I have found them, for the most part sober, steady and intelligent to a degree far above what might be expected from their humble situation. In their persons, clothing, and the appearance of their children the Barnsley weavers contrast favourably with the same class of person in Leeds and elsewhere.

This remark about Barnsley weavers is particularly complimentary in view of Keyser's comments on another page in the same Report, where he praises the qualities of weavers encountered in Leeds,

whose moral character is equally as good, if not superior to the generality of the labouring class.

The Barnsley families were evidently better still!   One of the manufacturers in 1840 had seen

a great disposition among weavers in Barnsley to bring up their children well and respectably,

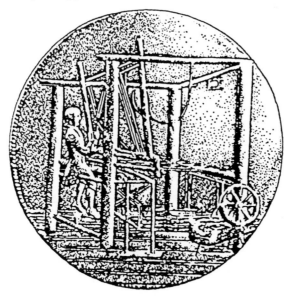

A penny 'token' issued by the firm of Jackson & Lister in 1811 for use in payment of weavers for their work. On view in Western Park Museum, Sheffield.

though the Report of that year comments further that

> *want of decent clothing operates in preventing many children from attending schools, and also from attending places of worship. They get but middling of schooling*, stated weaver James Hitchen, *but it is chiefly on Sundays.*[19]

Nevertheless a good many children in Taylor Row were attending some sort of school by 1851, since ten of the nineteen boys and fifteen of the twenty girls aged between three and sixteen are described as 'scholars' in the Census. By 1871 the proportions were to be a great deal higher.

Since 1824 there had been a primitive Methodist Sunday School in Heelis Street. The Wesleyan Sunday School in Sheffield Road, which opened in 1835, became a day school in 1843. A Baptist Sunday School, also in Sheffield Road, opened in 1849, and in the previous year St. John's Anglican Church had begun to operate a School in the Barebones area. By 1857 there was a 'Free Infant School' in Baker Street, supported by voluntary subscriptions.

Some children were more fortunate than others in the amount of education they received. The youngster John Dunk, mentioned earlier, had been asked about his schooling and his religious knowledge when interviewed by J.C. Symons and had replied:

> *I have been very little to school. I have been to a Sunday School when I do go. I don't know who made the world. I have heard them talk of God Almighty, but I don't know who he is. I don't know whether I have ever heard of Jesus Christ or not; I never pray, I'm not taught how; I don't often go to church, I have not the clothes to go in. I stop at house and do nought.*

However, George May could tackle 'Reading made Easy' and had 'a fair knowledge of Christianity', while his 13 year old sister, Mary, could 'read in the Testament', and had 'a little knowledge of Christianity.' The interview with another youngster is more detailed, 'though without the list of questions, apparently inconsequential:

> *I have been to Sunday School; I can read; I don't go to the evening school; I don't know who St. Paul was, nor St. John, but I know about St. Matthew. Jesus Christ was born in heaven, but I don't know what happened to him; he came on earth to commit sin, yes, to commit sin.' Can spell tolerably and can write a little. 'Scotland is a country, but I don't know where it is; I never heard of France.*

Such a set of replies speaks volumes about the state of education among working class children of the 1840's.

New work opportunities and the decline of handloom weaving.

By 1861 the number of handloom weavers in Barnsley had declined markedly, and the trend would continue. In Taylor Row, however, where the community had been more heavily dependant on the loomshop than in some other streets in the town's main weaving district, thirty out of the forty-four households were still headed by weavers. There were another seventeen loomshop workers among these families, as well as seventeen of the lodgers at the time of the Census.

Nevertheless noticeable changes had been taking place, perhaps the most significant being the presence of twelve 'power loom workers', all but one of them females, and mostly young women or girls. It was no longer the custom for all or most of the youngsters in the family to

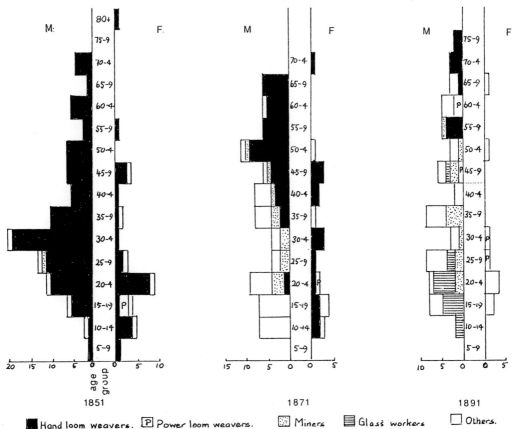

Occupations of the residents of Taylor Row, as recorded in the Censuses. (M=Males; F=Females.) Note the decreasing numbers and increasing ages of handloom weavers over the forty year period.

help in the cottage loomshop. All four daughters of Isaiah Exley, himself a handloom weaver, were power loom weavers.

As mentioned earlier, the power loom had been introduced into Barnsley in the 1830s. Despite this, there was still a role for the handloom. The fact that certain types of fabric could be more profitably made in the cottages than in the factory was among the reasons. Although built to house steam-powered looms, Taylors mill in Peel Street included a handloom shed for a time, until the firm realised that 'they took up too much space'. The mid-century map of the Townend area (Map Five) shows a cluster of mills with their ponds to feed the boilers. It was now truly the town's mill district.

The predominance of females among the mill workers reflected the fact that young men were now looking increasingly towards the expanding coal industry for employment, attracted by the better pay. Barnsley was on its way to becoming the 'Coal Capital' of south Yorkshire. Between 1851 and 1861 the number of colliery workers in Barnsley more than doubled, and would almost double again by 1871. The trend is clearly seen in the illustrations from the Census for Taylor Row in 1851, 1871 and 1891.

There were other alternatives to the loomshop too. The workers living in Taylor Row in 1861 included a brewer, a wire-drawer, a foundry worker, several stone masons, a sawyer and a painter's apprentice, the latter group reflecting the good opportunities in the building trades as the town continued to expand.

A number of men worked at the bobbin mill at Beevor, a short walk away from the Row in Pontefract Road. The 1861 Census records some of the tasks carried out there — tool making, wood turning, sandpapering and polishing. Ten-year old James Birtles was a 'Knocker off' at the factory!

Some of the long-established weavers themselves who lived in the Row were moving to new kinds of work. Jesse Barlow, a weaver in 1841 and 1851, was an agricultural labourer in 1861. John Cherry had found work at one of the nearby breweries by 1861, and John Peech, still a weaver in 1861, would be a collier ten years later.

It seems, however, that the older men tended to adapt to new kinds of work only with difficulty. By 1891 there would still be fifty 'handloom weavers' in Barnsley and the adjacent Worsbrough Common, with an average age of seventy one. Although desperately poor, they were too proud to be admitted to the Workhouse.[20] Robert Darling, who died in 1915 in his eighties, is reputed to have been the very last working handloom weaver in the town. There is evidence that he was still working at the loom in the early years of the twentieth century.[21]

By 1891 only nine of those in Taylor Row whose occupation is

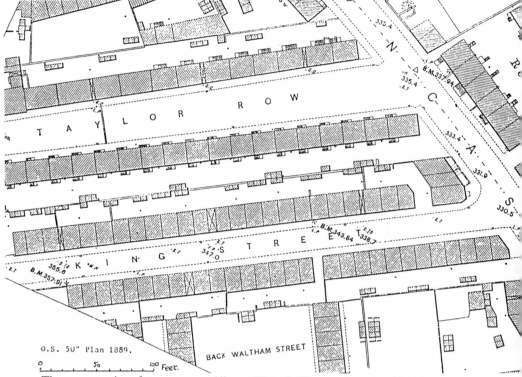

The concentration of steam-powered linen mills in the Townend area in mid-19th century. (O.S. 6″ map of 1851.)

recorded are described as handloom weavers. By this time employment in the local glassworks featured prominently among the variety of occupations, for the Oaks Glassworks and Wood Brothers works in the Hoyle Mill area, but a short distance from the Row, had both opened in 1872.[22] The foundries offered other work opportunities. By the 1870s there were nine of them in the town, two of them cheek-by-jowl with the main handloom weaving area, the Union Foundry in May Day Green, and the Nelson Foundry of Wilson & Longbottom. In the hard working community of Taylor Row sixty-five-year-old David Jackson, who described himself as 'Knocker-up, early morning', would be a key man every working day!

Even power loom operatives formed only a small group among the workers living in the Row by the time of this last census, for the linen industry in Barnsley and district had been facing serious problems for many years. The 'flax famine' of the 1850s, when the supply of flax from Russia was interrupted, had done nothing to inspire confidence in the industry. In the 1860s and '70s labour disputes may have deterred mill owners from investing in new plant, thus weakening the towns'

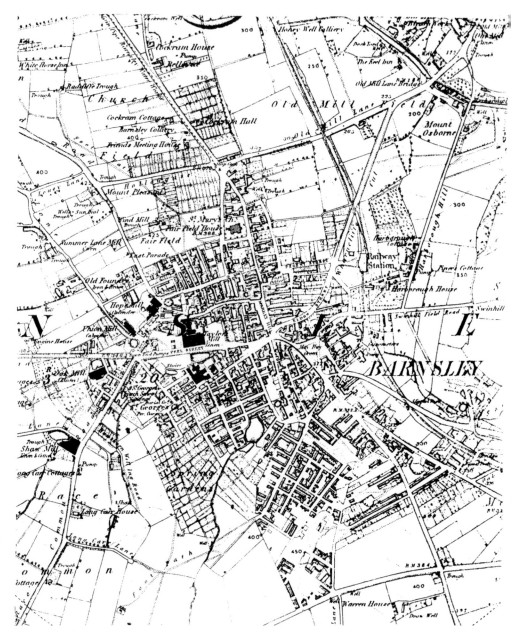

Taylor Row as shown on the Ordnance Survey 50″ plan of 1889. Note the steps to front and back doors of houses on the south side of the street indicating cellars. Cottages on the north side had no cellars but some needed steps to back doors because of the slope of the ground, 'ginnels' giving access to the back yards.

prospects for competing successfully with rivals in Scotland and in Ulster.

There had been labour disputes in the 1860s, but even more serious disagreements arose in 1872 — leading to strikes and lockouts, with power loom operatives out for several months. Eventually a compromised settlement was reached, but after such a length of time that the Barnsley Chronicle was prompted to print a comment that was remarkably prophetic:

Why could not such a settlement have been arrived at six months ago? Why should the sum of £500 odd have been expended in supporting weavers in idleness when they might have been earning their weekly wages and while the masters would have been retaining the linen trade, a considerable portion of which, we feel, has permanently gone from Barnsley.

A Barnsley Trade Directory of 1871 had listed over twenty 'Linen Manufacturers', but by the end of the century there were only seven in the town. By 1913 four of these had gone out of business.

Postscript

The cottages in Taylor Row survived until the 1960s. They had been purchased in 1929 from J. Thornely Taylor by Barnsley Corporation, with a view to the construction of a new link road on the site. The cellars still played a useful role in the domestic life of these small houses, compensating for the limited living accommodation by providing

Here we give our readers a last look at Taylor Row. In the picture the bottom house on the right hand side was occupied when this photograph was taken. As we write there are only one or two houses still occupied in Taylor Row —soon it will be deserted. We shall be sorry to see demolition begun, and this old row of weavers' houses—for so long part of this Parish—disappear.

space for food storage, for laundry work — using the 'copper' and the sink — and play areas for children on occasion. Washing the floor created no problems, apparently, despite the cellar depth, in some at least of these cottages, surplus water being carried away through a drain located in the centre. The replacement of gas by electricity — probably during the 1930s — improved the quality of these modest cottages. One of the last tenants, who had lived here for a very long time, remembered 'some happy years' in Taylor Row.

She remembered too the removal of 'machines' from the cellars during the 1920s. Could these have been the old hand looms making their last journey? And if only looms could talk, what a story these could have told!

Notes & References

1. The cottages appear in the 1825 Rate Valuation List.
2. Document LC 222 W.Y., Registry of Deeds, Wakefield.
3. The Taylor Family of Dodworth. (Typescript) Sam Sykes. Barnsley Local Studies Library (B.L.S.L.).
4. Burland's Annals of Barnsley (Microfilm), B.L.S.L. p.426
5. Report to the General Board of Health, Barnsley. 1852 (B.L.S.L.)
6. Burland. *Op. Cit.* p.235.
7. Hoyle, Eli: *History of Barnsley*, p. 299, B.L.S.L.
9 and 10. Parliamentary Report (I.U.P. 7) Children's Employment, 1842.
11. Keyser Report ('Reports from Assistant Hand-loom Weavers' Commissioners Part II, 1840) p.487.
12. Parl. Report, 1842. I.U.P. 7.
13. Burland, *op. cit.*
14. Roberts, R.A. *op. cit.*
15. Burland, *op. cit.*
16. Roberts, R.A. *op. cit.*
17. Kaijage, *op. cit.*
18. Hoyle, Eli *op. cit.*
19. Parl. Report, 1842. I.U.P. 7.
20. Kaijage, *op. cit.*
21. Photograph of Robert Darling (Barnsley Archives) shows electric light above loom.
22. Ashurst, D. *The History of South Yorkshire Glass*, 1993

Acknowledgements

I acknowledge the valuable assistance received from the staff of Barnsley Local Studies Library and Archives. I thank John Goodchild, Robert Roberts and Michael Stringer for advice or information on particular matters. I also owe a debt to former tenants of Taylor Row and their relatives who supplied details about the cottages: D. Smith of Gawber, K. Mitchell of Barnsley, K. Charnock of Monk Bretton, L. Hall of Dodworth, S. Dutton of Staincross and N. Jennings of Wombwell.

4. PAST FORWARD: TEACHING HISTORY IN BARNSLEY PRIMARY SCHOOLS

by Andy Atkinson

Introduction

THE NATIONAL CURRICULUM EXPECTS CHILDREN aged between five to eleven years old to have an understanding of their past. School teachers throughout the Barnsley area are especially fortunate to have such a varied historic landscape to draw upon to enthuse and excite their pupils. There is an expectation placed upon schools to use educational visits as an essential part of their teaching. The Barnsley Advisory Support and Inspection Service (BASIS) has developed a partnership with various individuals and agencies to help children come to terms with their roots and bring the dim and distant past forwards to the present. Young children require real examples that they can relate to in order to gain some understanding of the past. The following pages illustrate **a few** of the ways that are being used by Barnsley teachers to involve children in their heritage.

Barnsley Local Education Authority has within it boundaries a rich vein of historical buildings that are locally important and help to illustrate national events and changes. The great enterprising families of the nineteenth century can be studied at first hand. The Fitzwilliam's at Elsecar and Spencer-Stanhope's at Cannon Hall, Cawthorne are just two examples. The change that has taken place to town centres is well illustrated through a study of Church Street, Barnsley. Even when pupils are required to study the times of Henry VIII, Monk Bretton Priory offers a wonderful atmosphere to bring the past forward to the present. In this video age the rich resource that exists at Barnsley Central Library in the form of census returns and early photography allow children in primary schools to study their localities in a more interesting way. The use of the computer can help to bring this information into the classroom and make it more easily available to the children. The computer has much to offer the teaching of history.

An addition to the family: the Addy family of Elsecar

The village of Elsecar is famous. The Addy family of Old Row, Elsecar is not famous. Elsecar CE Primary School make considerable use of the rich variety of houses and buildings to help the children to understand some of the benefits of modern life. By paying attention to particular houses from 1841 to 1891 the children can imagine life through the

The Addy Family 1841. By using an artist impression children can begin to imagine family life during the Victorian period. *(drawing by Gary Dutton)*

reign of Queen Victoria. With the help of a computer database children in Jan Hopwood's class became historical detectives and traced a family history:

'Houses in Elsecar and The Addy Family of Old Row by Heather Williams and Lois Oliver aged eleven years, Elsecar C of E Primary School

Disease wasn't rare in the nineteenth century as in many homes conditions were poor. For example, dampness helped to spread Tuberculosis. Many

The Addy Family home as it is today by Michelle Copley aged 11 years. The 1841 to 1891 Census records the address as Old Row, a terrace of 15 households. However, The Addy family used to live on what is now called Wath Road.

people didn't have houses at all. The ones who did were very unhappy with them. One woman tells of the hole over the sewers letting the rats into the room.

The poorer people's houses were drafty because they had no carpets or heavy curtains. There was often one lavatory for twenty or more houses.

The buildings themselves were badly made. They were normally made of sandstone, which weathered well, and the window frames were made from wood, which could rot easily. In some parts of the country houses were built back to back, or in tenements. These houses were very unhygienic and it was not unusual to find people sharing their beds or even their room with pigs and rats!

In Elsecar the picture was very different. People lived in proper houses and had proper drainage. The houses had four rooms, a pantry, a small backcourt, ash pit, a pig sty and a garden. The houses were two shillings a week to rent, which was quite good value. The houses in Elsecar were, as a local report of the time says, "Of a class superior in size and arrangement..."

The Addy family were a large family who lived on Old Row. We have census records of them living on Old Row from 1841 through to 1891. From the records, we have worked out this plan:

In 1841, George and Hannah Addy had met and married each other, and had had six children. William Addy, (eighteen), Anne Addy, (ten), Sarah Addy, (six), Henry Addy, (five), Allis Addy, (three), and Mark Addy, approximately 0.11. We decided to follow Hannah and Mark Addy through the census to 1891.

In 1851, Hannah Addy was fifty-two and still married to George. Mark Addy was ten years old.

In 1861, Hannah Addy was sixty-two and a widow, as George had died between 1851 and 1861. Mark Addy was twenty and unmarried. Mark's brother, Henry, had died in a pit explosion at Elsecar Colliery between 1851 and 1861, aged seventeen. Records show Mark's sister Anne had had Ellen Addy at age thirty out of wedlock.

In 1871, Hannah Addy was seventy-two. Mark Addy was thirty and still unmarried.

In 1881, Mark Addy was forty and now married to Charlotte Addy (thirty-five). They had had two boys, George Henry, (eight) and Frank, (0.8). No records were found of Hannah Addy. Presumed dead.

In 1891, Mark Addy was fifty, Charlotte Addy was forty-five, George Henry Addy was eighteen and unmarried, Frank Addy was ten and Sarah Elizabeth, a new addition to the family, was five.

This information was collected from a computer database. Some information was unreliable and inaccurate, so has been altered.

Along with the Addy family, you may have found members of the Stitch family, the Hurst family, the Evans family, the Wigfield family, the Blenkinsop family, the Crawley family, the Rodgers family, the Litchfield family, the Rigley family, the Cooper family and many more.

The average number of children per family in each house on Old Row in 1841 was six. Altogether, a staggering ninety-eight people lived on Old Row between 1841 and 1851, aged from 0.5 to seventy-three years old.

If you come to Elsecar today, you will not find the Addy house on the row known today as Old Row. We know what was previously known as Old Row is now Wath Road.'

By Heather Williams and Lois Oliver, Year 6.

By involving children in real research they can begin to question the validity of records and make informed judgements about the past. Did Mark Addy name his first born son after his father and eldest brother? Why did Mark marry so late in his life? Why did Charlotte come from Hatfield to Elsecar to get married? Where are the descendents of Mark now?

Upstairs, Downstairs: working life at Cannon Hall

Cannon Hall at Cawthorne is the 'jewel in the crown' for schoolchildren if they wish to experience an aspect of the past. Cannon Hall is the former home of the Spencer-Stanhope family who sold the property to the County Borough of Barnsley in 1953. The basement area has been restored to a late Victorian kitchen and servant's working area. The Victoria Servant Day for Schools began in February 1995 and has met with universal acclaim. It is now possible for children to visit the 'big house' and bring the past forward to the present by reliving life as a

Apprentice servant Stephen Hey, aged 6 of Gooseacre Primary School, takes a lesson from head laundry maid, Mrs Walton who is normally a dinner supervisor at his school.

Working in the arches.
1. We got the Saddles out
2. Then we got the polish and clothes out
3. And then we started polishing with a Saddle brush.
4. We gave it a real good Scrub.

Working in the Arches at Cannon Hall: Natalie recorded her memories of "sprucing up the tack" for the groom at Cannon Hall when her class visited Cannon Hall Kitchens as part of their topic work on Victorian Britain.

downstairs servant. Many Barnsley schoolchildren have had the opportunity to be bossed around by Cook and the Butler. Children as young as four years old have had an experience and a taste of the past in the kitchens at Cannon Hall. Others have laid fires, black-leaded the range, cleaned boots and silverware, prepared food as well as planted out the potatoes in the historic walled garden.

The range of experiences at Cannon Hall offer many opportunities for follow up work and discussion about history. Taking young children back in time beyond the memory of their grandparents presents a particular challenge for the Primary teacher. By reconstructing the past in a particular setting gives the children a tangible experience that will allow the teacher to discuss the differences and similarities with some greater meaning.

Children at Dodworth Keresforth Road Primary School have visited the Cannon Hall Kitchens as part of their topic work on Victorian Britain. Many activities at the Hall allowed class teacher Matthew Harris to become involved in detailed follow up work about the late Victorian period. Natalie Noble, aged eight, decided to record her experience of cleaning and polishing a saddle.

Cawthorne CE Primary School have made full use of the proximity of the Hall to their school by drawing on the potential of the Kitchen area for their topic work. The children even went to the lengths of changing their names to be in sympathy with the Victorian period and the setting. Claire Wicks, aged nine, became Victoria for the day when she visited the Kitchens. The detail of her written work recorded in her 'diary' entry for 5th May 1892 is evidence of how involved she became with her reliving of the past...

Diary entry 5th May 1892...4:30am
I am Victoria Alice Wicks. I am 9 years old and I am a servant. I get up at 4 o'clock and get dressed because I know it is a special day. It is Miss Alice Mildred's wedding day. I have got a hard day's work ahead of me. I get up out of bed. All of the other servants are up. I walk out of the bedroom and go down the back stairs. I am working in the scullery. I have breakfast at 4:30.

I went to get the hot water ready and the butler came in.

"Haven't you got started yet Wicks? Make some snowflakes with the grater immediately. Here's some washing get cracking."

I grated the soap and poured the hot water into the tubs. I got three dolly tubs and two possers a dolly peg, a rubbing board and a mangle. I washed the day clothes in soapy water then mangled them, then I rinsed them. I mangled them again and hung them outside. It was time for my lunch. I had lots more washing to do... I went to bed at 11 o'clock.

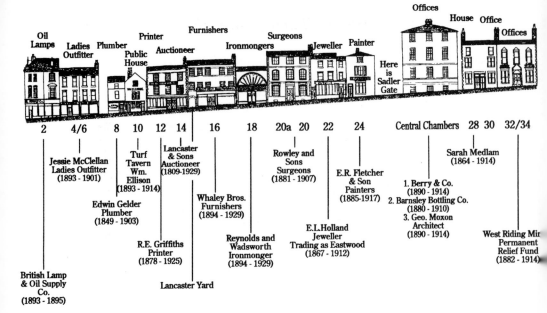

Church Street 1895. Teresa Carr from Planning Services spent many hours examining photographs of the period to draw up a fascinating profile of the buildings which were eventually demolished to make way for the Town Hall which was finished in 1933.

A changing townscape: Church Street, Barnsley

The streets of Barnsley Town Centre have changed in many respects over the last 100 years. Church Street, previously known as Kirk Gate, once resembled a street from York or Chester: narrow, jumbled and chaotic! Most of the buildings have since been demolished or improved to make room for the Town Hall or more modern forms of transport. With the help of Barnsley Council's Planning Services, the Church Street of the 1890s has been recreated in the form of drawings and a set of model buildings. Children can now rebuild the street and examine contemporary photographs to see how life has changed in Barnsley.

Year 6 class teacher, Lesley Schofield at Darfield Upperwood Primary School, enthused her children in a study of Victorian Church Street. She guided them into the lifestyles of those households living along the 1891 street by bringing to life the 1891 Census Returns and using the pioneering photography of the time. An example of their work is typified by a team effort including Matthew Larvan, Mellissa Merrills, Gemma Embleton and Jamie Jackson, aged ten, who investigated 21 Church Street on their class Apple Mac computer database. This group was asked to use their artistic talents and knowledge of the period to draw an impression of the household and make certain deductions from their investigations.

Find out all you can about the
Sadler family
who lived at
21 Church Street

Jot down the facts you discover and any inferences or deductions
you could make from them as to the lifestyle of the family.

**Here are some facts about the residents of 21 Church Street from the
Census of 1891.**

Michael Sadler was the head of the household. He was 57 years old. He was born in
1834 in Barnsley. His occupation was a Physician and Surgeon for M.D. Lond. At the time
of the census he was married and unemployed.

Anne Sadler was married to Michael. She was 51 years old. She was born in 1840 in
West Farrington, Lincolnshire. She was a housewife.

Mary Sadler was the daughter of Michael. She was 15. She was born in 1876 in
Barnsley. She was a scholar.

Evelyn was Michael's granddaughter. She was 5 in the census of 1891. She was born in
1886 in Cheltenham, Gloucester.

Aretha was Michael and Anne's other granddaughter. She was 5. She was born in 1886
in Cheltenham, Gloucester.

Michael was the grandson of Michael and Anne Sadler. He was 4 and born in 1887. He
was born in Cheltenham, Gloucester.

The Sadler Family had 3 servants:

Susannah Hornsby was a domestic servant, who was 26 and single. Susannah was
born in 1865 in Donnington on Baine, Lincolnshire.

Harrieta Bodger was a domestic servant and nurse. Harrieta was 26 and single. She
was born in 1865 in Elton, Huntingdon.

Emily Howard was 21 and single. She was born in 1870 in Pickhills, Yorkshire. She was
a domestic cook and servant.

We think that the Sadler family were quite rich. We will tell you about the reasons. They
have got 3 servants which was very unusual for those days. Another thing is that they
have got 9 people living in the house. So it must have been a big house. The last reason
is that their daughter, Mary, is still at school at the age of 15. We think that the Sadler
family were one of the richest in Church Street. We think that the grandchildren are there
either because they are on a visit or their parents have gone away. The 2 granddaughters
Aretha and Evelyn may be twins as they were both born in the same place and the same
year. Another puzzling thing is that Mary is the only child in the house so there must have
been another child who had Michael, Aretha and Evelyn.

Tell the class what you have discovered.

Facts and deductions about 21, Church Street 1891 by Matthew Larvan,
Mellissa Merrills, Gemma Embleton and Jamie Jackson, aged 10.

The Sadler Household

Michael Sadler — Anne Sadler — Mary Sadler — Evelyn — Aretha — Michael — Susannah Hornsby — Harrieta Bodger — Emily Howard

The Sadler household, 21, Church Street, 1891. Matthew Larvan, Mellissa Merrils, Gemma Embleton and Jamie Jackson, aged 10, have their impressions of the Sadler household. Notice the type of dress for Mr Sadler compared with that of the servants uniforms.

Schedule 117

Parish or District St. Mary

Address (street or road) 21 Church Street

Year of Census 1891

First name Harrietta

Surname Bodger

Sex F

Relation to head of household servant

Condition as to marriage single

Andy and Stewart
Connections at BASIS

Age 26   **Year born** 1865

Occupation Nurse domestic

Employment status employed

0226 281961

Place of birth Elton Huntingdon

Disability

Special comments

Census Record for 21, Church Street, 1891. The census records have been re-presented in a form that is more easily recognisable yet hopefully keeping true to their original integrity. Children can explore the information held on the database and become motivated to ask their own questions. For example, what types of jobs did women have 1891?

Street Games by Brueghel. The games in this painting give us a clue about life as a child during Tudor times here in Barnsley. Some of these games are still played in school playgrounds.

Let's have a brawl: Tudor Life.

Barnsley's past is long and interesting. The dim and distant past needs to be made fun especially when teachers are required to go back as far as Tudor times. Even this period has been brought forward with the help of imaginative teaching and timely visits to historic sites. Barnsley has a unique resource in the shape of Monk Bretton Priory which is under the care of English Heritage. Tudor England has certainly left its mark on Barnsley. What was it like to live next to the Priory at the time of Henry VIII?

The street games of the past can be replayed together with the music of the time by carefully selecting contemporary paintings and drawing on the expertise of period musicians. Hundreds of Barnsley schoolchildren have had a good brawl at the Priory! A medieval brawl was simply a rustic sing-a-long and dance session which over time has acquired its more modern connotations.

Children from Sue Rowlands class at Worsbrough Bank End Primary School found out at first hand what it was like to brawl and listen to

Tudor life. Children from Worsbrough Bank End Primary School bring the past forward to the present at Monk Bretton Priory. English bagpipes help to get things rolling along with the help of Tudor musician Rick Heavisides. *(reproduced courtesy of the* Yorkshire Post)

the sounds of medieval musical instruments including English bagpipes. Bagpipes first made their way into England when Crusaders returned from the Holy Lands. The more famous Scottish bagpipes are the **younger** cousins of their more southerly neighbour! The children dressed as Tudor children and were left with a lasting impression of the sites and sounds of Tudor Barnsley.

The Spirit of Ardsley: aspects of local history

Computers in primary school classrooms are beginning to have a meaningful impact on the teaching of history especially when the learning is set in a local context. Children at Ardsley Oaks Junior School used their Apple Macintosh Computers in a study of the local area. Ardsley is an ancient Parish with many interesting buildings and reminders of past forms of transport to draw upon. Over centuries Stairfoot has been the meeting place of cart, barge, steam, and rail. The Census Returns for 1881 became the starting point for some imaginative writing by Sean Popplewell and Darren Perry in Miss Anna Straw's class. Both young historians worked hard to get into the mind of William Smith, a master of the Royal Oak in 1881. Sean and Darren are ten years old and used their word processing skills to compose the following...

> *...It was William Smith's birthday and it was a cold and wet day. That night he was passing the Keel Inn on the Dearne-Dove Canal and he decided to call in for a decent meal and a soft and comfortable bed for a change. When he got into bed he felt really snug. It was better than his bed on the barge. In the morning he got up feeling sleepy. At first he did not recognise where he was. He went downstairs for breakfast. It was a pleasant change for him not to have to cook it himself. He didn't want to go back to his barge but he saw what a pleasant day it was - besides he could not live life on the land for long. He really liked his stay at the Keel Inn.*

The stimulus for this work came from the Census Record which was supplied to the School by the Barnsley Archives Service. The spirit of Ardsley lives on through the interest shown by such youngsters and their teachers.

Dressing children and adults in period costumes is always interesting. This is especially true when the clothing is real. Roy Young is such a collector of the most personal of antiques and was invited to Ardsley Oaks Junior School to involve the children in another aspect of the past. Each of the garments collected by Roy has a story to tell about the original owner. Through the use of real costumes children can see and feel for themselves just how much taller and bigger we are compared with 100 years ago. They begin to understand the difference between

Headteacher, Tony Heald, Sarah Winfield aged 9, parent Liz Jones together with Jack Hopper aged 9 and James Whyke, aged 8 at Ardsley Oaks Junior School bring the past forward to the present by dressing in authentic costumes provided by Roy Young. (Barnsley Chronicle: Town Edition 7/7/95)

garments worn for fashion and those designed for work. Smocks, aprons and overalls were designed to last. The work stimulated by Roy involves children in thinking about diet, technology, materials and the science of dyeing.

Conclusion

Barnsley teachers are full of enthusiasm about the many stories relating to the past character and events of the area. This enthusiasm is also found throughout the town and is a rich resource that manifests itself in the high number of local history and heritage groups. At times schools can be the focus of this energy so that the Barnsley story can continue to be told. The local historians of the future are the school children of today.

Acknowledgements

1. Elsecar:
Gary Dutton, Graphic Designer, Barnsley MBC; Christine Roebuck, Elsecar CE Primary School; Jan Hopwood, Elsecar CE Primary School; Matthew Lovatt, BASIS.
2. Cannon Hall:
Val Wilkinson, Cannon Hall; Peter Starling, Cannon Hall; Geoff Sawyer, Headteacher, Cawthorne CE Primary School; Matthew Harris, Dodworth Keresforth Primary School.
3. Barnsley, Church Street:
John Hislop, Conservation Officer, Barnsley MBC; Teresa Carr, Design Unit, Planning Services, Barnsley MBC; Lesley Schofield, Darfield Upperwood Primary School, Sally Horsfield, BASIS.
4. Monk Bretton Priory:
Heautbois: Helen and Rick Heavisides; Steve Poxton and Sue Rowlands, Worsbrough Bank End Primary School, Jim Watts, Monk Bretton Priory; *Yorkshire Post*.
5. Ardsley:
Tony Heald, Headteacher and Anna Straw, Ardsley Oaks Junior School; Roy Young, a collector; Barnsley Archives and Local Studies.

Barnsley for Kids | **Localising the National Curriculum**
Information Handling: Evidence:-Census material

Census records:-

We have put the details of the Census on to the computer by using a database program called ClarisWorks.

The headings are the same as the Census but it is easier to read and is more helpful to find out answers to our questions.

Census records like this are kept at Barnsley Central Library in the Archive Department. The people there are very helpful.

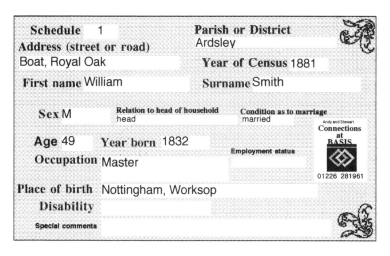

Census Return for the Keel Inn 1881. This entry was sent to Ardsley Oaks Junior School by the Barnsley Archives Service.

5. IRONSTONE MINING AT TANKERSLEY IN THE NINETEENTH CENTURY FOR ELSECAR AND MILTON IRONWORKS

by Melvyn Jones

WHEN MINING IN SOUTH YORKSHIRE is mentioned, most people think 'coal', but the first mineral to be exploited was ironstone, and miners ignored the coal seams and simply dug through them to get at the ironstone below. This was because the fuel for smelting the iron until well into the eighteenth century was not coal but charcoal made from the underwood and branchwood from local coppice woods. Mining for ironstone in South Yorkshire continued until the last quarter of the nineteenth century when a combination of dwindling supplies of easily exploited ore and the opening of new orefields at home and abroad made its further mining in South Yorkshire unprofitable. George Dawes, who had become the tenant of both the Elsecar and Milton Ironworks in 1849, 'imported' Frodingham ironstone from north Lincolnshire from the late 1850s to supplement and eventually to replace local supplies. Within a few years he set up a new ironworks, the Trent Ironworks, in Scunthorpe in 1864. He gave up the Elsecar and Milton operations in 1884, by which time local ironstone mining had already come to an end.[1]

This article is concerned with the exploitation of three seams of ironstone on Earl Fitzwilliam's[2] estate at Tankersley from 1795 until 1879 for Elsecar Ironworks, which was opened in 1795, and the nearby Milton Ironworks at Hoyland which was opened some time between 1799 and 1802. Ironstone had been mined at Tankersley (on the southern edge of the parish) before 1795 to supply the Chapel (Chapeltown) Furnace and a number of seams continued to be mined extensively to the west of the Tankersley Ironstone outcrop from about 1794 until about 1880 to supply Newton Chambers' Thorncliffe Ironworks.[3] As we shall see, there were arguments from time to time because of supposed infringements of mineral leases granted to the various tenants at Tankersley.

A feature of added interest is that much of the mining activity at Tankersley took place within a medieval deer park. The deer park was in existence by the early fourteenth century, contained about 250 deer in the 1650s, and when Daniel Defoe went on his *Tour Through the Whole Island of Britain* in the early eighteenth century, he said the park at Tankersley contained some of the biggest red deer in Europe.[4] Figure 1 shows the park in about 1730. As mining gradually encroached on

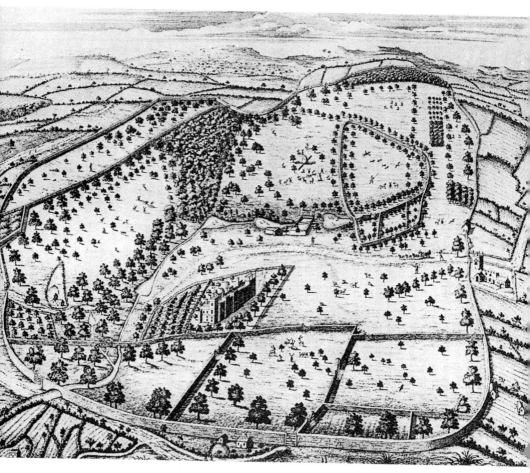

Figure 1. Tankersley Park from the east in c.1730. The artist has changed the orientation of Tankersley Church: it should be aligned east-west with the tower at the west end.

the park in the nineteenth century, the deer were restricted to an ever decreasing area and they were eventually relocated at Wentworth in the 1850s when the herd consisted of about fifty-five red deer.[5] The story of the extension of mining for ironstone at Tankersley is, as the following account will show, coloured by doubts in the 5th Earl Fitzwilliam's mind of the wisdom of allowing, at worst, the despoliation of the park or, at best, a change in landscape character to take place, something that was inevitable because of the mining methods employed.

GEOLOGICAL BACKGROUND

The geological context in which ironstone mining took place at Tankersley is relatively simple. Two of the ironstone seams in question — Tankersley Ironstone and Swallow Wood Ironstone — outcrop

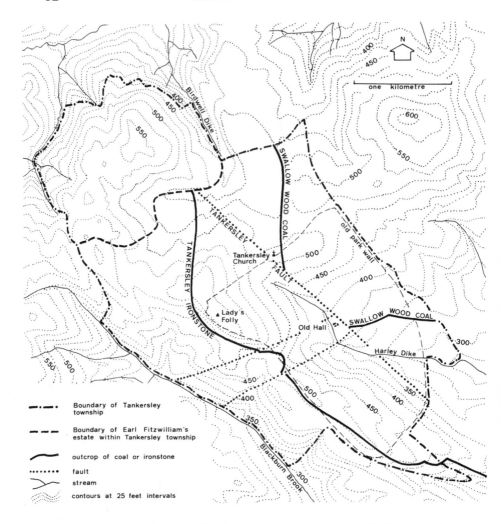

Figure 2. Tankersley township showing the outcrop of the Tankersley and Swallow Wood Ironstone seams.

within the parish and dip gently, at a gradient of about 1 in 12, to the north-east (Figure 2). The third seam, Lidgett ironstone, does not outcrop in Tankersley township. All three seams are affected by faulting, causing steps to occur in the dipping strata as shown in Figure 3.

The Tankersley Ironstone seam (also referred to in the nineteenth century as the Tankersley Mine, the Tankersley Park Bed, Musselshell Ironstone, Musselband Ironstone and Black Ironstone[6]) outcrops within the Fitzwilliam Tankersley estate in a broad arc extending from a point about 500 metres west of Tankersley School, southwards to the vicinity of the present Tankersley Manor Hotel, and then south-eastwards just outside the park wall until it reaches Warren Lane where it outcrops within the park boundary. From Warren Lane the outcrop runs across the Sheffield-Barnsley road (A6135) and leaves Tankersley just south of Barley Hole Springs. The broad arc of the outcrop is broken by two faults as shown in Figure 2. In a pit sunk in the nineteenth century the seam was forty-seven metres (fifty yards) deep 650 metres east of the outcrop and at Skiers Spring pumping pit in Hoyland about two kilometres east of the outcrop it was 137 metres (150 yards) deep.

Tankersley Ironstone is shelly, hence its alternative names of Mussellshell or Musselband Ironstone. It consists of between two and four bands of nodules separated by beds of shale; the ironstone and shale together vary in thickness from between two and eight feet (seventy to 234 centimetres). In pits near Hood Hill in the early nineteenth century the ironstone was about nine inches (twenty-three centimetres) thick; near the present Tankersley Manor Hotel it was twelve inches thick. On the Rockley estate it was eighteen inches (forty-six centimetres) thick. Because of it varying thickness, the yield per acre (the basis of the mining leases) varied, but averaged about 2,000 tons.

The Swallow Wood coal and ironstone seams take their name from a wood in the park at Wentworth. The ironstone occurs just above the coal seam. It is sometimes referred to as White Mine. The outcrop of the seam parallels that of the Tankersley Park Ironstone, about one kilometre to the east, from the northern boundary of the parish to the vicinity of Tankersley Church Yard. From there as far as the Old Hall, coinciding with the line of the Tankersley Fault, it does not outcrop,

Figure 3. Section across Tankersley township and Hoyland Nether from south-west to north-east showing the Tankersley, Swallow Wood and Lidgett Ironstone seams and the effect of faulting on the depth of the seams.

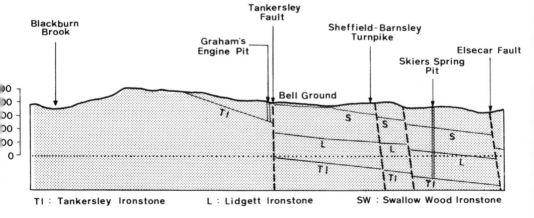

TI : Tankersley Ironstone   L : Lidgett Ironstone   SW : Swallow Wood Ironstone

but the outcrop reappears on Black Lane to the east of Tankersley Old Hall and runs generally eastward until it leaves the township just to the north-east of the old Wentworth railway station (Figure 2).

A sample of Swallow Wood Ironstone examined in the 1870s is reported to have consisted of 'balls of hard closely-grained light brown ironstone, embedded in shale'.[7] This ironstone occurred very near the surface east of the outcrop and at a shaft at Skiers Spring over 400 m to the east of the Tankersley parish boundary, it was still only 28.3 metres (thirty-one yards) below the surface. The average output per acre was about 1920 tons which would mean, on average, about 26.7 centimetres (10.5 inches) of workable ironstone in the seam.

Lidgett (or Lidgate) Ironstone, named after Lidgett Lane between Birdwell and Pilley, occurs above the coal seam of the same name (see Figure 3) and was mined for only a short period in the 1850s and 1860s from the Skiers Spring pit in Hoyland Nether township. In the estate account books the tonnages mined were always combined with those of the Swallow Wood Ironstone.

THE DEVELOPMENT OF IRONSTONE MINING AT TANKERSLEY, 1795-1879

Altogether more than 1,674,000 tons of ironstone were mined at Tankersley and in neighbouring parts of Hoyland Nether and Wentworth townships between 1795 and 1879. The geographical development of mining activity is summarised in Figure 4. Eight different areas of mining can be identified : six areas of mining for Tankersley Ironstone, one for Swallow Wood Ironstone and one for Lidget Ironstone.

Mining at Hood Hill for Elsecar Ironworks 1795-1836 (area A on Figure 4A)

During this period ironstone was mined over an extensive area from many small and shallow workings mostly inside the old park wall but in the last five years or so mining extended eastwards out of the old park and into Wentworth township. Until the year ending on Lady Day (25 March) 1827 the mining at Hood Hill was carried on by John Darwin and Co and after that date directly by Earl Fitzwilliam.

When Darwins' began their ironstone mining operations at Hood Hill, they were not working in an untried area. Systematic mining for Tankersley Ironstone right at the outcrop had preceded them by at least fifty years. An estate map, dated 1749, of the southern edge of Tankersley parish shows old and new ironstone grounds within the deer park including an area of pits in Hollin Delph (delph = pit).[8] In

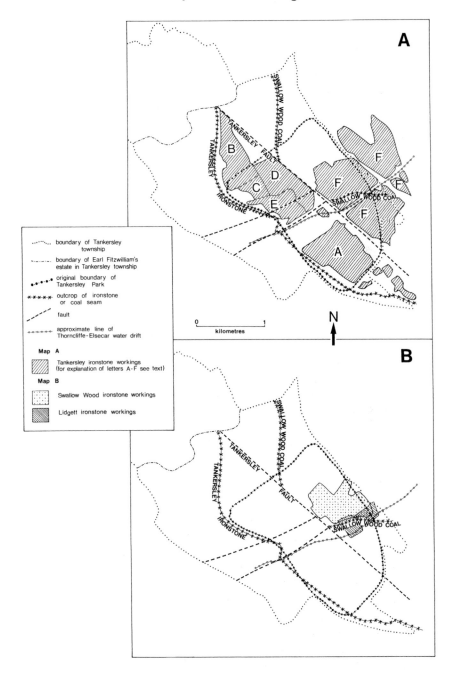

Figure 4. Geographical movement of ironstone mining in Tankersley township and adjacent parts of Hoyland Nether and Wentworth townships.

the same general area Fairbank in his 1772 survey noted an area 'Full of Old Pits' and another with 'Many New Ironstone Pits'.[9] Hollin Delph became Delph Hills in the ninteenth century and estate maps and the early Ordnance Survey maps show many small pit hills covering the whole area. More recently, in the 1950s, during opencast coal mining operations, many small ironstone pits, between eleven and twenty-one feet deep, were discovered to the west and further away from the outcrop than those already noted.

Smith, Stacey and Co who were negotiating to build a furnace at Elsecar and mine ironstone at Hood Hill in the early 1790s before the lease went to Darwins', were well aware that other ironstone miners had preceded them. On 24 December, 1793, Charles Bowns, Earl Fitzwilliam's legal representative, wrote to the Earl to say that 'Stacye & Co decline entering into an Article till they have found the bed of Iron Stone which they are now digging for in Shirt's Ground'.[10] Shirt's Ground was John Shirt's Farm which occupied much of what is now Hood Hill Plantation. Just over a month later on 29 January, 1794, Bowns wrote to the Earl again: '...Stacye and Co are sinking into Shirt's land, but have been much interrupted by the Old Hollows...'[11] The first ironstone rent - for half a year - was paid by Darwins' on Lady Day 1796. This was presumably for the period 24 September, 1795 to 25 March, 1796. The method of collecting ironstone rents from Darwins' until 1812-13 makes it impossible to state with certainty when the first ironstone was mined. Until that date they paid rent for one acre (which would have produced about 2000 tons of ironstone) whether they mined any ore or not. Darwins' paid the minimum rent for half of the year 1795-96, for the whole of the year 1796-97 and for the year 1798-99. In 1797-98 they paid one year's rent and rent for an additional two acres, one rood and ten perches, i.e. they mined three acres - one rood - ten perches in all. No doubt some ironstone was being obtained from late 1795, but in the early stages at least as much effort would be expanded on sinking shafts and making a sough as in mining the ironstone. As Darwins' Elsecar furnace was reported to have been in blast as early as 24 November, 1795, they were evidently obtaining substantial ironstone supplies from elsewhere in the first few years of their operation at Elsecar. From 1800-01 until 1811-12 Darwins' output was relatively consistent and averaged just over 10,000 tons per year from Hood Hill. Their lowest annual output was 6,113 tons in 1802-03. In two years - 1817-18 and 1822-23 - they mined no ironstone at all, and their average annual output from 1812-13 until they gave up the Elsecar Works was less than 2,500 tons.

The anxiety of Darwins' over their ironstone supplies towards the close of the first decade of the nineteenth century is reflected in a letter from Charles Bowns to Earl Fitzwilliam in December 1809:

> *Messrs Darwin are boring in different places in order to find Stone for Supplying their Furnaces, when that in Shirt's Farm is exhausted — they have some thoughts of erecting another Furnace on the north side of Skiers Spring not far from Stead to which they mean to bring ironstone from Mr Vernon's estate.*[12]

The Vernon estate was at Rockley in Worsbrough township where Tankersley Ironstone, as noted above, was reported to be 45.7cm (eighteen inches) thick. These plans never came to fruition. A letter written to Earl Fitzwilliam by William Newman, Charles Bowns' successor as the Earl's legal representative in South Yorkshire, in December 1818, gives a contemporary assessment of the likely life of the ironstone reserves at Hood Hill after more than twenty years' exploitation by the firm:

> *... but as there is every reason to believe that the remaining Bed of Ironstone in Shirt's Farm and at Hood Hill will be exhausted by one Furnace in five or six years... Messrs Darwin, however, should be requested to keep one Furnace constantly at work with your Lordships Ironstone.*[13]

In the event, ironstone was mined at Hood Hill for another decade after Earl Fitzwilliam took over the direct running of Elsecar ironworks in 1827 through an arrangement to mine under Widow Rawson's land on the eastern extremity of Tankersley township and beyond in Wentworth township. In the meantime, Hood Hill Plantation was created on the abandoned workings.

It seems, from occasional references in the estate correspondence that by 1836 ironstone for Elsecar Ironworks was being obtained from the Greasbrough area and this may well have continued into the next decade.

Mining at Upper Tankersley for Milton Ironworks 1801-1836 (*area B on Figure 4A*)

Mining was carried on successfully at Upper Tankersley by Walkers' (from 1801-1821), Hartop and Sorby (1821-1825), Hartop and Graham (1825-1829) and Grahams' (1829-1836). According to the estate account books, the lessees named above mined just over eighty-one acres at Upper Tankersley between 1801 and 1836 and this coincides almost exactly with the combined acreages of Potter Holes Plantation, Twelve Lands Plantation, Town Close (later Tankersley) Plantation and two paddocks — Newbiggin and Far Newbiggin — just inside the old park wall immediately to the south of Town Close Plantation. In the three plantations evidence of ironstone mining in the form of shale mounds is very clear and relatively little levelling appears to have been done before planting took place (which was under way by 1820). The pit waste in the two Newbiggin paddocks was levelled and the land returned to agricultural use after mining had ceased.

The first time ironstone at Upper Tankersley was mentioned was in early December 1796 when Charles Bowns reported to Earl Fitzwilliam that:

> *A shaft has been sunk in your Lordship's land between Hangmanstone Tollgate and Tankersley and a very rich band of the black as well as the White Mine of ironstone has been found at a depth of 13 yards with a good roof, which will render it as valuable as the seam now working by Messrs Darwin and Company.*[14]

Walkers' signed a contract with Earl Fitzwilliam the following year, the first annual rent for the furnace at Milton was paid in 1799 and the first annual rent for ironstone was paid on Lady Day, 1802. From sporadic mentions to drainage to agricultural land and to land taken in hand to be planted after the cessation of mining, it appears that the Walkers' began their operations in what is now Potter Holes Plantation and then gradually the scene of operations moved southwards along the outcrop towards the park.

The pattern and extent of mining at Upper Tankersley might have been different if faulting had not curtailed mining to the east. Late in 1809, when about eighteen acres of land had been mined along the outcrop, Walkers' sought permission to obtain additional ironstone supplies to feed a second furnace which they wished to build at the Milton Works. Bowns intimated to them that it was doubtful that Earl Fitzwilliam would agree to this, but permission was given and in November 1810 Walkers wrote to Earl Fitzwilliam to report on the progress of the borings — which were further to the east of their current workings, down the dip — and to request further permissions:

> *As the experiments for boring for Ironstone at Tankersley have thus far turned out favourably and promise a supply for an additional furnace at Milton, we wish to be preparing for Building also to begin as early as possible to drive a new Sough.*[15]

They went on to say that the onset of winter would delay work on the new furnace until Spring, but that the work on the sough 'might go forward immediately.'

A week later Bowns wrote again to the Walkers' informing them that the Earl wished to know the exact location of the ironstone that they intended to mine. Their reply, on 14 November, besides confirming

that boring was still continuing, gave details of their intended method
of draining the ironstone measures:

> ...*the range of the ironstone will be ascertained by the Boring now
> going on... There cannot be a doubt of a sufficient supply of Ironstone,
> the work of drying it points out itself, by a Sough up the valley from
> Birdwell.*[16]

They went on to ask permission to 'get the Ironstone up to the Park',
pointing out that the Rector of Tankersley had offered them the ironstone
in the glebe land, part of which lay between their current workings and
the park. The letter makes it clear that this permission was being sought
to provide an easily obtained supply of ironstone at the outcrop while
the deeper workings were being prepared. On 20 November Bowns
communicated to Walkers' that Earl Fitzwilliam and Lord Milton would
not agree 'for the Ironstone to be got in the two paddocks situated
between your present works and the park'.[17] The two paddocks in
question were the Newbiggin and the Far Newbiggin Paddocks which
had originally been part of the open parkland but had been enclosed
by walls sometime after 1750. The Grahams' were subsequently allowed
to mine in the paddocks.

By the end of December, 1810, Walkers' were boring 400 yards (366
metres) east of their workings along the outcrop and by early February,
1811, Joshua Biram, the Earl's colliery steward was able to report to
Earl Fitzwilliam that:

> *Messrs Walker seem much pleased with their success in boring at
> Tankersley having found the iron mine to their satisfaction for five
> hundred yards* [457 metres] *upon the deep of their first winning of the
> mine... I have been taking a Level for Messrs Walkers Borings at
> Tankersley this Day in order to ascertain the situation in the valley
> towards Rockley for beginning their new Drift for mining more of
> this Iron Mine upon the Deep of what they have already got...*'[18]

Later that same year these preparations for deeper mining of Tankersley
ironstone were abandoned because of the Tankersley fault (see Figures
1 and 2), whose existence did not seem to have been known when the
borings began. This turn of events was made clear in correspondence
in December 1814 in connection with a disagreement between Earl
Fitzwilliam and Walkers' over a second furnace at the Milton works
which, it was maintained on the Earl's behalf, should have been built
only in conjunction with the extension of ironstone mining at Upper
Tankersley, rather than by obtaining further supplies from elsewhere.
Charles Bowns wrote to Earl Fitzwilliam:

*The Ground in which the Iron Ore intended to have been demised for
the 2nd furnace is situate to the north west of that coloured red in the
sketch also enclosed, towards the Toll Bar, and in consequence of the
Treaty so made, the necessary Borings, Sough, drivings &c were began
and proceeded in until some time in 1811 when it was discovered that
the Iron Stone Bed was thrown down so much below the Level of the
intended Sough, that it could not be got by virtue of it, not without
an Engine, and on that account I was informed by Mr Jon W. that
they had totally abandoned any further pursuit of that Mine...*[19]

The sketch referred to in the letter has not survived. It is interesting
to note that the north-eastern boundary of Potter Holes Plantation,
which was planted on old ironstone pit heaps, coincides exactly with
the line of the Tankersley fault.

Because of the downthrow of the ironstone at the Tankersley fault
and the need to install a pumping engine to drain the ironstone to the
east of the fault, mining continued at the outcrop, progressing in a
southerly direction towards the park and presumably - there are no
documentary or cartographic records - to the east of already mined
areas, at greater depths. By December 1818 when a new lease was being
entered into by Walkers', in succession to the twenty-one year lease
they had signed in 1797, William Newman reminded the Earl that 'the
Lease that is now intended to be granted is only for ten years, because it
is calculated that the supply of Ironstone cannot possibly overreach
that period.' Later in the same letter he is even more pessimistic and
refers to the probable Failure of the supply of Ironstone even within
that Term...'[20]

On Lady Day 1821 Walkers' gave up the Milton works, and their
place as lessees of the iron works and the ironstone grounds at Upper
Tankersley was taken by Hartop and Sorby until 1825, Hartop and
Graham until 1829 and, by the Graham partnership alone until sometime
in 1835-36. By the latter date, although Grahams' were mining the
Swallow Wood Ironstone at Bell Ground on the eastern edge of
Tankersley Park, they were almost at the end of their 'get' in the two
Newbiggin paddocks inside the old park wall at Upper Tankersley
(shown in Figure 4A as that part of area B inside the original boundary
of Tankersley Park), and they were in some difficulties over future iron
ore supplies in the short term.

The Grahams' at the 'Top of the Park' 1836-1841 *(area C on Figure 4A)*

This short period witnessed the first entry of ironstone mining by the
Graham partnership into the northern half of the already greatly
shrunken park. It was also marked by the intense rivalry between the
Milton, Elsecar and Thorncliffe ironworks over local ironstone supplies.

At the centre of the drama — for that is how it emerges in the correspondence between the protagonists — was Tankersley Park, already greatly reduced, and threatened by complete disparkment. A letter from William Newman to Earl Fitzwilliam on 10 July 1835 contains the first reference to preparations for a major new ironstone mining development:

> *Their* [Grahams'] *supply of Ironstone in the Paddocks is now nearly exhausted, and I should advise your Lordship not to allow more to be gotten, until their arrears for Ironstone Farm and Cottage Rents at the least are discharged. Mr Hartops borings have not turned out quite so satisfactory as he expected, but even if the Winning be decided upon as he recommended, two years must elapse before it be available.*[21]

The 'Paddocks' referred to in this correspondence, as has already been pointed out, lay just inside the old park wall in the north-western corner of Tankersley Park. Being near the outcrop of the Tankersley Ironstone seam, the ironstone was obtained by means of many small pits and would have left the ground heavily disturbed. The paddocks were then levelled. In the 1841-42 survey books, the paddocks are described in the remarks column as 'been pits now reclaimed'.[22]

The borings referred to in Newman's letter were for the new deep ironstone pit between Tankersley Old Hall and St. Peter's Church which was to come into production in 1839 and would allow mining under the park without disturbing the surface (see below). It is not clear whether the borings (these would have been to test for the depth and thickness of the seam, not the actual sinking of a shaft) were being carried out by Henry Hartop or his son John, who had been appointed to assist him in 1833. It was John Hartop who supervised the sinking of the Skiers Spring ironstone pit between 1838-49 (see below).

The situation in the summer of 1835 must have presented a major dilemma to the Earl and his representatives. A decision not to grant more ground for ironstone mining could only result in a number of related and serious problems: the end of the Graham tenancy or loss of orders at Milton Ironworks or the need to search for ore or metal elsewhere — in all cases resulting in widespread unemployment amongst the ironstone miners and in the case of loss of orders or the end of the tenancy, the short-term closure of an important market for Elsecar coal and unemployment or reduced wages amongst the coal miners and ironmakers. On the other hand, a decision to allow more Tankersley Ironstone to be mined on the Tankersley estate immediately, meant allowing it to be obtained from near the outcrop where it could be won from shallow pits without the lead time that would be necessary for a deep pit to the east. But by this time, the only remaining areas of

Tankersley Ironstone near the outcrop lay between Hood Hill and Upper Tankersley within the park boundary, and, of course, the many small pits that would need to be sunk meant much disturbance of the ground and a further reduction in the grazing area for the deer. Moreover, a decision had to be made in the knowledge that the Grahams had arrears of coal, cottage, farm and ironstone rents amounting to over £26,000.

In late February 1836, more than six months after their original request, Grahams' had been granted no additional ironstone grounds at Tankersley and William Graham was forced to write to Benjamin Biram to ask him to obtain some minerals from Greasbrough where the Elsecar works was obtaining some of its supplies. The reply from Henry Hartop was uncharacteristically short and to the point: 'on further considering the subject of our ironstone stock at Parkgate I must for the present decline letting any part of it go to the Milton works.'[23] On March 2, after what was no doubt a difficult meeting with William Graham, Benjamin Biram put the problem to the Earl and suggested a course of action:

> *I beg to name to your Lordship that Mr Graham called upon me yesterday in great tribulation at the prospect of a deficiency of Ironstone... He has only six weeks consumption of Black stone before hand, and has not room to employ men to get a sufficient stock — If your Lordship thinks well to allow them to extend another pit-breadth in Tankersley park it would greatly relieve them, and I am of opinion it might be done and afterwards trenched in so as to do no injury either to the surface or general appearance of the park.*[24]

On 4 March the Earl acceded to Biram's proposals, but his misgivings were clear:

> *Under the circumstances stated by Mr Graham, I shall have no objection to his getting another pit breadth in the park, but care must be taken that the work is so carried out as to ensure the perfect making up of the ground broken into — you may communicate this to Mr G.*[25]

Shortly after this agreement was reached and the test borings at the bottom of the park had been completed, rumours reached the Grahams' that Newton Chambers were to be allowed to obtain Tankersley Ironstone in Tankersley Park. Benjamin Biram saw William Graham at Milton Ironworks on March 15, 1836, and then wrote to the Earl:

> *In compliance with a note from Mr. Graham, I called upon him this morning at Milton Iron Works. He had understood that the Thorncliffe Co. had leave to get the Tankersley Mine by drifting from their black*

*mine level, and drawing the mineral by an Incline without the park,
thereby not disturbing the park. Messrs. Graham were concerned that
as your Lordship had given them permission to sink on the deep side of
the park, whereby they could as effectively get the mineral without
disturbing the park as the Thorncliffe Co. on the opposite side, —
they therefore had a prior claim on the stone in the park, especially
as their engine would be likely to drain it, and the quantity could not
be more than sufficient to keep them in ironstone to the expiration of
their lease. ... I happened to be with Mr Newman when Messrs.
Chambers asked if he thought your Lordship would object to their
getting part of the Tankersley mine, provided it could be done without
entering the park. Mr Newman thought there would be no objection but
I think his impression was, as was mine, that they merely wished to get
a little of the basset edge of the mine, and not by taking advantage of
their black mine level, drive a drift at the expense of £1,000 or
upwards which would dry a breadth of 8 or 900 yards. I am sure that
if the Thorncliffe Co. have contemplated such a proceeding, it has
been with the belief that Messrs. Graham could not, or might not do
the same thing on the opposite side. Nothing has yet been done by the
Thorncliffe Co. and I am satisfied they will not wish to go beyond the
limits which may be set for them.*[26]

The letter confirms that the test borings at the park bottom had been
successful and that the Graham partnership had been given permission
to sink a deep pit — with a pumping engine to drain off the water —
to work under the park, hence their unease about hearing of its possibly
being mined from the other direction. The Earl's reply two days later
made it clear that the Grahams' were to have the lion's share of the
remaining Tankersley Ironstone under the park, to the west of the
Tankersley fault, but that a previous agreement with Newton and
Chambers would stand:

*Mr. Graham must understand that any permission to get ironstone in
T. park must be taken in such a manner as will be consistent with
any engagement previously entered into with Thorncliffe.*[27]

This letter was followed by a meeting between the parties at Wentworth
Woodhouse on 29 April. At that meeting Earl Fitzwillam agreed to
Newton Chambers' getting Tankersley Ironstone inside Tankersley
Park, provided that they did not enter beyond a certain point under
the park — what the Earl referred to in a later letter as 'the rule of sixty
yards within the park wall'.[28] On the day after the meeting, William
Graham, obviously still smarting from what he considered to be an
injustice, wrote to Benjamin Biram, again pleading for more pits while
business was good:

> *From the determinaton of his Lordship last night to grant to the*
> *Thorncliffe Company to get the Tankersley ironstone as far in the park*
> *as our first row of pits — it will most seriously inconvenience us as to*
> *the quantity of our present gettings — we must therefore request you*
> *to state to his Lordship the difficulty we shall be under to carry on the*
> *two furnaces without leave to open another row of pits, indeed there*
> *appears no probability of keeping them both in blast up to their full*
> *power without his permission. and we are therefore induced to solicit*
> *you to point out to his Lordship the serious evil that must follow to us*
> *at these times when the iron trade may be affording compensation to*
> *those engaged in it — we would not have made this request but from*
> *the conviction upon our minds that we must otherwise either put one*
> *furnace out of blast or curtail the produce to an equal degree in both.*[29]

Such was his anxiety that he wrote again just two days later, ending
his entreaty with 'we are... losing the opportunity of taking full advantage
of times that may not last forever...'[30]

In late May he went with his mineral agent, Richard Hinchcliffe, to
inspect the ironstone got out of the new pit at Jump and in June he
reported on an inspection of ore from a trial pit at the old coke ground
at Milton. The latter was not of very good quality and he suggested
another trial pit 'on the lower side of the fault above our pond'. But
this did not solve his immediate problem and he repeated his request
for more pits at Tankersley:

> *... we are getting worse every day and have for some time been*
> *compelled to reduce our make in the furnaces for want of ironstone.*
> *and unless his lordship permits our working another row of pits*
> *immed[iatel]y one of the furnaces must be put out.*[31]

Some relief was at last afforded in July 1836 when the Grahams were
allowed to sink another row of pits in the park. There is then a silence
in the correspondence on the subject of ironstone for almost a year and
a half until December 1837 when another crisis developed and William
Graham wrote to Benjamin Biram stating that they wanted:

> *all the ironstone at Greasbro for about six months after which we*
> *might give up our part for the following six months — we have been*
> *compelled this morning to suspend the blast upon our furnaces for want*
> *of ironstone. Our present confined space in the park not supplying us*
> *with sufficient quantity to carry us on. and we shall be forced to do*
> *so again (I fear) occasionally unless we can find assistance from some*
> *quarter.*[32]

The surviving correspondence for 1838 makes no further reference to
the problem of ironstone supplies, but on 3 January, 1839, presumably

in reply to a request at the end of 1838, the Earl wrote with finality to Benjamin Biram:

I shall not agree to any more rows of pits more to the eastward in T. park.[33]

The Ordnance Survey One Inch Sheet 87 (surveyed between 1838 and 1840) shows three rows of pits at the top of the park, served by a tram road extension of the the Tankersley Park mineral railway, but by the time an estate map of Tankersley was compiled in 1840-41 the tram road extension had been removed and the levelling of the ground, which had been a condition of the development of the pits, had been completed. The last entry in Benjamin Biram's notebooks for ironstone from the top of the park is for the period from Lady Day 1840 to Lady Day 1841.[34]

Grahams' engine pit in the park, 1840 - c1850 *(area D on map 4A)*

When their take at the top of the park was exhausted, and having been refused permission to sink more small pits within the park, the Grahams' had to rely on the opening of a deep pit on Black Lane between the Parish Church and the Old Hall, just to the west of the Tankersley fault (see Figure 2). This new set of workings, which had been alluded to for the first time in the letter between William Newman and Earl Fitzwilliam on 10 July 1835 quoted above, had the disadvantage of requiring several years for its development and substantial development costs, but the advantage of having no impact on the park landscape beyond the immediate environs of its spoil heaps. There were four shafts with steam engines variously engaged in draining the workings, lowering the miners to and raising them from the pit bottom, and raising the ironstone to the pit surface. The pits are clearly shown on an estate map compiled in 1840-41 part of which is produced as Figure 5.[35] When the sub-commissioner for the Children's Employment Commission (Mines) visited Graham's pit in the early 1840s he reported that it was fifty yards deep and dry and free from gas.[36] In 1849, twenty-eight miners, in two undertakers' teams, were employed at the engine pit. It is not clear what the lifespan of the engine pit was, but the fact that shallow working of the Tankersley Ironstone from small, shallow pits had resumed by the early 1850s suggests that the pit may have been abandoned by then.

Mining for Swallow Wood Ironstone at Bell Ground 1823 - 1858 (?) *(Figure 4B)*

Swallow Wood Ironstone was very near to the surface within the park and was mined from a large number of small bell pits, hence the name

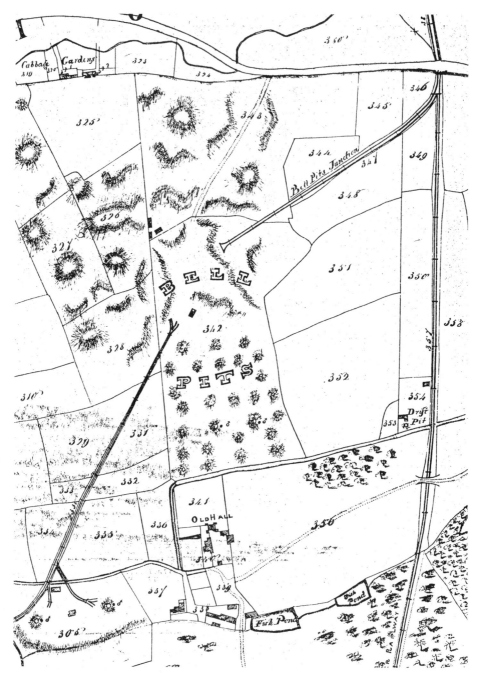

Figure 5. Extract from an estate map of Tankersley compiled in 1840-41 showing Grahams engine pits, and bell pit activity for Swallow Wood Ironstone at Bell Ground. *Source: Sheffield Archives, Wentworth Woodhouse Muniments, A-1647-14*

Bell Ground. The first entry in the account books for Swallow Wood Ironstone is for the year beginning 25 March 1823 but because Swallow Wood Ironstone was mined concurrently at Bell Ground and Skiers Spring in the 1850s, and was entered in the account books just as Swallow Wood without indicating location, it is not possible with certainty to say when mining for Swallow Wood Ironstone ceased at Bell Ground. Ironstone was certainly being mined at Bell Ground until the end of 1852 but by 1865 it was being referred to as 'the Bell ground, formerly ironstone pits.'[37] John Atkinson, in his paper on local ironstone mining, confidently asserts that mining took place at Bell Ground until 1858, but gives no source for his assertion. As he also says it was being mined by 'a man named Graham' until that date (Grahams' went out of business in 1848), his date should, in the first instance at least, be accepted with caution.[38]

The first edition O. S. One Inch Sheet 87, surveyed between 1838 - 40, shows pits near the outcrop beside Black Lane and further east at the edge of the park beside the main Barnsley-Sheffield road. The estate map of 1840-41 shows two working pits near the outcrop and one working pit near the turnpike (Figure 5). By the time the Tankersley area was surveyed for the O. S. Six Inch Sheet in 1850-51, mining had ceased near the outcrop location of 1840-41 and the land had been levelled. At the same date mining had begun in a new area near the outcrop to the north of the Old Hall. During the 1850s this area extended northwards, covering altogether almost thirty acres. The total output of Swallow Wood and Lidgate ironstone (they were not shown separately after 1853) between 1851 and 1858 was almost 39,000 tons. The acreage of that part of Bell Ground known to have been mined after 1850-51 would have yielded, if mined in its entirety, about 55,000 tons. Using the bell pit method at least a quarter would be left untouched. These figures, therefore, suggest that the late 1850s is a likely date for the cessation of mining at Bell Ground.

The resumption of mining for Tankersley Ironstone from shallow pits in the park in the 1850s *(area E on Figure 4A)*

Despite earlier misgivings about extending shallow mining in the park, by the time of the survey for the First Edition Six-Inch O. S. map in 1850-51, a new complex of such pits had appeared south of the area worked out by the Graham partnership in 1840 (area C on Figure 4A). The new pits were a mixture of very shallow bell pits near the outcrop in the west in which the miners were lowered and the miners and ironstone were raised by windlass, giving way to pits with horse gins ('gin pits') further down the dip. The pits were connected to the main Elsecar-Thorncliffe Railway by a series of tramways and Tankersley

Park mineral railway. The spoil from these pits was never levelled, tree planting never took place and these are the giant mole hills that grace Tankersley golf course to the present day (Figure 6).

Ironstone mining at Skiers Spring Pit 1849-79 (*for Tankersley Ironstone as shown in area F on Figure 4A and for Swallow Wood and Lidgett Ironstone as shown in Figure 4B*)

Skiers Spring ironstone pit, was located to the west of Skiers Spring Wood. It opened in about 1849. John Hartop, who had supervised its development, wrote to Earl Fitzwilliam in 1849, when George Dawes was about to take over the lease of the Elsecar and Milton Ironworks:

> *I trust your Lordship will be able to allow me to continue the management of the Ironstone works [ie, the mining of the ore], for I have now with some little trouble got the new Winning about complete, the entire arrangement of which has passed through my hands...*[39]

From its six deep shafts, Swallow Wood, Lidgett and, most importantly, Tankersley Ironstone were mined at depth (the pumping shaft at Skiers Spring was 150 yards deep) as shown in section in Figure 3. Figure 4A shows how Tankersley Ironstone was mined as far west as the Tankersley fault under the park from the Skiers Spring pit. Uninterrupted production was facilitated by the fact that the workings were drained by the Elsecar-Thorncliffe Drift, a massive engineering project completed in 1844, which consisted of a drainage level driven from Elsecar to Thorncliffe designed to drain large areas of the Silkstone, Fenton and Parkgate coal seams and the White, Claywood, Tankersley, Lidgett and Swallow Wood ironstone seams.

With the closure of the Skiers Spring pit in 1879, ironstone mining at Tankersley for the Elsecar and Milton Ironworks came to an end.

THE MINING POPULATION AND THE ORGANISATION OF THE INDUSTRY

A casual browser among the Wentworth Woodhouse Muniments in Sheffield Archives could be forgiven for believing that ironstone mining on the Earl Fitzwilliam's estate in South Yorkshire in the mid-nineteenth century was a very small industry indeed. The 1853 wage books, for example, list only about forty men and boys at the ironstone grounds.[40] For the most part, the persons named in the wage books were members of a small staff, headed by a mineral agent, who maintained the pits by pumping out water from the workings, laying and repairing wagonways, erecting and dismantling headgear at the gin pits and tending the steam engines at the deep shafts. Absent from the 1853 wage books, because they were technically self-employed, were the

Figure 6. Spoil heaps in Tankersley Park indicating the positions of gin pits and bell pits dating from the 1850s. *Source: Cambridge University Collection of Photographs, BHW-46*

nearly 300 men and boys who actually mined the ironstone.

The mining, whether in small, shallow bell or gin pits or in a deep pit, was organised on an 'undertaker' basis, a type of organisation widespread in the British Isles in coal mining and lead mining as well as ironstone mining. In this system, undertakers or contractors were appointed to work a small pit or a particular section of the workings in the case of a larger, deep pit. They then undertook to 'get' the ironstone and 'hurry' or 'tram' it to the bottom of the shaft in the case of the deep pits, and to the surface in the case of small, shallow pits. Each undertaker was paid an all-in price per ton or dozen (about forty-two cwt) for the ironstone he got and out of this he had to pay the workers he employed. Although no written contracts for the period under discussion appear to have survived, a number prepared about fifty years earlier by Newton Chambers, who were mining coal and ironstone about a mile to the south, have survived in transcript. For example:

5 July 1805 John Shelton and John Parkin.[41]

To work 2 pits in the Black Ironstone Mine at Thorncliffe and get all the Ironstone 31 yds more or less up on the end from the level to the Bassett in both pits, to be got, hurried, hung on and Drawn on to the pit hill, to be set up 22″ high, 18′ x 3′ and shall be reckoned one Doz to be led away in carts and D/D C ft 81 and paid at the rate of 22/- per Dozen, and to allow to L[ondgen]. N[ewton] & Co 6/- per Dozen for all the levels new driven by instalments of 1/- per dozen of the stone. To find their own tools, except Ropes, corves and Gin, also to employ sufficient hands to get 12 Dozens per fortnight and to work for no one else during Agreement.

Witness	John Hollings		His	
	5/- Ernest	John		Shelton
		John		Parkin
			Mark	

Given the organisation of the industry, its rural setting and its location in a largely unpopulated part of the Wentworth estate away from established settlements, a number of interesting quetions spring to mind: did the ironstone miners live in isolation or were they drawn from the established villages and hamlets in the area? How far and from which directions did the miners commute to work? Did kinship play an important role in recruitment into undertakers' teams? To what extent did incomers find employment in the small, tightly-knit work units?

Two lists of Wentworth estate employees, when used in conjunction with the enumerators' books of the 1851 census, provide clear answers to these questions.

The nature of the estate records

The first list is an enumeration of the 100 men and boys who were employed at the ironstone grounds in September 1849.[42] The workforce was divided into fourteen undertakers' teams, twelve working in small bell pits at Bell ground and two at the deep pit in the park, with the undertakers (ten) or partnerships of undertakers (four) clearly indicated at the head of each team. For each miner the full name and place of residence are given and, in the case of those under twenty years of age, their ages.

In 1849 only one of the two ironworks in Hoyland Nether was in blast, but two months later both works were leased to George Dawes, a Staffordshire ironmaster, and the demand for ironstone grew quickly and the number of ironstone miners increased accordingly. The relatively small and fluctuating numbers of ironstone miners in the 1840s and the rapid expansion in the early 1850s were recorded with great accuracy in detailed lists compiled by the various heads of department on the Fitzwilliam South Yorkshire estate for the purpose of distributing the St Thomas' Day charity donation on 21 December each year and the Collop Monday charity in March each year.[43] It is not clear when these two charities began or when they ceased and this is the subject of further research. Detailed lists have been located for 1768, 1811-28 and 1841-56.[44] The charities are mentioned in the account books for other years but no other detailed lists appear to have survived. At the back of the 1849 list there is a 'Rule of Admissibility' to claim for the St Thomas' Day donation: 'Any person regularly employed in the Service of Earl Fitzwilliam and employed at that time. Persons employed at that time at a merely occasional job are not entitled'.[45] The note also instructed each head of department to attend 'to identify his men'. A quantity of meat and a sum of money were given on St Thomas' Day and meat only on Collop Monday. It is the St Thomas' Day list for 1850 that has been analysed for the purposes of this study.[46] The complete list names 1,242 persons grouped according to occupation, and in some cases, principally miners, by place of work. The list includes 606 men and boys employed at collieries, 271 men and boys employed at the ironstone pits, seventy-seven employees at the estate workshops and on a railway, forty-one farm workers at the home farm, twenty-eight carpenters, twenty-six woodmen, sixteen grooms and sundry gatekeepers, masons, slaters, quarrymen, bricklayers, painters and glaziers, millers, saddlers, smiths and former employees and widows of former employees living in almshouses. A few names among the lists of male workers were of women, denoting widows on estate pensions.

The 1850 St Thomas' Day list was compiled on 16 December, just three and a half months before the 1851 census (which was conducted on the night of 30/31 March) and then adjusted for the Collop Monday charity three weeks before the census (Collop Monday was on 10 March in 1851). Seventy-nine of the 100 ironstone miners named in the 1849 list, and 251 of the 271 named in the 1850 list, have been identified in the 1851 census.

Ironstone miners' places of residence

Figure 7 shows the distribution of the places of residence of the 251 Tankersley ironstone miners who were identified in the December 1850 St Thomas' Day list. They lived in substantial numbers at Pilley in Tankersley parish, Birdwell in Worsbrough township, Hoyland Common in Hoyland township, and Thorpe Hesley in Kimberworth township, with a fairly dense secondary scatter throughout Tankersley parish and Hoyland and Wentworth townships. The small number of ironstone miners in the northern part of Ecclesfield parish close to Tankersley Park is explained by the fact that Newton Chambers and Company provided an alternative source of employment for iron workers, coal miners and ironstone miners at their Thorncliffe Works in that area.

The wide dispersal of the homes of the ironstone miners is partly explained by the fact that the ironstone was being mined largely under Tankersley Park where, apart from one or two cottages and the farm attached to the ruined hall in the centre of the park, there were no settlements. The pattern also reflects, to some extent, the historical development of ironstone mining in the area and in particular, its relocation during the previous half century from the southern to the northern and then to the central part of the parish. At various times, therefore, during the first forty years of the nineteenth century the pits working the Tankersley seam near its outcrop, were within easy reach of Thorpe Hesley in the south, and Pilley and Birdwell in the north, all of which were important locations of the homes of ironstone miners in December 1850. As the workings had retreated towards the middle of Tankersley Park and to Skiers Spring so the workforce had lengthened its journey to work so that Birdwell, Pilley and Thorpe Hesley retained their importance as centres where Tankersley ironstone miners lived even though journeys to work had doubled by mid-century. In 1850 only 4 per cent of the coal miners at Earl Fitzwilliam's collieries in Hoyland and Elsecar lived more than two kilometres' walk from the colliery at which they worked. By contrast, over 45 per cent of the ironstone miners in 1850 walked between three and four kilometres to

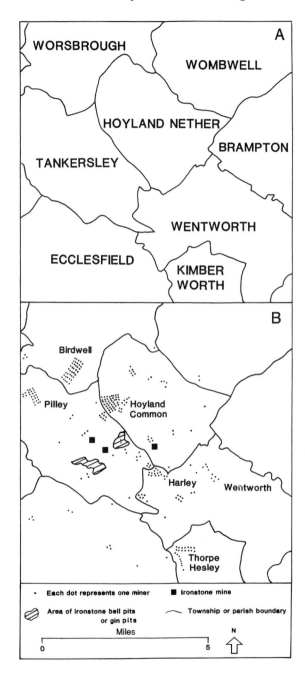

Figure 7. Distribution of the places of residence of the 250 ironstone miners working at the Tankersley ironstone grounds in December 1850.

work, with as many as 95 per cent walking at least one kilometre.

Although largely segregated from other miners employed on the Fitzwilliam estate, who were concentrated in Hoyland, Elsecar and Greasbrough, the ironstone miners did not live in complete residential segregation from other miners and from families engaged in other occupations. Figure 8, summarising the occupations of employed males in 1851 in the main settlement centres in which the ironstone miners lived, shows that although these settlements, with the exception of Wentworth whose estate village function is very clear, could be described as mining villages, they did not contain a residentially segregated ironstone mining population. Indeed, only the hamlet of Harley and the village of Hoyland Common had more than a third of their employed male population in ironstone mining.

Kinship and Teamwork

Though not segregated residentially from other miners, agricultural workers, self-employed metalworkers and workers in iron manufacturing, there was, nevertheless, a certain closeness among the ironstone miners. Every working day, unlike most of their neighbours, they left their villages to walk a fair distance to their workplace, often in another parish, and when they arrived they spent their day working in isolation in a close-knit team under an undertaker. On the other hand, the overwhelming majority of local coal miners worked in their home village, in bigger teams. Moreover, the boys who worked in the coal pits as trappers and horseboys were employed and controlled by the pit manager rather than an undertaker.

In putting together his team an ironstone undertaker would try to ensure the greatest efficiency and therefore the greatest profit. This meant having a getter or getters to mine the ironstone, hurriers or trammers to take it in corves (wagons) from the working place to the pit bottom and, in the case of small, shallow pits, coupling the corves onto ropes or chains (called hanging-on) to be wound up the shaft by a gin boy who operated a pulley system by leading a horse or pony round a circle at the pit top (Figure 9). It was then taken away from the pithead to be banked prior to being taken to the furnaces. Getting was normally done by experienced miners in their prime. According to the evidence collected in south Yorkshire by the sub-commissioners of the Children's Employment Commission (Mines) in 1842 some getters were as young as seventeen or eighteen, but typically they were in their twenties, thirties and forties. Older men helped to fill the corves and were employed as hangers-on and banksmen. Teenagers were used as hurriers and the youngest of all — including nine year olds in 1851 — were employed as gin boys.

Occupations of employed males in 1851 in selected settlements in the Tankersley area.

	Birdwell		Pilley		Hoyland Common		Harley		Wentworth		Thorpe Hesley	
	no	%	no	%	no	%	no	%	no	%	no	%
Agriculture	35	19.7	23	20.7	15	12.9	7	17.1	72	25.9	45	12.5
Mining (Ironstone mining)*	89 (42)	50.0 (23.7)	67 (21)	60.4 (18.4)	70 (53)	60.3 (45.7)	23 (21)	56.1 (51.2)	32 (7)	11.6 (2.5)	154 (100)	42.8 (27.8)
Building	19	10.7	4	3.6	11	9.5	1	2.4	47	17.0	15	4.2
Manufacture	13	7.3	9	8.1	13	11.2	10	24.4	54	19.5	103	28.6
Transport	4	2.2	0	0	1	0.9	0	0	3	1.1	4	1.1
Dealing	7	4.0	4	3.6	2	1.7	0	0	8	2.9	6	1.7
Industrial service	10	5.6	3	2.7	4	3.5	0	0	0	0	26	7.2
Public service and professional	0	0	0	0	0	0	0	0	10	3.6	2	0.5
Domestic service	0	0	0	0	0	0	0	0	51	18.4	1	0.3
Property owning and independent	0	0	1	0.9	0	0	0	0	0	0	4	1.1
Indefinite	1	0.5	0	0	0	0	0	0	0	0	0	0
Totals	178	100	111	100	116	100	41	100	277	100	360	100

Notes: * = Employment in ironstone mining is expressed as a sub-total of the main category of Mining. The classification adopted here is that of Charles Booth (1886) modified and described by W.A. Armstrong in, E.A. Wrigley (ed), **Nineteenth Century Society**, 1972, pp.226-310.

Figure 8. Occupations of employed males in 1851 in the main settlement centres in the area surrounding Tankersley Park.

Figure 9. Horse gin and gin boy.

The ironstone miners would obviously go through an occupational life-cycle, starting as gin boys, progressing to be hurriers, becoming getters in their prime, and then, as their health and strength declined, taking on the less arduous roles of hangers-on or banksmen. Figure 10 shows the structure of the Tankersley ironstone mining labour force in 1850-1 arrived at by combining the names given in the December 1850 St Thomas' Day list with the ages and occupations stated in the March 1851 census returns.

Teams were likely to be made up on the basis of a number of criteria. Skill, work rate, reliability, availability, sentiment and profit would all have played a part. Because of the heavy nature of the work and the ageing process, teams must have been constantly changing as miners fell ill, died or moved into other teams as lighter or heavier work became available, or moved into other occupations. The appointment of new undertakers from the mining population would also have caused the disintegration of existing teams as would the formation of their new companies of workmen.

In a deep pit there was less need for young boys than in a small pit. Corves here were trammed over larger distances but only to the bottom of the shaft, so that gin boys were not required. Nor were boys employed as trappers, to open and close airtight doors, as they were in the deep coal pits where gaseous explosions were a constant threat. There were more opportunities in the small pits for youths and boys. In such pits, teams were small, consisting of between four and eight members, and as many as half of them were young boys employed as trammers and gin boys.

There were certain advantages for undertakers in employing members of their own families. The main advantage was that earnings were kept within the family. If they were young they could also be more easily controlled and directed than other employees; they could possibly also be worked harder at no extra, or even less, expense. Evidence in government enquiries at the time suggests considerable abuse occurred in situations where undertakers employed their own children, with an insistence on very long hours and unrealistic output targets. The mineral agent at Thorncliffe only a mile or so from Tankersley told the sub-commissioner of the Children's Employment Commission (Mines) in 1842 that:

Those [undertakers] who have got their own children at work with them use them worse than the others. I am quite sure of this. Where the lads are hired by the undertaker, they will stick up for themselves and will not work more than the time agreed on, but where the undertakers employ their own children, they can make them do as they like.[47]

In the same report, a boy of seventeen, who worked for his undertaker father as a getter, the most demanding job in a pit, said:

> *I get and have been getting for two years. I find it very hard work indeed; it tires me very much; I can hardly get washed of a night till 9 o'clock, I am so tired. My father always tells me what to get. I and another boy have to get 35 corves a day; each corve holds nearly 4 cwt. We work from five in the morning till nearly five in the evening and have about ten minutes for dinner.*[48]

Whether an enlightened manager and a caring father or a bullying tyrant, an undertaker's ability to recruit family members varied according to personal circumstance. Obviously undertakers in their forties or fifties with large families, and perhaps a large number of

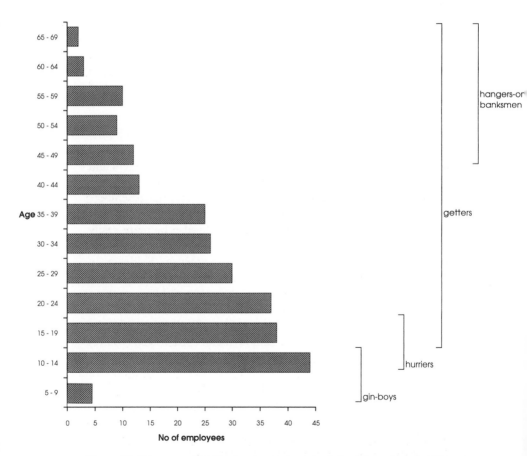

Figure 10. Structure of the Tankersley ironstone mining labour force in 1851.

Team	Size of team	Age of under-taker	Make-up of team		Number related to undertaker
			men	boys	
Bell pits/gin pits					
Pit 1	5	42,44*	4	1	3
Pit 2	5	45	3	2	2
Pit 3	5	27	3	2	0
Pit 4	6	29	5	1	1
Pit 5	8	30	5	3	0
Pit 6	7	56	4	3	3
Pit 7	8	44	6	2	5
Pit 8	4	44	3	1	1
Pit 9	6	24	3	3	1
Pit 10	4	37	3	1	0
Pit 11	8	23,23*	5	3	0
Pit 12	6	30	3	3	1
Engine pit (deep shaft pit)					
Team 1	20	33,30*	18	2	1
Team 2	8	56	8	0	3

Notes: * = two undertakers in partnership; in these cases the figure in the last column shows those persons related to one or the other or both of the undertakers.

Figure 11. Characteristics of ironstone undertakers' teams at Tankersley in September 1849.

nephews, were in a much better position to introduce their kin into their work teams than relatively young undertakers whose brothers were probably already established in other teams or occupations and whose own children were too young to be recruited.

Attention may now be turned to the undertakers' teams working at the Tankersley ironstone grounds in September 1849. Selected characteristics of the teams are summarised in Figure 11. Bearing in mind what has already been said about the differences in the undertakers' responsibilities between the deep pits and the smaller pits, it is interesting to note the virtual absence of boys (under fifteen years old) from the two undertakers' teams at the deep pit. Indeed, there were only five miners under twenty-one in team one and one under twenty-one in team two at that pit. In team two, four of the eight team members were related, a father of fifty-six (the undertaker) and his grown up sons aged thirty-five, twenty-eight and twenty-six.

It is clear from Figure 11 that in the small bell pits and gin pits there was a relationship between the age of the undertaker and the number of kin in his team. In three of the four instances where there were no relatives of the undertaker in a team, the undertakers were aged thirty or under. Conversely, in all four cases where between two and five subordinate team-members were relatives, the undertakers were in their forties and fifties.

Figure 12 gives further details of a representative sample of five of the twelve teams operating in September 1849. The team in pit one was the only one in which all members were related. The team was headed by two brothers-in-law. The nephew of one (William Smith) was the gin boy (Figure 13); James Burgon, the other undertaker, was childless according to the census of 1851. The other members of the team were the brother of one of the undertakers and his son.

In pit two the middle-aged undertaker was accompanied by his two

Examples of undertakers' teams in the bell pits and gin pits at Tankersley in September 1849.

Name	Age	Assumed role	Known relationship to undertaker
A - Pit 1			
James Burgon (undertaker)	42	getter	brother-in-law of WS
William Smith (undertaker)	44	getter	brother-in-law of JB
Thomas Smith	51	banksman	brother of WS; brother-in-law of JB
Ezra Smith	15	hurrier	WS's son; JB's nephew
William Smith	9	gin boy	TS's son; JB's and WS's nephew
B - Pit 2			
James Trippett (undertaker)	45	getter	
Thomas Sylvester	54	getter	none
George Smith	15	hurrier	none
Edward Trippett	11	hurrier	son
Henry Trippett	10	gin boy	son
C - Pit 6			
William Bennett (undertaker)	56	getter	
George Bennett	24	getter	son
Thomas Bennett	21	getter	son
James Bennett	19	getter	son
Henry Smith	14	hurrier	none
William Bell	13	hurrier	none
Samuel Platts	9	gin boy	none
D - Pit 3			
William Bennett Jnr (undertaker)	27	getter	
Henry Wroe	*	getter	none
David Holden	15	hurrier	none
Charles Ward	13	hurrier	none
Samuel Ward	11	gin boy	none
E - Pit 10			
William Jubb (undertaker)	37	getter	
William Hunter	43	getter	none
Charles Smith	16	hurrier	none
John Senior	14	gin boy	none

Notes: * = individual not located in 1851 census returns.

Figure 12. Examples of undertakers' teams in the bell pits and gin pits at Tankersley in September 1849.

Figure 13. William Smith and his wife Millicent. William Smith was a gin boy at Tankersley in 1849. *Mrs M Smith*

young sons, the elder of the two probably hurrying and the younger acting as a gin boy. The other two members of the team were another middle-aged getter and a teenager, George Smith, who probably acted as a hurrier. George Smith was a near neighbour of the undertaker.

William Bennett, the undertaker who headed the team in pit six, was also accompanied by his sons, but in this case two were in their twenties and undoubtedly getters. The structure of the undertaker's family in 1849 (he then had four sons aged twenty-seven, twenty-four, twenty-one and nineteen and a daughter aged sixteen) meant he had to look outside his immediate family for two hurriers and a gin boy. William Bennett junior, the undertaker in pit three and the eldest known son of William Bennett of pit six, was only twenty-seven years old, unmarried and still living with his father. He had almost certainly learned his trade as a member of his father's team. None of the other three members of his team who have been located in the census were his relatives.

The team in pit ten was also made up of unrelated individuals. Although thirty-seven years old, William Jubb, the undertaker, still had a very young family (his five children were aged nine, six, four, two and one) and the eldest two were girls. In Jubb's case he made up his team by employing two near neighbours, William Hunter and John Senior, and sixteen-year-old Charles Smith, who could not be accommodated in the team in which his father worked. His father was Thomas Smith in pit one, and the place Charles might have filled was already taken by his cousin Ezra Smith whose father was one of the undertakers in that pit.

Birthplaces of Ironstone Miners

The Tankersley ironstone miners were overwhelmingly locally born, a not surprising circumstance in view of what has already been revealed about the organisation of the industry. More than 97 per cent of the 251 men and boys employed at the ironstone grounds in December 1850 and who have been located in the 1851 census were born in the West Riding, of whom 236 (94 per cent) were born in South Yorkshire within fifteen kilometres of the ironstone grounds, and 195 (78 per cent) were born in Tankersley parish and the adjacent townships of Worsbrough, Hoyland Nether, Wentworth and Kimberworth within six kilometres of the ironstone grounds. All sixteen (out of eighteen) of the undertakers leading teams at the ironstone grounds in September 1849 who have been found in the 1851 census enumerators' returns were born in the same narrow area. Of the seven ironstone miners born outside the West Riding of Yorkshire, six had originated less than fifty-five kilometres from Tankersley. Two of these, from

Nottinghamshire, were young nephews of undertakers who may have been specially brought to South Yorkshire to fill gaps in teams. They were aged eleven and thirteen, were probably gin boys, and worked in teams headed by young undertakers with no boys of their own of those ages.

CONCLUSION

Tankersley Park and its immediate surroundings today forms a quiet island of countryside enjoyed by walkers and horseriders, by golfers, and by those with specialist interests in botany and ornithology.[49] Yet it is a landscape with a most complicated history, not least that resulting from the mining activity for ironstone in the period extending from the early 1790s until the end of the 1870s described above. It is not difficult to imagine the procession of boys and men in the heyday of ironstone mining converging on the park in the half light of a winter's morning (they worked six days a week from eight till five) and then their weary trudge home in the evening towards Pilley, Birdwell, Hoyland Common, Thorpe, and even further towards Rockley. Because so many worked on or near the surface for much of the period in question, and because of the related work on the tramways and mineral railways, it must have been a hive of activity, noisy, and messy in wet weather. Now it is silent and the testimony to their toil has to be searched for in the bumps and hollows of the landscape; in the grey shale that they brought to the surface in their search for the precious raw material that provided so many jobs in neighbouring Hoyland and Elsecar; and in the churchyard at Tankersley where many were buried (Figure 14).

IN MEMORY OF

RICHARD HINCHCLIFFE, WHO DIED
Feb 2nd. 1851, AGED 70 YEARS.
HE WAS MINERAL AGENT AT THE
TANKERSLEY MINES
TO MESSRS WALKERS 13 YEARS
TO MESSRS HARTOP SORBY
-----------& Co. 8 YEARS-----------
TO MESSRS GRAHAM & Co. 21 YEARS
AND ASSISTANT AGENT TO THE
RIGHT HON. EARL FITZWILLIAM
18 YEARS. AND FILLED HIS
VARIOUS ENGAGEMENTS WITH
GREAT PUNCTUALITY AND ATTENTION.

Figure 14. Gravestone inscription in Tankersley Churchyard.

Acknowledgements

I am grateful to Olive, Countess Fitzwilliam's Wentworth Settlement Trustees and the Director of Sheffield City Libraries for permission to quote from the Wentworth Woodhouse Muniments in Sheffield Archives.

Notes and References

Abbreviations: WWM — Wentworth Woodhouse Muniments; MD — Miscellaneous Documents. Both in Sheffield Archives.

1. For further details of George Dawes at Elsecar and Milton ironworks and at Scunthorpe, see 'The Dawes Brothers at Milton and Elsecar' Ch XIV, pp. 64-69 in *Hoyland Nether* by Arthur Clayton, Hoyland Nether Urban District Council, 1973; 'The Elsecar and Milton Ironworks' in unpublished typescript also by Arthur Clayton, a copy of which is deposited in Sheffield City Libraries (Local Studies Library); 'The Elsecar and Milton Ironworks', Ch 4, pp. 45-63 in *Aristocratic Enterprise* by Graham Mee, Blackie, 1975; and *The Heavens Reflect Our Labours, an illustrated account of Scunthorpe's early iron and steel industry and the men who worked in it*, Scunthorpe Museum & Art Gallery, 1974.
2. Two different Earls Fitzwilliam are referred to in this paper: William, the 4th Earl, (1748-1833) who succeeded to the estates of his uncle, the 2nd Marquis of Rockingham, in 1782, and Charles, the 5th Earl (1786-1857).
3. For a popular account of Newton Chambers & Co see: Mel and Joan Jones (eds), *'A Most Enterprising Thing': an illustrated history to commemorate the 200th anniversary of the establishment of Newton Chambers at Thorncliffe*, Chapeltown and High Green Archive, 1993.
4. Daniel Defoe, *A Tour through the Whole Island of Great Britain*, published 1724-26, Folio Edition, 1983, Volume 3, p. 59.
5. WWM, Stewards' Papers (Stw. P.) 16 XV, Benjamin Biram's diary, entry for 15 January 1855.
6. It was called Black Ironstone in Benjamin Biram's notebook for 1848 (WWM, Stw. P. 17 (q) (v)) when there can be no doubt that he was referring to the Tankersley Ironstone. Confusion can arise because of the Thorncliffe Black Mine Ironstone which was mined at Tankersley throughout the period under discussion by Newton Chambers, and was referred to normally just as Black Mine.
7. A. H. Green and others, *The Geology of the Yorkshire Coalfield*, HMSO, 1878, p. 317.
8. WWM Add, Map 67 — 'A Map of the Ironstone Ground at Hollin Delph and Tankersly (sic) Park.'
9. Fairbank Collection.
10. WWM, F106/33.
11. WWM, F106/34.
12. WWM, F106/59.
13. WWM, F107/98.
14. WWM, F71. The terms black and white mine appear to refer to bands within the Tankersley ironstone.
15. WWM, F106/62.
16. WWM, F106/62.
17. WWM, F106/62.
18. WWM, J. Biram's drafts, February 8, 1811.
19. WWM, F106/65.
20. WWM, F107/79.
21. WWM, G49/27a.
22. The top soil of Far Newbiggin Paddock is a marked blue-grey colour from the shale that was brought to the surface in the 1830s.
23. WWM, Stw. P. 15 (xi) H/34.
24. WWM, G40/88.
25. WWM, Stw. P. 14 (ii)/93.
26. WWM, G40/90.
27. WWM, Stw. P. 14 (ii)/95.
28. Newton Chambers had begun preparing to mine Tankersley ironstone under the park by June 1836 (WWM, Stw. P. 15 (ix) G/80). The pit lay 'between two throws about opposite to Newbiggin' (WWM, Stw. P. 14 (ii)/101) immediately outside the park wall and worked the mineral in a north-easterly direction. William Graham complained in a letter to Benjamin Biram on June 17, 1836 that he understood that the objection to their opening more pits in the park was 'to disturbing the surface' and yet their neighbours (Newton Chambers) were 'doing so at the very commencement of

their new workings' (WWM, Stw.P. 15 (ix) G/80). Almost exactly a year later he complained that Newton Chambers were 'beyond the limits fixed upon by Earl Fitzwilliam at our meeting at Wentworth House' and were below their level in the park. 'This encroachment', he went on, 'should be stop't immediately, or they will be getting our stone our limits for which are not very extensive...' (WWM, Stw. P. 15 (ix) G/104). The estate account books show that Newton Chambers first paid rent for Tankersley Ironstone in 1836 - 37. It was then mined continuously until 1841/42. Tankersley Ironstone was also recorded as being mined by Newton Chambers in the year 1846/47.

29. WWM, Stw. P. 15 (ix) G/75.

30. WWM, Stw. P. 15 (ix) G/76.

31. WWM, Stw. P. 15 (ix) G/80.

32. WWM, Stw. P. 15 (ix) G/118.

33. WWM, Stw. P. 14 (iii)/78.

34. WWM, Stw. P. 17 (a) - (iv).

35. WWM, Map of the Tankersley estate, compiled 1840-41 and accompanying survey book (A 1647-14).

36. *Children's Employment Commission (Mines)*, vol. XVI, report by J. C. Symons, the sub-Commissioner for the Yorkshire coalfield, 1842, Appendix 5N, pp.223-25.

37. WWM, A 426.

38. MD 3591, 'Ironstone Workings near Rockingham colliery', John Atkinson, n.d.

39. WWM, G45/8a.

40. WWM, A1557.

41. MD 3590(d). The abbreviation D/D means delivered, and C ft 81 means 81 cubic feet.

42. WWM, G-45.

43. In the supplement to his Sheffield Glossary (1891), Sidney Oldall Addy stated that on Collop Monday, the day before Shrove Tuesday, 'poor people go to their richer neighbours to beg a collop or slice of bacon, to supply the fat in which pancakes are baked on the following day', p.13.

44. WWM, R2A-42; A1543; A1412-1424.

45. WWM, A1412.

46. WWM, A 1419.

47. *Children's Employment Commission (Mines)*, 1842, witness no 60, p. 237.

48. *Children's Employment Commission (Mines)*, 1842, witness no 67, p. 240.

49. For a series of self-guided trails around Tankersley parish, see Mel Jones, Joan Jones and Bob Warburton, *Tankersley Parish Walks*, Tankersley Parish Council, 1993.

6. THE DEARNE AND DOVE CANAL

by Roger Glister

THE ROAD SYSTEM IN THE WEST RIDING of Yorkshire during the late eighteenth century was in a dangerous state. The situation eventually became an embarrassment to the Don Navigation Company in particular. Since the opening of their waterway to Tinsley, near Sheffield, a transhipment depot had been established at Swinton for the transfer of goods to and from the district of Barnsley. They were now in the difficult position of having an efficient and convenient method of taking cargo up to and away from Swinton and an inefficient and highly inconvenient system of horses and carts on mud tracks for the remaining nine and a half miles to Barnsley.

As early as 1773 the Marquess of Rockingham had tentatively pursued the idea of making the river Dearne navigable towards Barnsley but nothing came of his deliberations. It was not until 1792 that during a share-holders' meeting of the Don Navigation Company the subject was raised once again. This meeting agreed to a proposal that a cut be made from Tinsley up to Sheffield and also resolved to create a navigable waterway to Barnsley. It was now becoming increasingly important to provide a sensible means of transportation to serve the blossoming coal mining and iron working industries of this area. Time was of the essence to the Don Navigation Company as the Aire and Calder Navigation Company to the north were already making a survey based on their intention to build a canal from Wakefield to Barnsley and on to Barugh. Consequently it was only three weeks later that another shareholders' meeting was convened. There it was agreed that a subsidiary company be formed that would be responsible for a navigable cut 'from the river up to Barnsley', and would be made for about £50,000; and Robert Whitworth Snr was asked to do the survey under William Jessop's supervision.

Barnsley was now in the fortunate position of having two proposed canals heading towards the town. Much horsetrading ensued between the two companies with regard to branch lines, tolls and water supplies. When both routes were settled the required Acts of Parliament were applied for and both were granted on the same day in June 1793.

The Dearne and Dove Canal was to run for nine miles and five furlongs from Swinton through Wath-upon-Dearne and Wombwell until finally meeting the Barnsley Canal at Hoyle Mill. Two branches were to be built, one to Elsecar of two miles one and a half furlongs and another to Worsbrough of the same length. There were to be

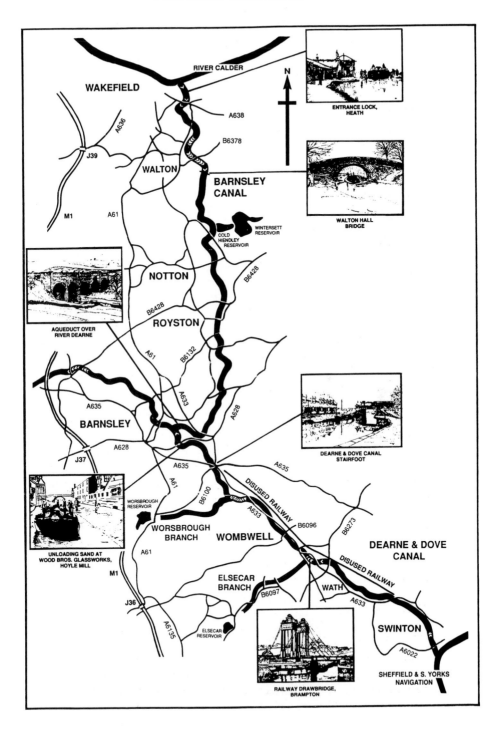

Barnsley's network of canals. (*Barnsley Canal Group* [hereafter BCG])

nineteen locks on the main line, lifting the canal by 127 feet from the river Don. Six locks were needed on the Elsecar branch to lift it forty-eight feet to the terminus basin. Two reservoirs were planned at Elsecar and Worsbrough, and one tunnel of 472 yards at Adwick-on-Dearne.

By December 1798 the canal was open to Elsecar and carrying started from the colliery at once. This early revenue was very welcome as the company was experiencing a shortage of funds due to increased construction costs and unforeseen works. On 12th November 1804 the stop lock leading to the Barnsley Canal was flooded and the Dearne and Dove declared open. The waterway could accommodate craft fifty-eight feet long by fourteen feet ten inches wide drawing four feet six inches. These dimensions were slightly less than those of boats capable of passing locks of the Don Navigation right up to Sheffield.

The Barnsley Canal had by this time been open for nearly three years and had built up a good trade. However, when the Dearne and Dove became operational, nearly half of the tonnage shipped from Barnby Basin, which was the terminus of the Barnsley Canal some four and a half miles north-west from Hoyle Mill, was soon travelling down the new canal. After settling down, the two concerns worked together in reasonable harmony for some years. Any changes in tolls were agreed between them, and the Barnsley, always suffering from water shortage, was supplied from the Worsbrough reservoir between the months of December 1804 and February 1805 with water that was surplus to the Dearne and Dove's needs. This generous offer was not repeated as the Dearne and Dove was itself stopped for lack of water during the summers of 1805 and 1806. An attempt was made to overcome the problem in 1826 by increasing the depth of the Worsbrough reservoir by four foot six inches and extending the acreage from twenty to forty-two.

In 1810 the first dividend paid to shareholders was 4.46% and in the same year 2,334 boats used the canal. By 1928 almost 150,000 tons of cargo, mainly coal, had been sent down the Dearne and Dove to the tide-way and all in all the canal was proving to be quite prosperous. Then the bane of canals raised its head of steam and rolled along the Dearne valley. The North Midland Railway opened in 1840: in 1845 the Don Navigation Company, trying to protect its trade, attempted to buy both the Dearne and Dove and Barnsley canals. The deal with the Barnsley fell through and this canal was eventually leased to the Aire and Calder Navigation Company. The Dearne and Dove, however, was taken over by the Don Navigation on 1st January 1846.

For the next forty years the canal continued to serve the coalfields of the Barnsley area with fluctuating fortunes. Various tactics were used to coax traffic away from the Barnsley Canal in order to make the

Boats in the pool below number 4 lock at Swinton, 1949 BCG

waterway viable in the face of railway competition. During these years the parent company was involved in many attempted take-overs and amalgamations as the railways increased their stranglehold on the region's transport system. In 1889 they were in the ownership of the Manchester, Sheffield & Lincolnshire Railway Company when an Act of Parliament was obtained enabling an operating company to be set up governing all four of South Yorkshire's canals. These were the Sheffield Canal, the Don Navigation, the Stainforth & Keadby and the Dearne and Dove. The company so formed took the now familiar name of the Sheffield & South Yorkshire Navigation.

Five years previously the industry which had given the Dearne and Dove its prosperity began to exact payment as the first sign of the cause of the canal's demise started to appear. A twenty-five yard section of the Worsbrough Branch collapsed due to subsidence from the colliery workings nearby. It took six months and £19,000 to reinstate the canal to navigation. This was only the beginning; in 1906 the situation in this part of the coal field was so bad that the Worsbrough Branch was closed completely because of unsupportable maintenance costs caused by the land settlement. Following this closure, the company reluctantly agreed to allow extraction of coal from directly below the canal thus effectively signing its death warrant.

In 1928 the Elsecar Branch was closed also due to subsidence and the high costs involved in protecting navigation. It became increasingly difficult to keep a navigable depth of water in the main line and in 1934 the last boat made the passage to Barnsley. The Dearne and Dove

Barges alongside Manvers Main Colliery, c.1910 (*BCG*).

The Dearne & Dove Canal between Station Road Bridge and Common Bridge at Wath, 1949 *(BCG)*.

Remedial work in very icy conditions: 'downstream' from Station Road Bridge at Wath, 1949 *(BCG)*.

was now closed except for a short length at either end. By 1942 the selfsame malady had closed the Barnsley Canal as well and in a further ten years the remaining traffic on the Dearne and Dove, from Manvers Main colliery at Wath to the Don, ceased. Final abandonment came in 1961 apart from the first four locks which were kept open by back pumping to serve a boat yard and a glass works. The Barnsley Canal had received its abandonment warrant some years previously in 1953.

After closure the infrastructure of the canal continued to be affected by the land settlement and many bridges were lowered when they became unsafe. The main industries of this region, coal and glass, were still in a state of development and land was needed for expansion. The canal which ran close by was a ready source of such land which was greedily swallowed up. Of the original length of the main line, nine and a quarter miles (sixty-seven percent of the channel) is filled in and obstructed. Surprisingly only one and a quarter miles (thirteen percent) is built on. Of the two branches, the Elsecar has fared best. Some forty percent of the channel is still in water, forty-seven percent exists but not in water and the remainder is infilled but not obstructed. The Worsbrough branch also has no obstructions but some fifty percent has been filled in.

Thus the Dearne and Dove languished in abject misery, its once ingeniously engineered channel suffering the indignity of being covered up with asphalt car parks or filled in with rubbish. Even today the vandalism continues with parts of the main line disappearing under road building schemes.

Then, early in 1984, a glimmer of light appeared in the gloom with the formation of the Barnsley Canal Group. This enthusiastic band promptly undertook an exhaustive survey of the state of the Barnsley Canal and published a detailed study of the waterway entitled *The Barnsley Canal, a Forgotten Waterway?* The Dearne and Dove was then given the same treatment which resulted in a companion study, *The Dearne and Dove Canal, the Vital Link.* This excellent report gives a very concise description of the condition of the canal and the case for full restoration is very convincingly put as are the ways and means of accomplishing this.

In comparison to the main line, the restoration of the two branches is fairly straightforward. The Worsbrough basin has already been restored along with a short length of canal which is fed from the reservoir and has an overflow into the river Dove. The Elsecar Branch with its six locks presents very little problem to full restoration. Only one quarter mile of the channel is infilled and all the locks are recognisable, though heavily affected by subsidence.

Since its conception the Barnsley Canal Group has fought several

The unusual railway drawbridge at Brampton, 1949 *(BCG)*.

Barges at Elsecar Basin: From an early photograph, c.1900 *(BCG)*.

planning application battles in an effort to protect the line of both canals. There have been successes but there have also been failures. An important objective is to bring the three councils involved — Wakefield, Barnsley and Rotherham — together with the group to decide upon a common policy with regard to the future of the two canals.

In 1991 the canal group commenced restoration work on the canal basin at Elsecar in conjunction with another conservation scheme taking place in this former mining village. The Elsecar Project is establishing an industrial and social museum in the original Earl Fitzwilliam workshops adjacent to the canal basin. The complex will also boast a Newcomen steam pumping engine which once kept the mine workings dry. It is intended that this formidable beam engine is restored to working order.

Following a successful application for an Urban Development Grant

Station Road Bridge at Wombwell, 1949 *(BCG)*.

Fishing at Worsbrough Basin, 1948 : The leisure potential already well-established *(BCG)*.

The Worsbrough Branch of the Dearne and Dove : Upstream side of Lewdin Bridge, The Boatman's Rest in the background, 1948 *(BCG)*.

a full feasibility study was undertaken of the Elsecar Branch by consulting engineers Ove Arup. This comprehensive report confirmed the opinion that restoration, though expensive, was practicable. Subsequently the basin and top pound of the branch have been restored to navigation and an annual trail boat rally is held on this three hundred yard length of canal when many small boats are launched down the newly constructed slipway.

The Elsecar flight of three locks are in the process of being excavated prior to re-building and re-gating. There are three major obstructions on the Elsecar Branch: Tingle Bridge at Hemingfield and Cobcar Bridge at Elsecar have both been lowered (and the water culverted beneath the road) and a large diameter gas pipe restricts height at Cobcar Lock. None are insurmountable, given the necessary funds and the will of the Authorities.

At last, after many years of neglect and vandalism, there is perhaps a change of fortune for the derelict waterways of South Yorkshire. Now that this work has started it is essential that the momentum is maintained thus ensuring the complete restoration of the Dearne and Dove Canal.

How long will it be before the hire boat companies' brochures are advertising a cruise around 'Yorkshire Ring'?

Notes and References

1. Copies of the two studies mentioned above and details of the Barnsley Canal Group (£2.50 each post paid) may be obtained from: Roger Glister, 2 Moorside Court, Cowpasture Road, Ilkley, LS29 8UF (01943 600026).

Acknowledgements

The Editor would like to express appreciation to Alan Hall and the Barnsley Canal Group for loan of photographic material used in this article.

The Dearne and Dove at Stairfoot : From an Edwardian postcard *(BCG)*.

Number 6 lock at Stairfoot, 1949 *(BCG)*.

Stairfoot Bridge, 1949 *(BCG)*.

Beevor Bridge at Hoyle Mill, built in 1837 and restored in 1927. Two small adjacent dams impounded a small length of the canal for the use of the Beevor Bobbin Works, 1949 *(BCG)*.

Hoyle Mill Bridge, 1949 *(BCG)*.

Unloading raw materials for Woods Glass Works, Hoyle Mill, c.1910

Watering hole and datestone '1817' near Stop Lock and junction with Barnsley Canal.

7. THE NEWCOMEN-TYPE ENGINE AT ELSECAR

by Arthur K. Clayton

With an Introduction by Brian Elliott

On 15 May 1963 Arthur Clayton of Hoyland Common took time off from his work as a miner at Rockingham Colliery to read a paper at a special meeting of the Institute of Mechanical Engineers and Newcomen Society, held at the Science Museum, London, in celebration of the tercentenary of the birth of Thomas Newcomen. The audience of about eighty included a Fellow of the Royal Society, four professors, many professional engineers and academics; as well as individuals with a keen interest in the history of technology. Mr Clayton was invited to speak to the meeting because of his detailed research on the Newcomen-type engine at Elsecar.

The atmospheric engine was built to pump water out of Earl Fitzwilliam's Elsecar New Colliery which began working on 25 September 1795 and coincided with the foundation of the Elsecar Ironworks and the cutting of the Elsecar branch of the Dearne and Dove Canal. More efficient technology was of course readily available due to the improved designs of Smeaton and Watt but Newcomen's invention remained a popular choice for mine owners because fuel costs were of little importance and the engine had a proven record. The fact that the engine worked successfully for such a long period of time confirmed the judgement of Fitzwilliam and his advisors; and also testified to its good design.

Since 1972 the engine has been classified as a Scheduled Ancient Monument and therefore now subject to the regulation of English Heritage who would view any future proposals within very strict conservation limits. Locally, it is a credit to the Fitzwilliam family, the National Coal Board and its engineers, Barnsley MBC and volunteers such as members of the Cortonwood & Elsecar Project that this splendid example of eighteenth century engineering has survived virtually intact and *in situ*.

Much has been discussed and written about Elsecar's Newcomen-type 'atmospheric' engine, especially in the context of the recent development of tourist facilities based on the Elsecar Workshops; but Arthur Clayton's pioneering paper is a most welcome addition to the *Aspects* portfolio, and we have no hesitation in recommending it to a wider local readership. It is also an opportune time for inclusion, since 1995 is the bicentenary of the building of the engine, a situation that we would not be fully

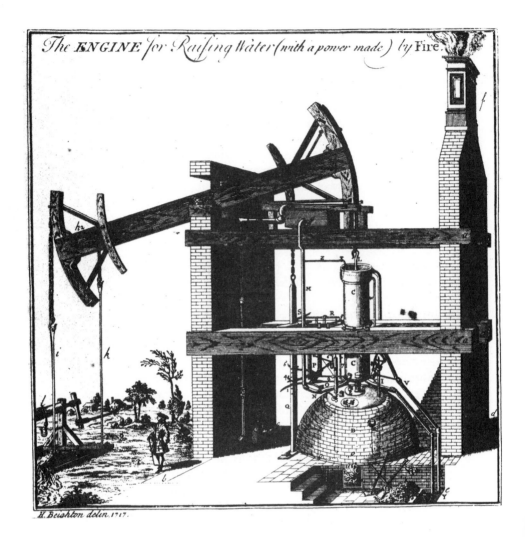

Beighton's 1717 engraving of an early 'Newcomen Engine'. The Newcomen-type engine installed in 1712 at Dudley Castle in the Midlands, for pumping water out of a coal mine, is generally regarded as the first commercially successful example.

aware of but for Arthur Clayton's painstaking research, undertaken more than thirty years' ago.

I am very grateful to the Newcomen Society for permission to reproduce Mr Clayton's original article. Some new illustrations have been added and every effort has been made to trace all copyright owners of other illustrations.

THE NEWCOMEN-TYPE ENGINE AT ELSECAR was built towards the end of the eighteenth century (when James Watt's patent was still active) and operated continually until 1923, that is, for at least a century and a quarter. It was brought back into service in 1928 when the

This photograph, taken in 1934, shows the Elsecar engine more or less as it was when in operation *(F.D. Woodall)*

Arthur Clayton (centre, wearing jacket) outside the entrance to the Elsecar engine in September 1986 — and the suspect '1787' datestone that, after hundreds of hours of detailed research, led him to conclude was probably added incorrectly from memory at a much later date *(Brian Elliott)*

electrical pumps which had replaced it were overwhelmed and drowned by a flood. In 1931, on the occasion of the Newcomen Society Summer Meeting in Sheffield, its working was the subject of a special demonstration. Since then it has remained on its original site at present under the respectful care of the National Coal Board's engineering staff, a monument *in situ* to the reliability and longevity of the atmospheric engine for its original purpose of mine drainage. It has long been supposed that the engine was erected in 1787, for that is the date on the lintel of the engine house. It is desirable that the birth and career of such industrial ancient monuments should be established: that is the purpose of this Paper in which it will be shown that the correct date for starting is 1795.

We know that in the first half of the eighteenth century Newcomen engines were erected in the inland coalfields of South Staffordshire,

Warwickshire, Leicestershire and South Derbyshire to drain mines which supplied the industrial towns of the Midlands, and in the Tyneside and Wearside collieries which supplied London, the eastern and the southern coastal towns with coal. The populations in the northern counties did not attain great densities until the mid-nineteenth century when their industrial development was brought about by the building of railways. The Yorkshire Coalfield (now one of the greatest) was not developed extensively until the second half of the nineteenth century except in favourable situations. Such a favourable situation was found in the Sheffield-Rotherham area, particularly after the river Don had been made navigable from the Humber estuary through Rotherham to Tinsley, halfway between Rotherham and Sheffield. This was achieved by 1740. It gave an outlet to coal from Parkgate collieries (about two miles from the river Don and the same distance from Wentworth Woodhouse, the seat of the Earls Fitzwilliam). In 1769 it is estimated that 300,000 tons a year from this area were sold in the large towns on the river Trent which discharged into the Humber estuary.[1]

The canal from Chesterfield to Gainsborough, planned by Brindley in 1769, was completed in 1773 and coal from the Chesterfield area could then compete in the towns of the river Trent with that from Parkgate. This competition was countered by cutting, from the river Don to Greasbrough[1] near Parkgate on which work was begun in 1775. The next step, undertaken jointly by the 'River Don Navigation' and the 'Aire and Calder Canal Company,' was to cut a canal from Wakefield through Barnsley to the river Don.[1] In 1793 the *Dearne and Dove Act* authorised a canal from Swinton to Barnsley with cuts to Elsecar and Worsbrough[1]; that to Elsecar was completed in 1796 (Map 1). It was

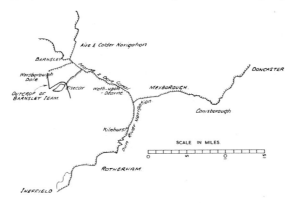

Map 1: Canal Connections with Elsecar.

these canals which enabled Earl Fitzwilliam's coal-bearing lands to be developed. Sir John Fitzwilliam had authorised the working of coal on his estates as early as 1367; in 1370 he leased his mines at Cortworth for thirty years; these early grants, like so many other early ones, being each limited to 'three picks' from which the annual production is unlikely to have exceeded 1000 tons.[2] The seam which outcropped near Wentworth Woodhouse and Elsecar was the Barnsley seam, 9 ft. thick with a band of hards, ideal for making coke for blast furnaces, by the hearth process of that day.

Most of the subsequent records on which this Paper is based are taken from the Fitzwilliam (Wentworth Woodhouse) Muniments lodged in 1949 in the Sheffield Central Library [Now Sheffield City Archives]. The records used are chiefly Household Vouchers kept by the Steward of the Household of the Earls Fitzwilliam who, until 1857, also overlooked or managed the Earl's collieries. When these vouchers are used the dates are supplied. Where records from the Colliery Accounts are used the reference of the Sheffield Central Library [City Archives] is used.

In 1781 the Fitzwilliam pits were Elsecar with only three or four hewers, and Low Wood with twelve hewers. These pits worked the Barnsley seam along the outcrop, Elsecar pit being on the northern side of the stream and Low Wood on the southern side. The stream that runs north-east, and formerly ran under the reservoir which was built to feed the canal, was the boundary between the parishes of Hoyland (to the north) and Wentworth and Brampton Bierlow to the south. Adits or soughs (drainage levels called the Deep Levels) were driven to the stream to drain the two pits. In 1790 the Low Wood Deep Level was in poor condition and the pit was not being properly drained. The Earl sought the advice of Mr J Stephenson, a mining engineer of Walker's Kimberworth Park colliery, who, on 1 March 1790, advised against sinking a new colliery because of insufficient assurance of the sale of the coal.[3] He recommended the taking of levels down the valley to test the possibility of obtaining drainage by sough for a further belt of the seam which dips about one in fourteen from the outcrop. Following this advice, in May 1790 three holes were bored which struck the Barnsley seam at depths of 24 and 34 yards in the first two but failed to reach it at 53 yards in the third. The bores were, on the 'deep' of Low Wood Deep Level, spaced about 230, 170 and 150 yards apart. The irregularity in the third bore was due to a fault with a downthrow of 25 yards between the second and third bores. Michael Hague, manager of the Elsecar colliery, computed that a sough from below the coal at the second bore to run for 400 yards parallel to the contemporary drainage level would drain 145 acres of coal (over 1½ million tons).[4]

The 'Newcomen Engine' when under the care of the National Coal Board, photographed in September, 1983 *(Brian Elliott)*

A recent photograph of the Newcomen Engine, taken in July 1995 *(Brian Elliott)*. Notice the workers' cottages to the right side of the engine in this and the 1983 view. This area, known as Distillary Side after a short-lived tar works (1814-18), included another short terrace, and a school which closed in 1850 when the railway made access impracticable.

As the cut from the river Don to Elsecar was being made, the Earl decided to sink a new collliery. On 21 July 1794 Michael Hague drew a sketch plan of the 'proposed mode of working the colliery from Elsecar'[5] proposing to drive a sough on the deep side to carry the water to a sump at the pit bottom from which an engine would pump the water. The site of the shaft was near the second bore, for a voucher on 24 April 1794 recorded a payment of £7-2-0 to John Hague and Richard Watson for 'Boreing for coal near where the Engine Pit is to be at Elsecar in Francis Hardy close West Corner of Simon Wood,' the bore being 35½ yards. They were also paid 2/6d each per day for 22 days in boring 13 holes to ascertain the direction of the throw or fault. This bore of 35½ yards to the bottom of the seam, which was 9 ft. 4 in. thick, was also noted by Charles Bowns, the Steward of the Earl's estates and collieries on 29 January 1794. He added that this bore was 'at the spot where the Fire Engine is meant to be fixed which is in the corner of the close opposite to Michl. Hague's house near the Dyke' (stream). He also stated that 'the place where the furnace etc. is proposed to be ereceted by Stacye & Co. is in the close adjoining where the Engine is to be, nearer to Wentworth on the Brampton side of the water.... I am in daily expectaion of receiving John Bargh's estimate for the intended Fire Engine, which he will undertake to erect.'[6] John Bargh was an engineer who lived near Chesterfield. Michael Hague's house is now dismantled, but the rent books show that he occupied it from 1771 to 1794; it is shown on a Fairbank plan[7] of 1771 to be on the site of the present Gas Office at Elsecar. Almost opposite, on the Brampton side of the now subterranean boundary stream, is the site of the Newcomen engine. These sites are shown in Map 2; also those of the proposed furnace and the existing engine house. This plan gave to the author the first hint that the date on the engine house was incorrect.

The sinking of the engine pit was begun about July 1794; a voucher of 5 July records an account for sod ale, earnest for the sinkers, and ale for removing the gin (a horse gin) and setting it up at the engine pit. Fourteen men with wages of 2s. 2d to 3s 0d per day sank the shafts, one the engine pit and the other a 'by pit' for coal winding. Gunpowder was used to blast the rocks, flannel suits were issued to the men because of the water encountered; Michael Hague supervised. By December 1794 the coal had been reached. Vouchers for the period 6 to 13 December record payment of £8-8-0 to 'William Sellers & Co.' for making a sump 3 ft. 6 in. below the coal and finishing the Engine pit, and of £2-5-5 for a feast to celebrate the same. A further voucher for 15 December was 'for an entertainment for masons etc. for Elsecar Colliery New Works.' Quarries were opened in Simon Wood and Low Wood for stone for the engine house and workshops; bricks were

'The Newcomen Beam Engine' and its architectural details, from *A Study in Conservation* (c.1982), Barnsley MBC Department of Architecture and Planning with acknowledgement to A.K. Clayton for his study *Hoyland Nether*.

supplied from a brickyard at Low Wood as well as from a new one at Elsecar. Men were paid on 18 September 1794 for felling and dressing trees in adjacent woods for the Elsecar engine, and sawyers were paid on 1 October for 'Engine Beam Slabbing.'

Work on the engine house began before the end of 1794 and parts of the engine were supplied from October 1794 to October 1795, by Longden, Chambers & Newton (later Newton, Chambers & Co.) of Thorncliffe, about three miles from Elsecar. The account for this company includes a cylinder, bottom and other cast iron and brass fittings. The total weight was 16½ tons; carriage cost 15-0d per ton. This account was approved by John Bargh, the engine builder. There was an account from John Darwin & Co. of Sheffield (who, and not Stacye & Co. as first proposed, built the first blast furnace in Elsecar) for 'Sundry Goods for Elsecar Engine' to the value of £581-13-7. The chief item was 'A steam pan Large' costing £239-1-3; this would be the wrought-iron boiler. Other items such as 'engine chains,' beam straps and piston rods show these to be wrought-iron work. There was also "a condenser for cylinder Bottom." This account was also approved by John Bargh. John Booth & Co, of Park Ironworks, Sheffield, supplied the pump pipes (including a working barrel, bored), clacks and other pipes: the total account, also approved by John Bargh, was for £153-18-6.

On 1 September 1795 £8-11-6 was paid for bucket leathers for the engine and a few days earlier George Sellers had been paid for walling the sump in the engine pit and putting in stays for the engine pipes. The engine was complete at this time and ready for use — for opening out the colliery. Charges for ale were paid after each major operation, e.g. laying foundations, setting the boiler, hanging the engine beam and erecting the cylinder. The final payment, on 14 September 1795, was the payment of the account of John Bargh, the engine builder:

To erecting an engine at Elsecar with	
42 inch cylinder at £1-1-0	*£44-2-0*
To travelling expenses and extra attendance	*25-0-0*
	69-2-0

This payment was entered into the accounts for the same sum with the statement: 'John Bargh for erecting a steam engine to drain the coal.'[8] The engine minder had been paid on 5 September 1795 for six weeks at 14-0d. per week 'for tending his Lordship's Engine at Elsecar' i.e. from the last week in July. By November a second minder was being paid, so that it was probably working continuously. On 9 December

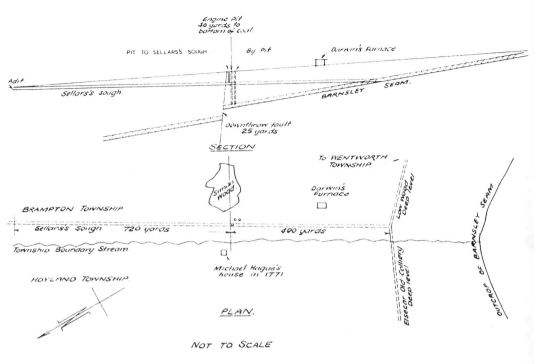

Map 2: Plan and Section Through the Engine.

Michael Hague reported that the 'Engine at Elsecar has nearly dried the Low Wood Level at the head of the sough, through a body of coal about 400 yards in thickness'[9] (see Map 2).

When the engine was ready, work proceeded underground. On 12 September 1795 a payment was made for 20 yards 'bord gate' (tunnelling from the Engine pit to the By pit at 3-0d. per yard. This distance agrees with the present distance, but is less than Hague's planned 30 yards. For 7 yards 'endway' and for boring a further 10 yards in the By pit, 2s. 0d per yard was paid. Payment was made for drawing the coal between the two pits. Further payments were made in September-October 1795 for driving a level for a lodge for the water in the engine pit, for the purchase of candles, and for a horse to work at the pit bottom. One other payment is important, for it shows that the engine house with the date 1787 was, in fact, erected in 1795. It was made to Francis Hardy & Co., for £167-19-3¼ for building an engine house, workshops and a bridge near the engine. Other payments were made for slating the engine house, workshops and for building the chimney stack. Messrs. John Darwin & Co. of Sheffield built the first coke blast furnace (Map 2) at Elsecar in 1795 when supplies of coal for it could be ensured.[9]

In 1796 it was the intention of the Canal Company to bring the cut from the Dearne and Dove Canal only as far as Cobcar Ing, 600 yards from Elsecar New Colliery. At that stage the Earl thought of making a connection, and in March 1796 paid a man for levelling the route of

A close view (July, 1995) of the Engine House, a rectangular three-storey building with a slate roof. Note the distinctive long and short ashlar quoins or corner stones, contrasting with the sandstone masonry; also the two short chimneys — unlike the typically tall chimneys of Cornish tin mines. Part of the modern former NCB workshops can be seen in the background *(Brian Elliott)*

a tramway from the canal in Cobcar Ing to the colliery near Simon Wood in the close where the Engine stands. Actually the Canal Company extended the cut to the colliery.[10]

The original winding of coal from the By pit was by horse gin, but from 3 November 1795 to 5 July 1796 Messrs. Jarrett, Dawson & Hardy of Low Moor Ironworks, near Bradford, were supplying 'cast metal goods for the machine for drawing coals at Elsecar colliery.' These included a cylinder and bottom (£19-19-0) a piston, ring and shaft, two spur wheels and a flywheel at a total charge of £158-8-7½. John Darwin & Co. of Sheffield provided a boiler for £45-15-1½ and Jonathan Woodhouse, an engineer from Ashby de la Zouch, superintended the building of the 'whimsey' or winder; his fee was £31-10-0 as noted in a voucher dated 10 September 1796. This winding engine was called the 'Little engine' and the atmospheric steam engine the 'Great Engine.'

In 1797 it was proposed to sink a pit in George Copley's Close which a Fairbank plan of 1771 shows to be adjacent to Michael Hague's house. In May 1798 stone masons were paid for '18½ roods of stone wallilng at the new whimsey by Michael Hague's house' and in 1798 payments were vouched for digging the foundations for the new whimsey. A second whimsey as bought for £178 from the Low Moor Company, and on 19 December 1798 Jonathan Woodhouse was paid £32-11-0 for erecting the new winding engine and repairing the old one. This pit worked until 1869[11] but is now covered by sidings.

Estimates were recorded on 2 September 1797 of the performance of the Great Engine by Joshua Biram, who in 1804, became the steward of the Earl's household and collieries. He recorded on 2 September 1797 of the performance of the Great Engine by Joshua Biram, who in 1804, became the steward of the Earl's household and collieries. He recorded (in ale gallons per minute) the flow of water along the soughs: his figures have been converted to Imperial Standard gallons (1 = 0.965 gallon) in the following abstract:

	Imp.gall./min.
1794, April 19 before the engine put down at Elsecar	
Low Wood colliery sough	*128.8*
Elsecar colliery sough	*60.7*
Total	*189.5*

1796, 24 March after the Engine was put down

Low Wood sough	21.5
Elsecar sough	10.0
	31.5

The difference is 158.0 gall./min. 'It is reasonable to suppose the Engine has to dra' at 386 gallons per minute. It will take 9h. 49 min. pumping per day, therefore, to keep the pit free from water.

1797, 2 Septem. Water discharged at Low Wood sough   *12.5*   [12]

The lower clack in the pump shaft broke in 1799 and the colliery was flooded. John Bargh repaired this for a fee of 10 guineas. In 1801 the 42 inch cylinder was replaced by one of 48 in. by Jonathan Woodhouse at a cost of £189-9-0, the new cylinder etc. being supplied from Butterley Ironworks. The only comment that need be made on this change is that no condenser was fitted on the new engine; the condenser on the old engine, (perhaps just a pickle-pot) was apparently of little significance at a colliery where coal was so cheap. Just before the large cylinder was fitted new soughs were cut. The details for these have been supplied by Mr G T Newbould.[13] They were for 400 yards at 14s. 9d per yard from the engine to 'where it would foot the coal' (which in Map 2 is taken to be the junction of the two deep levels near the outcrop); and for 736 yards at 7s. 0d per yard from the Engine pit to the sough pit.

In 1811 the beam of the Great Engine needed replacement. Also in that year the Steward, Joshua Biram, stated in a letter to the Earl that the engine was big enough to work an additional pump to discharge either into Low Wood sough or into the canal, and suggested that Jonathan Woodhouse be asked to advise on the work.[14] Work, which may have been for such additional pumps, was carried out by the Coalbrookdale Company for there is a letter as follows:

Coalbrookdale 8th Mo. Aug. 31st, 1812
Respected Friend,
Johsua Biram
We have to acknowledge the rect. of thy favor last evening covering Walker, Eyre & Stanley's Drafts value one hundred and ninety two pounds 3/3d. which we place to the credit of Earl Fitzwilliam, and is in full for Engine work furnished thro. our friend Jonathan Woodhouse

for which we are much obliged and remain respectfully.

Richd. Darby

For the Coalbrookdale Co. & "Self"

On 26 February 1812 Biram stated that the Elsecar engine was reckoned to draw forty gallons to one stroke, to make thirteen strokes per minute and to draw 748,800 gallons per 24 hours. The engine then worked twelve hours per day. This rating is approximately 500 Imperial gallons a minute compared with 386 for the 42 in. cylinder in 1796.[15] On 15 November 1812 he reported that the Great Engine worked three pumps, one of 13 in. diameter and two new ones of 8 in. diameter all raising water to the Low Wood old sough, totalling about 600 Imperial gal./min.[16]

In July 1836 Benjamin Biram, son of Joshua, and who on the death of his father in 1835 had replaced him as Steward of the Household and Collieries, reported that the wooden beam was cracked and that the pumps were corroded and need renewing.[17] Messrs Graham, of the Milton Ironworks, ¾ mile from Elsecar, gave an estimate in the same month for a cast iron beam, parallel motions, piston, and 30 yards 9 in. of 21 in. pipes (including a 20 in. working barrel) etc for £385.[18] Unfortunately the Household vouchers for 1836 have not survived to give details but in 1836 Graham & Co. were paid £1621-14-8 for castings for Elsecar New colliery; in 1837 they received £595-12-2 for extraordinary expenses and £726-0-2 for ordinary expenses for castings. It seems that these payments covered the conversion to the present cast iron beam of the Great Engine. It should be noted, however, that the present working barrel is of 18 in. diameter, and the rising main 18½ in. In its last working days in 1923 the engine only made six strokes a minute.

One further point which has been established is that Longden, Chambers and Newton, of Thorncliffe, did not make the cylinder, bottom and piston included in their account. This firm was formed in 1792 by Thomas Chambers, formerly an employee at the Walker Ironworks, Rotherham and George Newton, a manufacturer of spades and trowels, of Sheffield, who set up at the Phoenix Foundry there in that year, with the help of £2000 capital contributed by Maskew, a tea merchant of London. When in 1793 Maskew withdrew, Henry Longden, a razor maker, replaced him. It was not until 1795 that they blew in their first blast furnace at Thorncliffe, on land leased by Earl Fitzwilliam, and 1802 before they moved their foundry from Sheffield to Chapeltown.[19] It would have been impossible for such a firm to cast the large cylinders supplied on 4 April 1795 and the records of the firm confirm this. These have been searched for the period 1794-5 but there is no record for cylinder, bottom or piston, though the entry for the four pillars for the cylinder occurs on the same date. When in 1798 Longden, Chambers and Newton required an engine to sink to the thin coal they bought an old one for £116.[20] Longden, Chambers and Newton must therefore have acted as factors on behalf of their landlord, but where the cylinder was cast cannot be ascertained.

With regard to the date 1787 on the lintel, the simplest explanation is that this was not cut when the engine was erected but was added from memory later, perhaps in 1836 when extensive repairs were made to the engine. The actual date for this fine old engine must henceforth be recorded as 1795.

Notes and References

1. G.G. Hopkinson, *Transactions of the Hunter Archaeological Society,* 1957.
2. R.A. Mott *National Coal Board Magazine,* July 1947, 10.
3. F. 70.h. Wentworth Woodhouse Muniments, (W.W.M.), deposited in the City Library [City Archives], Sheffield.
4. F. 100. W.W.M.
5. F. 70.i. W.W.M.
6. F. 106.b. W.W.M.
7. Fairbank Collection in the City Library [City Archives], Sheffield.
8. A. 51. W.W.M.
9. F. 70.i. W.W.M.
10. F. 71. W.W.M.
11. Memoirs of Paul Morrell of Hoyland: Private Typescript.
12. F. 70.i. W.W.M.
13. Private communication from notebooks in his possession.
14. Wentworth Stewards' Correspondence and Papers, 1771-1905. 5 (11) W.W.M.
15. Wentworth Stewards' Correspondence and Papers, 1771-1905. 5 (111) W.W.M.
16. *ibid*
17. G.40. W.W.M.
18. Stewards' Correspondence and Papers. 15.G. (IX). W.W.M.
19. T.S. Ashton, *Iron and Steel in the Industrial Revolution.* 1924. 157.
20. Copied by the writer from a Thorncliffe Memorandum Book, under date 9th February, 1798 (The book was in the private possession of Mr. R. Smith of Harley).

Acknowledgements

I wish to make grateful acknowledgement to Earl Fitzwilliam and the Trustees of the Wentworth Estate for permission to use information from the Wentworth Woodhouse Muniments, now in the City Library [City Archives], Sheffield. I am also indebted to Dr R A Mott for his help in writing this Paper, and to senior officials of the National Coal Board. I would also like to acknowledge, with thanks, the late Mr Gerald T Newbould of Stubbin Colliery, the late Mr W Foster of Pilley and the late Mr E Wilkinson of Hoyland Common for their help and kindness.

8. FLAT IRONS, BEST SUITS AND FAMILY JEWELS: A CENTURY OF PAWNBROKING IN BARNSLEY, c1840-c1940

by Brian Elliott and Margaret Holderness

Part One
by Brian Elliott

FOR MANY ORDINARY FAMILIES 'POPPING' a precious possession was a regular and necessary requirement a generation or two ago.[1] Doing business at the sign of the three brass balls was nothing to be ashamed of, but simply a convenient means of obtaining a short-term loan. For the better-off, a visit to the pawnshop, where discretion and privacy was assured, was not only a quick and easy way to obtain cash but also a relatively cheap and secure place to store valuables. Considering the social and economic importance of the pawnbroking trade it is surprising that so little has been written on the subject.

The seedier side of pawnbroking was portrayed by Charles Dickens in his early work, *Sketches by Boz* (1836). Pawnbrokers are shown, as can be seen in Cruikshank's illustration (Figure 1), as smartly dressed, debonair figures in contrast to the grim faces representing the masses of the London poor. Yet despite caricatures and literary references the trade was fast becoming both trustworthy and regulated. The *Pawnbrokers' Gazette and Trade Circular* appeared in 1838, a generation before *Exchange and Mart* was published. Its long-serving second editor, Alfred Daniel Keeson, gave evidence to the Parliamentary Committee on Pawnbroking in 1870 which explored some of the many ramifications of the trade, including associations with the criminal world. The resulting *Pawnbrokers Act of 1872* established a code of regulation and practice that stood the test of time until 1960.[2]

Pawnbroking existed in China more than two thousand years ago and was introduced into England by the Lombards in the thirteenth century. The traditional symbol of the three gold or brass balls originated from the amorial bearings of the Medici family, the richest money-lenders of Florence. By Victorian times the practice had become common place at a time when personal possessions were more abundant than ever before.[3] The pawnbroker preferred goods of high value and small bulk, like jewellery, watches and silverware.

A pawnbroker was (and is) a dealer licensed to lend money at a specified rate of interest on the security of a movable article (usually personal property). The article was redeemed (returned to the ticket-

Figure 1 The Pawnbroker's Shop; a London scene from *Sketches by Boz*. A drawing by George Cruikshank.

holder) on repayment of the loan — plus interest. The pawnbroker would normally offer money on about one-third of the value of the article, keep it for a year and a day (nowadays six months) and charge, say, ten percent interest per month. Thus a bracelet worth £60 would generate an advance of £20 which, after three months, would require £26 for redemption. Where possible unredeemed property would be sent to other branches for resale in order to save embarrassment for the customer, otherwise would be placed on sale in the 'shop' part of the business or, for valuable items, sent for auction.

An advertisement of 1874, shown as Figure 2, placed in the *Barnsley Illustrated Weekly* by W.G. Horsfield who describes himself as

M ONEY LENT on Gold & Silver Plate.
    MONEY LENT on Gold and Silver Watches.
MONEY LENT on Silver Spoons and Jewelry.
MONEY LENT on Silks, Piece-goods, &Wearing Appl
MONEY LENT on Feather Beds and Bedding.
MONEY LENT on Guns, Oil Paintings, Timepieces,
MONEY LENT on Pianos and Furniture.
MONEY LENT on every description of Valuable
                    Movable Property.

Sums above £10 by Special Agreement, at 1¼ per cent.
                    per month.

W. G. HORSFIELD,
PAWNBROKER AND SILVERSMITH,
59, *Sheffield Road, Barnsley.*

Milner's Fire and Thief-Proof Safes for Valuables.

Figure 2 An early advertisement by W G Horsfield, from the *Barnsley Illustrated Weekly*, 13 June 1874.

'PAWNBROKER AND SILVERSMITH' shows the great variety of goods accepted for loans. The reference to 'Fire and Thief-Proof Safes' was also an important asset, reassuring potential customers that precious items such as jewellery, watches and silverware would be kept in secure storage.

Sheffield Road was the main location for pawnbrokers' shops. Trade directories show that from the early nineteenth century until the 1960s at least eight pawnshops (with associated businesses) operated from this area (Bailey, Barton, Blakey, Grimwood, Guest, Hargreaves, Harral and Horsfield). Within town, New Street (Bailey, Clough, Guest and Wike) and Shambles Street (Harral, Mellor) had notable pawnshops. There were also shops on Doncaster Road (Barton, Foundhere).

Pawnbrokers often sold new goods in associated areas such as clothing, footwear, jewellery, watches and clocks. In 1898, as can be seen in Figure 3, W.G. Horsfield sold musical instruments, opera glasses, telescopes, in addition to a wide array of unredeemed pledges and a 'HANDSOME BRITANNIA METAL TEAPOT' was given away with every purchase of a wedding ring. Part of Horsfields operated as a 'CLOTHING AND BOOT FACTOR', selling a variety of men's and children's wear. The 'splendid variety' of 'SHAWLS! SHAWLS!! SHAWLS!!!' were a fashionable but functional item for women millworkers whilst 'CORD AND MOLESKIN TROUSERS' had the hardwearing qualities needed by working men. Similarly, at John Guest and Sons (Figure 4) customers were assured of 'THE LARGEST & CHEAPEST STOCK' of clothing and footwear from 'The People's Clothing Stores'. Guests, established in 1870, was one of the largest pawnbrokers in the area, having branches in Wombwell, Hoyland,

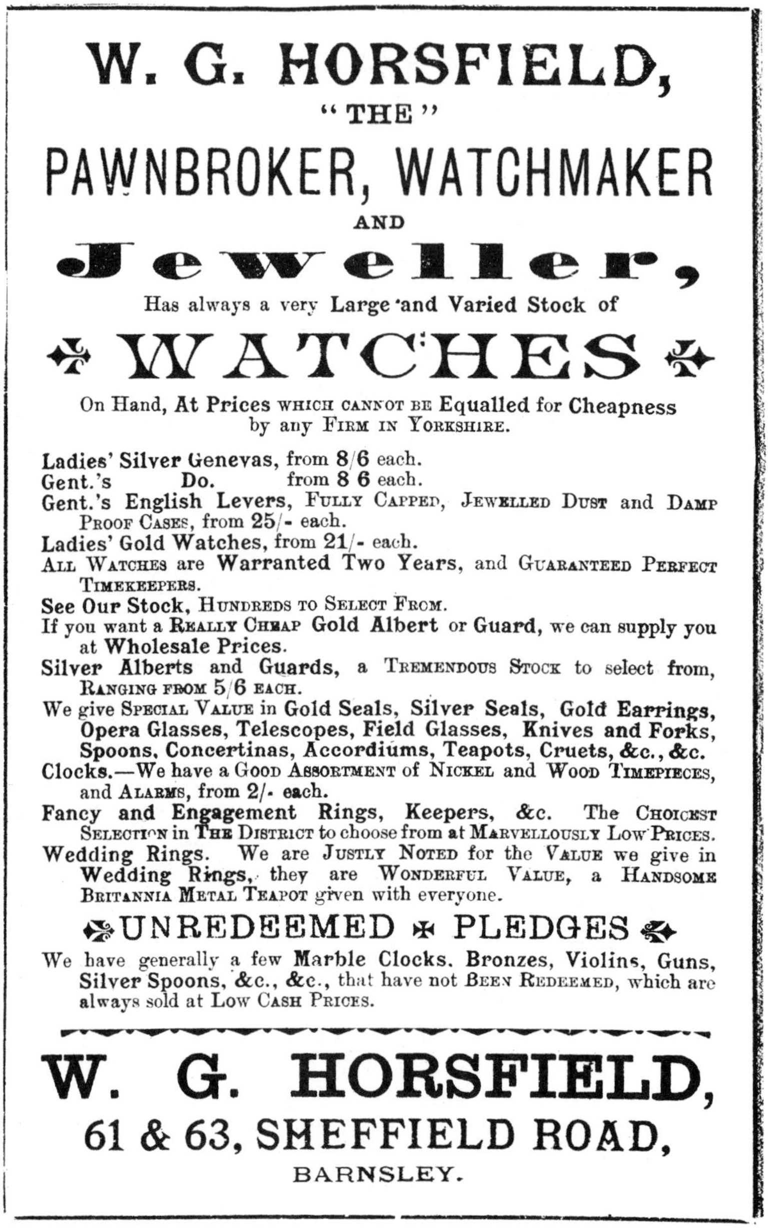

Figure 3 A double-page advert for W G Horsfield, from the *Barnsley Chronicle Almanack* of 1898.

28 & 30, New St., Barnsley

Corner of Baker Street.

THE LARGEST & CHEAPEST STOCK

OF

CLOTHING

IS AT

J. Guest's

The People's Clothing Stores,

20 & 30, NEW STREET,

BARNSLEY.

CORNER OF BAKER STREET.

Figure 4 An 1885 advertisement for John Guest, pawnbroker, clothier etc, from *Whitworth's Almanack*. Notice the impressive shop front, facing New Street. Entrance to the pledge office was by the side door, on Baker Street. The three 'brass' balls are also in view.

Normanton, Stocksbridge and Goldthorpe. Although each business had a considerable local following there was a great deal of competition in advertising goods and services through newspapers, trade directories and spectacular shop window displays.

As well as licensed pawnbrokers there were also several established businesses dealing in unredeemed pledges. In 1899, for example, Atkinson's Shops (Figure 5) of 68 Sheffield Road and 60 New Street were advertised as 'the best shops to buy FORFEITED PLEDGES'. Jewellers and watchmakers such as Benjamin Gaunt and Sons of May Day Green also sold items from the pawnbroking trade. Some pawnbrokers established departments or branches as 'House Furnishers'.

Two Pawnbroking Pioneers
1. William Bailey

William Bailey was one of the more successful of Barnsley's Victorian pawnbrokers. He was born in Ripon in 1819, the son of an auctioneer, moving to Barnsley during the 1830s to take up an apprenticeship with well-known stationer and printer George Harrison whose premises were located on Market Hill.[4] Four years after gaining his indentures he married, at St George's church, the daughter of Joseph Hargreaves who had a well-established pawnbroker's business on Sheffield Road. William assisted his father-in-law in the shop and by 1847 had become a business partner, assuming full responsibility when Hargreaves died in 1860.

For a short period Bailey retired from the pawnbroking trade, leaving his son, John Hargreave Bailey, in charge of the shop whilst he took a farm in the Doncaster area. On his return he was active in the business for a number of years, eventually retiring to Hopwood Street, off Victoria Road, where he resided until his death, aged eighty, in 1899. John Hargreave appears to have run the family business from premises on New Street from 1899 to 1919. 'J H Bailey', according to an advertisement of 1914 (Figure 6) preferred to be known as 'Clothier & Outfitter'. However, on an early photograph (Figure 7) of the shop, a torn poster for Bailey, displayed on the gable-end of an adjacent property, 'PAWNBRO[KER]' is just discernable. A postcard of New Street of c1910 (Figure 8) shows that the old properties had been replaced, and the shop was situated across from J Lodge's stationers shop and next to John Guest's clothiers and pawnbrokers. J H Bailey also operated as House Furnishers, as can be seen in an early photograph of the Kendray Street Market (Figure 9).

William Bailey was active in public affairs, being one of the principals in establishing the Board of Health in the town during the early 1850s.

For the WORKING FOLK of Barnsley.

The Cheapest Stores in this Town for MEN'S, YOUTHS', and BOYS' Ready-made

CLOTHING & BOOTS,

BLANKETS, QUILTS, SHEETS, &c., &c.,

ARE

ATKINSON'S WELL-KNOWN STORES,

MAY-DAY GREEN.

☞ WE GIVE THE BEST VALUE IN YORKSHIRE. ☜

DO YOU KNOW?

KNOW WHAT?

WHY! That the best Shops to buy FORFEITED PLEDGES are

ATKINSON'S SHOPS, 68, SHEFFIELD ROAD, and 60, NEW STREET.

If you are seeking Half-Crowns for Two Shillings you will deal at the above Shops.

Figure 5 Shop proprietors, perhaps with a bit of help from publishers, were able to produce ingenious advertising copy. Here 'Atkinsons Shops' are well-portrayed in the *Barnsley Red Book and Directory* of 1899.

J. H. BAILEY,

Clothier & Outfitter,

14, NEW STREET, Barnsley.

This advertisement is intended as a personal invitation for you to come and examine our stocks.

We are confident we can offer you

Men's, Youths' & Boys' Clothing

at fully 25% less than you have been paying elsewhere.

No purchase too small to receive prompt attention.

OUR MEASURE DEPARTMENT

is replete with Cloths selected from five of the largest Cloth Manufacturers in England.

Man's Suit, Black or Tweed, from 17/11.

,, Trousers, ,, ,, 6/11.

Come and choose the material you prefer and the fashion you desire and we guarantee you a perfect fit.

NO EXTRAS.

Figure 6 John Hargreave (J H) Bailey's advertisement, taken from the *Barnsley Chronicle Almanack* of 1914. Here you could get a made-to-measure suit for less then eighteen shillings (90p) — providing it was black or tweed!

Figure 7 J H Bailey's pawnbroker's (and clothier's) shop, New Street, 1890s. The property looks old and run-down.

Politically a staunch Liberal, he was a leading member of the Franklin Club, in fact served a term as President and was on the inquest jury for the Oaks Colliery disaster of 1866. He also campaigned for the purchase of the rights of the trustees of the Duke of Leeds with regard to ownership of the ancient freeholds of Churchfield and May Day Green.

2. W.G. Horsfield

W.G. (William George) Horsfield was a near contemporary of Bailey but died somewhat prematurely, at the age of 57, in 1895.[5] Believed to have been a native of Rotherham, he entered the trade of pawnbroking through the apprenticeship system, serving his time with a Sheffield master. Horsfield set up business on his own account after moving to Barnsley in the early 1860s. His premises were in that part of Sheffield

Road formerly known as Crow Well Hill, and numbered 59-63. Horsfield also described himself as outfitter and silversmith.

He was successful in business, being able to establish another branch in Wombwell (in partnership with a Mr Hall of Sheffield) and like other Barnsley business figures, resided on Huddersfield Road. After his death 'W.G. Horsfield' continued to flourish as a family concern, offering a very wide variety of goods. Eventually the shop was described simply as 'Horsfields' or 'Horsfields Store' as can be seen in a 1947 advertisement (Figure 10) imploring customers to 'Meet me under the clock where Horsfields sell nearly everything'. The store continued to operate until about 1971 and was therefore one of the longest established pawnbrokers in Barnsley, with over a century of continuous service.

Like Bailey, Horsfield was a Liberal, serving as secretary to the S E Ward Committee that interviewed potential election candidates. He was himself elected to the town council on three occasions: in 1881, 1884 and 1892. Horsfield presided over the formal opening of the new

Figure 8 New Street in c1910. Mostly re-built and refurbished properties. J H Baileys next to John Guest & Sons. There was probably strong competition between these shops — notice the range of wares on display in front of the shop windows. (*Dancerama*)

Figure 9 J H Bailey's 'House Furnishers' shop, Kendray Street market. *(Harry Brookes)*

Barnsley Cattle Market, Kendray Sreet, in 1884. Always interested in public affairs, he helped to found the Barnsley Agricultural and Horticultural Society (1881), the Barnsley and District Mutual Plate Glass Assurance Association and was an overseer of the poor for six years. He was described by his obituarist as 'a most agreeable companion, full of fun and anecdote, and free and open-handed to a fault.' Six mourning coaches attended his funeral. Businessmen such as William Bailey and William Horsfield were not the shadowy figures as portrayed in literary caricatures but were respected and public spirited citizens of Victorian Barnsley.

Life as a Pawnbroker's Apprentice : Lionel Bedford

An audio recording of a conversation with Mr Lionel Bedford (see Figure 11), born Wakefield, in 1902, provides us with very interesting information about what life was like as an apprentice pawnbroker.[6]

Figure 10 A 1947 advertisement for Horsfields, illustrating the wide range of goods on sale. Notice the reference to 'Checks and Coupons' (See Margaret Holderness's article in Part Two, below). From the *Penistone Almanack*.

Lionel started his seven-year term at the age of fourteen, on 4 July 1916, and received seven shillings a week, his meals and a bed in the basement of the shop premises. His master was William Richards who, with his brother Hardy, ran a busy pawnbrokers by the market place at Wakefield, access to the pledge office being via Zetland Street. Richards appears to have been a well-established firm, described in a 1906 trade directory as 'pawnbroker, jeweller, clothier etc' and later operating as 'house furnisher', according to a 1922 directory.[7]

Shortly after successfully completing his apprenticeship, Lionel was introduced by William Richards to the important Barnsley pawnbrokers, John Guest and Sons, whose large and imposing headquarters were located on New Street. He was subsequently appointed as manager of their Hoyland branch.

After about six months Lionel moved on, possibly to a shop at nearby Elsecar and certainly by the late 1920s was managing a shop at Royston, owned by a Mr McLintock who had a similar business in Cudworth.

Lionel sensibly retained references and testimonials in support of his job applications. Mr McLintock would almost certainly have been shown the following reference from 'William Richards Limited', dated 3 December 1925:

> *Dear Sir*
>   *Lionel Bedford was in our employ from 1916 until 1925. He came as a boy and was with us until he was well over 21. He left our employ to better himself and we were sorry to loose his services.*
>   *We found him a straight, honest, industrious lad and man and are very pleased to bear testimony to his character, ability and willingness.*
>   *We give him this reference with the knowledge that he will give satisfaction.*
>   *Yours etc*
>   *William Richards Ltd*
>   *& J. Hardy Richards (Directors)*

A testimonial, on headed-notepaper, from John Guest & Sons Ltd., also survives in family papers (Figure 12) showing that Guests were very pleased with Lionel's short stint at Hoyland.

Lionel Bedford had to leave the pawnbroking trade in the 1930s when McLintock's Royston shop was taken over by a Sheffield firm, at a time when pawnbroking was beginning to decline. Although Lionel's recollections are mainly in the context of his Wakefield experience they are relevant to other settings, including Barnsley.

As a young school leaver Lionel saw a notice in the Richards' shop window, 'Wanted. A Good Ticket Writer. Apply Within'. He applied,

ESTABLISHED 1870.

ALL COMMUNICATIONS TO BE ADDRESSED
DIRECT TO THE FIRM.

Telephone: BARNSLEY 489.

John Guest & Sons, Ltd.,

HEAD OFFICE:
NEW STREET,
BARNSLEY.

BRANCHES:
HIGH STREET,
WOMBWELL.
KING STREET,
HOYLAND.
WAKEFIELD RD.,
NORMANTON.
MANCHESTER RD.,
STOCKSBRIDGE.
DONCASTER RD.,
GOLDTHORPE.

Clothiers, Jewellers, Boot and Shoe Manufacturers,
and General Outfitters,

28 and 30, New Street,

Barnsley.

15th December 1925.

TO WHOM THIS MAY CONCERN.

Mr. L. W. Bedford, of 233 Lower Kirkgate, Wakefield,
recently on the staff of this Company, has asked us to give
him a testimonial.   We have always found Mr. Bedford
thoroughly honest and trustworthy, and during the 6 months
he has been with this firm he has given every satisfaction
as Manager of our Hoyland Branch.

FOR JOHN GUEST & SONS, LIMITED.

W. Marston.

Secretary.

Figure 12 Lionel Bedford's testimonial from John Guest & Sons Ltd. *(Maureen Hambrecht)*

assuming that the job entailed writing out information about shop goods on price tags! William Richards must have been pleased with the lad since he arranged to meet his parents and all were happy with an apprenticeship agreement. Lionel described aspects of his early work experience:

> *There were two lads* [apprentices], *two bosses* [W & H Richards] *and a manager, Mr Shepley. He frightened me when I was first introduced to him; he had a big white beard and wore a skull cap and an alpaca jacket. I started work at five* [a.m.] *and finished at about nine* [p.m.] *but we weren't allowed to pull the shop shutters down so long as there was anyone around who might pledge something. My first task was to make a fire in the fireplace, and then we opened up.*

'Opening-up' must have been a daunting experience for the young apprentice, for a large queue would have assembled outside the shop, especially on a Monday morning. Lionel described an amazing catalogue of movable objects awaiting inspection, including flat irons, men's Sunday suits, sheets, pillow cases and of course family jewels. Such was the demand that Richards employed a man on 'crowd control' every morning, whose principal job was to ensure an orderly flow into the pledge department. After the rush had died down, about three hours later, Lionel and his fellow apprentice had a well-deserved breakfast, but there was a very long day ahead. The shop stayed open 'as long as there was anyone in the street', so this usually meant eight or nine p.m., especially in the summer and on market days. He had a half-day off, on Wednesdays, but had to work a long day on Saturdays.

Lionel's tasks included a great deal of physical work, moving articles between the pledge office and storage areas:

> *We had a big warehouse. There were two flights of steps. As a warehouse boy I had to go to the top floor and every time a bell rang had to go to a chute, pull on a piece of string, open a bag containing perhaps six tickets and my job was to find the articles and send them down the chute. The manager would give them to whoever bought tickets and take the money. I had to take all the articles up to the top floor.*
>
> *My job on Saturday nights, at seven, was to empty all the shelves, cart the articles upstairs and pack them all away. Some of them were very heavy, so it was hard work.*

We can also gain further insight with regard to the business-side of the pawnbroking trade by reference to Lionel's early experiences:

> *Jewellery was the most common item pledged. The long counter rested on about six safes, used for different types of jewellery — watches, rings, bracelets, necklaces, silver cups etc. Sometimes 'posh' people*

such as actors and actresses would pawn their jewellery, We had a private box or door for them to use. Some people pawned with us because it was safer and cheaper than using a bank.

We charged a commission of five pence [2p] per £1 per month. There was also a ticket charge of ½d for up to ten shillings [50p], a little more for more valuable items. Goods were kept for twelve months and seven days before we could sell them.

There was a shop assistant in our Jewellery Department and another in the Clothing Department.

Lionel's work included a considerable amount of 'book keeping', entering information into huge ledgers. He was also able to describe the system of 'grading' articles according to their valuation:

I was a ticket writer but had to stand on a wooden box to write in huge ledgers, otherwise I couldn't reach. I had to turn pages over and fill in each column how much had been lent, number of articles etc. I also had to wrap the article, if required, pin the ticket on one half of it and slide the other half of the ticket on to our long counter. The counter was an enormous length. It was highly polished, so things would fly along it. The manager would look at the ticket and pay it out. There were 'lows', 'highs', 'agreements' and 'auctions' on these tickets. A 'low' went up to ten shillings. We were compelled by law to send to auction valuable items, usually to Hepper & Sons of Leeds, but we always put a price on them, so that if it wasn't sold it came back to us.

The recollections of Lionel Bedford help us to appreciate what life must have been like working in a pawnbroker's shop in the early years of this century. There must have been similar experiences in the Victorian period, and his reference to 'living-in' and 'opening all hours' have links with shopkeeping as far back as the seventeenth century.

Appendix

SOME BARNSLEY PAWNBROKERS

BAILEY, William	Sheffield Road	1862-1889
BAILEY, John Hargreaves	" "	1862-c1914
BAILEY, Joseph	New Street	c1870-c1914
BARTON, N	Doncaster Road	c1900-1938
BLAKEY, James	Sheffield Road	c1860-c1880
CLOUGH, James/Jasper	New Street (Oxley's Yard)	c1850-c1870
FOUNDHERE, W	Doncaster Road	c1900-c1914
GRIMWOOD, W H★	Sheffield Road	c1900-1914
GUEST, John and Sons Ltd	New St/Sheffield Road	c1865-1959
HARGREAVES, Joseph	Sheffield Road	c1830-1864
HARGREAVES and BAILEY	" "	1847-c1862
HARRALS STORES LTD	Shambles Street	c1870-1966
JUBB, Joshua	School Street	c1820-?
MELLOR, George	Shambles Street	1860s
WIKE, Ruth Mrs	New Street	c1840-1870s
ATKINSONS★	Sheffield Road/New St	c1880-1900
BROWN, Herbert	Peel Street	1991-present

★ Pledge Shop

Notes and References

1. There has been a small revival in the pawnbroking trade in Barnsley, with the recent establishment (in 1991) of a branch of Herbert Browns at 28 Peel Street, based mainly on jewellery. Cash loans are offered in the traditional way, private and confidential arrangements via the door at the side of the shop. Interviewed by the *Barnsley Chronicle* in 1993 shop manageress Christine Smith described how some regulars came to the shop every Friday 'to raise a bit of money to tide them over the weekend. Then they will come back on Monday and buy it back'. Browns were established in 1840, now have 13 branches, with headquarters in Castleford.
2. Briggs, Asa *Victorian Things*, 1988 p 41
3. *ibid*
4. Bailey's obituary can be found in the *Barnsley Chronicle*, 13.5.1899
5. Horsfield's obituary can be found in the *Barnsley Chronicle*, 12.3.1895
6. Recorded at Mr Bedford's home, Isle of Wight, by Maureen Hambrecht, 28.12.1989. Mr Bedford died in 1993.
7. Courtesy of John Goodchild, 19.8.95. The Richards shop is listed as at 34 Teal Street in 1906 and 30-32 (pawnbrokers) and 34-36 Teal Street in 1922, then known as WRS Limited. The firm is not listed in a 1936 directory so may well have ceased trading.

Acknowledgements

I am extremely grateful to Maureen Hambrecht for permission to use extracts from her recording of her Uncle, Lionel Bedford, and also for loaning photographic and documentary information. I would like to thank John Goodchild for background information relating to the Richards of Wakefield firm. My thanks also to Herbert Browns of Barnsley.

Figure 13 W G Horsfield's pawnbrokers and outfitters shop, Sheffield Road. It must have been a long job every morning to put up the street window display. Notice the PLEDGING OFFICE, entrance via side of the shop, a typical arrangement. *(Barnsley Archives & Local Studies)*

Part Two
'My First Job and How I Got It'

by Margaret Holderness

IN 1940 TO TRY AND 'SPEAK FOR' a job yourself, was an incredible thing to do for anyone, still less a girl approaching her fifteenth birthday. The straitened circumstances in which we lived, plus my determination to get the sort of job I wanted, were the reasons for my previously unheard of behaviour, especially amongst families living in poverty.

Longcar Central School which I attended from the age of eleven years was, for its time, a very progressive school. Not only committed to teaching the three 'Rs' but also teaching pupils about life beyond school. For example, two years before the Second World War, Longcar adopted a ship. Through an exchange of letters from the pupils and the officers and men on board, we learned of the duties and day to day activities of the ship's personnel. Visits for the day were arranged when the ship was anchored in the Manchester Ship Canal. This was my first experience of afternoon tea, sitting at a table covered with a crisp, white cloth on which were matching cups, saucers and plates. We were waited on by some of the ship's personnel dressed in immaculate white jackets and smart black trousers. I never forget the excitement and joy of this visit. When, early in 1940, Mr Williamson our Headmaster, told us our ship had been sunk and many killed including the Captain, we felt as if a member of our family had died. The war had touched our school in a very sad way.

For six weeks, during the second term of our last year at school, the girls and boys swapped places. For two lessons a week, the girls were taught woodwork and the boys cookery. In the last few weeks at school, we were all encouraged to discuss with our teachers what job we felt was within our competence. The headmaster and senior teachers liaised with the various shops, offices and businesses in Barnsley. Each pupil,

Figure 14 Benjamin Gaunt & Sons Jewellers Shop faced May Day Green at the junction with narrow Queen Street — a prime site for trade. Notice the clock and 'cobbled' street. This view probably dates from the 1930s, perhaps photographed on a Sunday or in the evening since the street is almost deserted and no shops are open. *(Barnsley Archives & Local Studies)*

after an interview with the respective managers/manageresses of a suitable place of employment was given a week's trial during term-time. To be chosen for a week's trial was considered a good mark both for the school and ourselves. To be given a job after the week's trial was even better.

My determination not to be a servant or maid led me to say, 'Working in a shop', when asked what job I would like. Days Music Shop in Shambles Street chose me and a very attractive girl called Joyce for an interview and subsequent week's trial. I enjoyed my week, running errands, dusting and putting the hundreds of records in the right order on the many shelves, even though I instinctively knew Joyce would be given the job.

I returned to school after my week, telling no one of my inner humiliation and sense of failure, at not relieving my Mother's hardship by becoming the family wage-earner. Greater than the humiliation was the fear of being forced to accept a job as a servant. This fear led me to do what was strictly forbidden. That was to ask for a job myself!

II

My fifteenth birthday was only a few weeks away and a continual row had been going on between my mother and me. The row was serious, I was a widow's elder daughter and had to face the inescapable fact that I was soon to become the family breadwinner. There were only two situations open to me, 'in service' or shop work, and this is what the row was about.

Having been a rebel since birth, albeit a quiet rebel, I nervously stated my views, showing all the pigheadedness that only a frightened fifteen year old can. The issue was simple, there was no way I was going into service, it just did not appeal. Film star, wife of a rich man or 'mistress' of same (I had no idea what 'mistress' meant, I hasten to add, but always wearing furs and diamonds appealed strongly to my romantic and book-loving mind). I was proud to work, but servant — Never! I was adamant.

My mother was an excellent dressmaker who sewed for anyone, even if they couldn't pay. The well-to-do customer, used to charge accounts, sometimes forgot to pay as well, so it was a meagre living. One of my mother's nicer customers had promised to 'speak for me' not only to find me an opening in a respectable house but by giving me a reference too. This pleased my mother; her reference, together with one from the Vicar, would assure my future.

When I told my mother that I could not accept, her face went grey and I nearly gave in. For me to turn down the offer was bad enough, but would my mother lose a good customer and, worse, would I ever get the chance of another job? I decided then that something had to be done and only I could do it.

On several occasions I sat in this lady's house to answer the telephone, whilst she and her husband attended a function. It was during one of these evenings that I found the courage to tell her that I had only refused her offer because I wanted something better. This was very radical thinking in the daughter of an impoverished widow, but she seemed to understand, delighting me by also promising to mention me to the manager of a leading departmental store.

I rushed home to tell my mother all was well, her daughter was going to join the ranks of genteel black-clad ladies who earned their living by helping the better-off choose their underwear and haberdashery. The lady, alas, was the very busy wife of a solicitor, and as the weeks went by and no letter came, my heart sank into my shoes.

My mother's face began to look grey again, and although she never said a word, two weeks before my birthday I realised that desperate measures were called for. Although I somehow trusted the lady to keep her word, I dared not risk being without a job. My mother had carried her burden of poverty alone for too long.

During my walks to school, and at playtime, I began to make enquiries, and to my delight found a girl whose father was manager of a big shop at the other end of town. She had no idea what kind of shop, except that it was big. We figured he must be an important man because he went to work in a dark grey suit and always wore a hat.

Together we laid our plans, me shivering with nervous excitement at the enormity of what I proposed to do. Protocol was unknown to us, but I was fully aware of the fact that no fifteen year old ever 'spoke for herself'.

We decided that Thursday dinner time half-day-closing would find Father at his most amenable. At last the moment came, I stood on his doormat shaking in every limb.

'Sir', I said gabbling incoherently.

'Speak up, Miss', he said.

Encouraged by the grown up 'Miss', I rushed into speech.

'Sir, please sir, I leave school in two weeks, I'm tidy and punctual, my mother is a widow and I must have a job.'

There was a dreadful silence for what seemed eternity and then Mr Brown spoke.

'Does your mother know you're going to ask me for a job?'

'Yes,' I said.

'Can you stand swearing?'

'Yes,' I said, raising my eyes to heaven and hoping God would forgive me those two lies.

BENJ^N. GAUNT AND SONS,

WATCHMAKERS

AND

JEWELLERS,

DEALERS IN

FANCY GOODS, &c.

The LARGEST Stock of WATCHES, CLOCKS, JEWELLERY, SPECTACLES, ELECTROPLATE, & WEDDING RINGS, at the CHEAPEST Prices.

The Largest Stock of **WATCHES** to Select from :

Silver Geneva Watches, from 18/6 each.

English Levers (Sound & Strong) from £3 each.

Everyone Warranted for FIVE YEARS.

CLOCKS in every Style and Description of Case.

30 hrs. Clocks, from 2/6 each.

8-days' Striking Clocks, from 13/6 each.

Marble Clocks, from 15/- each.

Every Clock Warranted

SPECTACLES for every defect of the Eyesight.   Agent for Henry Laurance's, London ; and Chadburn Brothers, Sheffield.

WEDDING RINGS of Guinea Gold.   The Largest Stock in South Yorkshire.   A Present given with each.

The Largest and Best Assorted Stock of LADIES' and GENTS' GOLD and SILVER GUARDS & ALBERTS, at Prices which cannot be equalled.

B. G. & S's. beg to announce that their FANCY GOODS DEPARTMENT is now replete with every Description of Goods in LEATHER, WOOD, BRONZE, PLUSH, GLASS, &c., Suitable for Presents of every kind.

OUR ONLY ADDRESS :

3 & 4, MAY-DAY GREEN, BARNSLEY.

Figure 15 An advertisement for Benjamin Gaunt & Sons, taken from an 1888 Almanack. The FANCY GOODS DEPARTMENT many have been a recent addition. *(Brian Elliott Collection)*

'Tell your mother I will see you at nine sharp Tuesday morning and bring two references with you.'

The shop was big; four departments in all, in a poorer part of the town. It appeared to sell everything; I caught a glimpse of clothing, bedding, shoes, watches and clocks as I walked by. It didn't look very elegant but nothing was going to stop me now, and in I went. I was so busy praying that I got this job that I failed to see the three large brass balls hung outside.

A young lady ushered me into a small office. My references seemed to be in order and Mr Brown said I could start the following Monday. My duties were to help serve in Gents Outfitting, when I was not helping him; 'helping him' was to be my main duty, and he offered to show me where I would work.

Walking through the shoe department, past a cash desk where money was sent in cups along overhead wires, we entered a very large room. It had a long counter in the middle, running the whole length of the room. Blinking in the dim light, I saw that all the walls on this side of the counter were covered with shelves up to twenty feet high, full of brown paper parcels with tickets on; at intervals there were long ladders

Figure 16 Sheffield Road, looking north towards the junction with Doncaster Road, c1956 *(Barnsley Archives & Local Studies)*

stretching up to the ceiling. Slowly it dawned on me, it was a pawnshop. What *was* I going to say to my mother?

Mr Brown explained that the pawnshop got very busy, and he needed an assistant (me) to fetch each parcel matching the ticket he gave me; I was to learn to run and be quick. I was also responsible for moving the parcels along in strict rotation of days, weeks and months, and there were two more rooms on separate floors upstairs. As the law stood, we had to keep the parcels not redeemed for one year and one day.

I had not only to find the parcels but to be responsible for seeing that none were ever lost. The importance of this rotation was soon revealed to me as later I ran up and down continuously, supplying Mr Brown as quickly as possible with the right parcel.

My Mother's face was a study when I bravely said that I'd got a job in a pawnshop. Stressing my five shilling wage and the good discount on any goods bought, allayed her fears, even if it didn't mine. Seeing her face gradually light up quelled my own doubts and I said goodbye to my dreams of black-clad elegance for ever.

On Monday morning I arrived at 8 a.m. I soon became absorbed in putting away parcels from the Friday before. For a moment I envied the girls in the shop laughing together, but felt it was not so bad.

Soon I became aware of a strange rumbling noise outside the tightly shut doors of the shop and an occasional thumping. This increased until, promptly at nine o'clock, Mr Brown looked at his pocket watch and nodded to a tall youth standing by, who unlocked and opened the big doors.

Nothing in my experience had prepared me for the rush of women of all shapes and sizes who pushed their way to the counter, shouting 'Morning, Brown', these were the bold regulars; the shy nervous ones sat on a bench at the back. 'Are you in a good mood, Brown? Gie'ing owt away? Rent's due and t'lad needs boots'. Calmly saying, 'Settle down ladies, one at a time, please. No rushing this new lass', Mr Brown started to work. All eyes suddenly focused on me and the laughing and ribaldry came quickly. 'My God, Brown, where's tha got this white-faced ginger'un from this time? Tha's scraped t'bottom of t'barrel this time!' Turning back to me, they said 'Tha'll have to run like hell, lass, no waiting for us, no posh little 'uns wanted here.' Thankfully the parcels came thick and fast, and time fled by. Soon I became absorbed in this strange job, and wondered about the lives of these women. What lay behind the pawning of these suits, blankets, and, sadly, many, many wedding rings? I learned to joke with them and to respect and understand why they came.

My eighteen months in the pawnshop gave me a great insight into human nature. I enjoyed meeting and talking to these women, who did their best through poverty and hardship.

I only moved to the cash-desk at sixteen and a half years old because it was such a big step up and meant more money for my mother, and I loved this new job working with figures. One of the bonuses was that my cash-desk backed on the pawnshop. I could still hear those familiar voices laughing, joking, swearing, as they pawned their only decent bits for food, rent or drink for their men.

I came to respect Mr Brown; he was a fair man. While appearing to drive a hard bargain, he could, at a glance, perceive desperation and, without letting those women lose pride, add a halfpenny or a penny, just that week, which made all the difference to that family's food and comfort.

I thank God today that those brass balls have largely disappeared, and many people scarcely remember them and the desperation of those times. I remember with happiness, though, learning my first lesson of life as it was lived then, among those brown paper parcels.

To end happily, my nice lady did not let me down. On that first Monday morning when I started my job at the pawnshop, I received a letter offering me a position at that leading department store. It was then that I made my first grown-up decision; I wrote back thanking her for her kindness, but explaining that I had got a job which I was happy to continue.

III

I did not regret this decision, because working at Horsfields in Sheffield Road not only gave me, a girl brought up in a quiet, strict, all female household, a knowledge of people which proved invaluable, but during the two-and a-half years I worked there Horsfields and Sheffield Road were a continual source of wonder and fascination.[1]

Horsfields was owned by Benjamin Gaunt, a well known jeweller and clockmaker.[2] He inherited the firm from his wife, Miss Litherland. He was a wise, kind if somewhat autocratic boss who took a great interest in the staff and how the shop was administered.

Always referred to as 'the shop', Horsfields was in fact four shops; each with its own separate glass door and prominent window display. Gent's Outfitting, Jewellery, Hardware and Ladies Fashion; a department which sold ladies underwear; blouses and accessories downstairs, ladies coats, suits and dresses upstairs.

The large pawnshop, so important to the many people with little or no income, was at the back of these departments, with a separate door in a back street behind Horsfields.

Mr Wilson managed Horsfields in a quiet, efficient and disciplined way. He, together with the department managers/manageresses and the various shop assistants, taught me how to keep stock neat, clean and tidy — *and* how to serve each customer in a polite and pleasant way, whether they were paying cash or using checks.

Horsfield sold cheap, reasonable quality goods and clothing, displayed inside and outside the shop. Before the war checks were the means by which hundreds of families paid for such necessities. These checks were paper certificates, (approximately 4″ x 6″) issued by *Provident and Mutual* (the two largest check companies) and several smaller companies. They were worth in spending power, sums ranging from £1 to £5 (in multiples of 10/- [50p]) and, less frequently issued, sums from £5 to £10. People who were accepted by the check company, had to pay the required sum each week in return for the check. Most shops, including Horsfields took *Provident and Mutual* checks as payment, fewer shops

Figure 17 Queueing outside the Alhambra c1940. *(Stan Bulmer)*

would accept the small company checks. The very large Co-op shops did not; they issued their own checks, usually to people who were 'better off' than Horsfields' customers.[3]

The two methods of payment, and the acceptance of such a variety of checks, meant Horsfields was a very busy shop. The continual flow of people inside the shop, was matched only by the continual throng of people in Sheffield Road walking to and from the town centre, especially on Friday and Saturday evenings. My Mother's concern that I would see a lot of drunken people when I worked late on those evenings (7.30 pm and 8 pm) was allayed when I told her, my only thought, was visiting the 'pictures', especially the Alhambra. I was wise enough not to add, that I thought the strong smell of beer which permeated the air in Sheffield Road, just added to its interesting atmosphere.

The Alhambra picture house (formerly a theatre) was situated only a few minutes walk away from Horsfields, and after I was sixteen years old, I was allowed to go to a second house performance at 8 pm. The Alhambra was everything I dreamed about when I read a rare copy of *Picturegoer*, left occasionally by my Mother's more affluent dressmaking customers. Each visit to this 'posh cinema', with its plush seats and equally ornate inside decorations, added 'glamour' to my life and fulfilled all my most romantic dreams through the films shown.[4] Each time I ran down from Horsfields to join the long queue of people waiting to see a second house performance, I felt 'rich', grown up and a little daring!

There were shops (and several pubs) on each side of Sheffield Road, and on the same side as Horsfields, higher up the road was a photographic studio, which was owned by Mr Irving.[5] Mr Irving was one of the two most important photographers in Barnsley. When I passed this studio, with its large, black glass window and distinctive gold lettering, I viewed it with some awe, knowing my Mother and Father's important engagement photograph had been taken there. When, just after my seventeenth birthday, and a few months before I left Horsfields to go nursing, I had saved the money for a sepia photograph of myself, I felt I had reached the pinnacle of grown-up importance as I walked through the door of Mr Irving's studio.

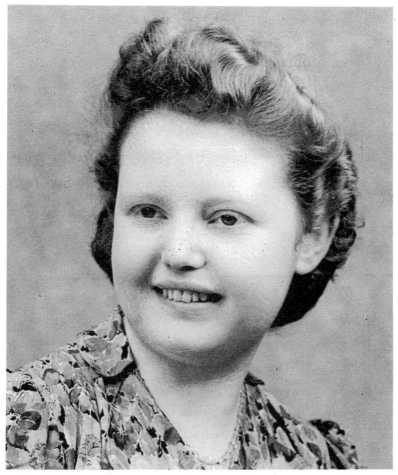

Figure 18 Margaret Holderness, aged seventeen, a typical studio photograph of the period.

Notes and References

1. Houses now stand on the site where Horsfields was situated.
2. [Benjamin Gaunt, the founder of the firm, was born in Barnsley in 1835. He served his apprenticeship to well-known Barnsley clockmaker Thomas Allen of Queens Street, setting up in business himself in about 1862. After his death, aged 53, in 1888, the business was initially run by his sons. By 1914 the firm claimed to have 'the longest, and most comprehensive Watchmakers and Jewellers Stock in South Yorkshire'. A Methodist, Conservative and Freemason, Gaunt lived on Huddersfield Road. One of W G Horsfield's daughters married one of his sons, so there was a family connection between the two businesses — Editor].
3. The edge of the clock face outside Herbert Brown, pawnbrokers of Peel Street, Barnsley has the legend 'USE MUTUAL CHECKS' and 'ALWAYS RICH'.
4. The equally 'posh' well lit and comfortable Alhambra Shopping Centre was built on the site of the Alhambra cinema in 1991.
5. Mr Irving's studio was demolished in the 1950s to provide a new road. Sepia (photographs in brown and white) were considered to be the most 'high class' photographs in the 1930s and 1940s.

9. THE JOSEPH MITCHELL MEMORIAL HALL: A SAD TALE

by John Goodchild, M. Univ

IT WAS IN THE EARLY WEEKS OF 1876 that Joseph Mitchell, engineer and colliery owner, died at sixty nine. His body was interred in the graveyard of St. Thomas's Church at Worsbrough Dale, but — unusually — his memory was kept fresh by a decision to erect a publicly-useful Memorial Hall. Within the West Riding coalfield such a proposal was itself unusual, but the story of the building and opening of the Hall, and its ultimate failure, as a public institution are apparently unique.

The recent find in a secondhand bookseller's shop of a copy of the minute book of 'The Mitchell's Memorial Fund', together with the use of other papers which are all in the John Goodchild Collection at Wakefield, allow the story of this unusual memorial venture to be studied in some detail. What was proposed, backed by Mitchell's sons and brought into being by an active group of the workmen of the foundry and the three collieries in which Joseph Mitchell had had an interest, was a building which could house a proposed Worsbrough Dale Mechanics' Institution, Reading Room and Library and also be let for lectures and concerts.

But first, who was Joseph Mitchell? He was a self-made man: apprenticed at the Milton Ironworks near Elsecar, he had subsequently been a journey man at Barnsley and elsewhere before taking a small foundry at Worsbrough himself when in his early thirties. Here he had prospered, in an area where the exploitation of the Barnsley bed of coal was prospering and where there were glassmaking, iron smelting, boat building, lime burning and coalmining, and a branch canal — and later a branch railway too — to bring in such raw materials as were not available locally, and to take away some of the finished products. Mitchell had manufactured boilers and been a general ironfounder, later taking up railway waggon building in addition; he took a coal lease in 1852 and two years later took partners in forming what became the Edmunds and Swaithe Coal Company: he was the managing partner. He received some blame for the disasters at those collieries in 1862 and 1875 respectively, and he died some thirteen months after the latter of them. Meanwhile, in the autumn of 1875 the Barnsley coal was reached in a new colliery called Mitchell's Main, in the development of which he had again taken partners.

THE EDMUND MAIN COLLIERY, NEAR BARNSLEY.—SKETCHED FROM THE BANK NEAR THE MASONS' ARMS.

The idea of commemorating Mitchell is said to have been that of his sons Joseph and John, but it was enthusiastically supported by the workmen of his foundry and three collieries, and men from all four were on the commitee which was set up to consider the matter in detail. The first meeting of the promoters of 'the Mitchell's Memorial Hall' was held at the Mason's Arms Club Room at Worsbrough Dale early in March 1876, where it was agreed to build on a site which was described as adjoining the Co-op Stores New Wesleyan Chapel. A committee was set up of three men from each of the four Mitchell concerns, with power to invite three further members. The public was to be informed of the decision to build, and within a few days agreement had been reached to buy land at 1s 3d (5.25p) a square yard; ultimately 400 square yards were bought at 1s 3d and 280 more at 2s 6d (10.5p). When acquired, the land was put into the hands of three trustees, headed by Joseph Mitchell junior.

The committee of the new Hall was very active, and although occasionally a Mitchell brother would attend, the venture seems to

Mitchell Main Colliery. *Barnsley Canal Group*

have been primarily a working men's venture in its implementation.
Subscriptions for the site and buildings were initially sought from
Mitchell employees, apparently alone, but it was soon decided to widen
the appeal via 1000 circulars which were to be printed. By ten weeks
after the committee was set up, Tacon & Rawson had prepared plans,
and others were invited to compete for a design. It was Wade & Turner,
architects of 10, Pitt Street in Barnsley whose design was selected and
who were awarded the premium of fifteen guineas, and it was their
design which was used, although in what was described as a 'curtailed'
form. Tenders for the new building were sought and obtained: Lawton
& Schofield of Duke Street, Barnsley, successfully tendered for the
principal, the masons' work, at £950, or less if the stone were given
and delivered, and there were tenders for the joinery, slating, plumbing
and glazing, plastering, etc.

But not all was going well. Money came in slowly in a difficult period
for the coal industry regionally. Mr Edmunds, the local landowner,
offered to give a lecture in aid of the funds, but the fund grew only
slowly, and for a long period there were no committee meetings. Then
in April 1879, some two years after the original tenders had come in,
new tenders were sought, and the tenderers were bargained-with:
eventually, £850 was agreed with Marvell & Aspin of Worsbrough
Bridge for the stonework, and the trustees of the late Joseph Mitchell
were asked to advance £1000. The corner stone of the Memorial Hall
was laid with Masonic honours in July 1879 by Henry Josse of Grimsby

and Paris, coal shipper, a partner in Mitchell's Main, assisted by the officers etc of the Friendly Lodge at Barnsley. An apparently sumptuous banquet was indulged in, as usual on such occasions.

A year later, it was decided that subscriptions to the new Mechanics' Institute be sixpence (2.5p) monthly, in advance, that an opening tea be provided and that a concert (there was a stage, stage curtain and stage carpet) be considered: the hall was to be opened. The Institute was to be open from 8.30am to 10pm, Mrs Jagger was appointed Hall keeper at five shillings (25p) a week, and it was decided to take four daily newspapers and three weeklies, plus illustrated sporting papers. What were described as the Barnsley Rules were to be adopted for Worsbrough Dale Institute, and in August, 1880 the committee met in its own Reading Room. Membership was quite small, despite the production of a handbill soliciting membership, and there were only twenty four members (twenty of those with the address of Worsbrough Dale), with a committee of seventeen.

A year later, in July, 1881, Drs. Sadler and Blackburn were to be asked to provide lectures on the St. John's Ambulance, and later in that year a series of Penny Readings was to be arranged, and some concerts. The Hall was to be let for outside events at a minimum of fifteen shillings a night, including gas. The last entry in the minutes relates to the organisation of a social, to be held in the last weeks of 1881.

The Institute had in fact only a short further life. The money borrowed to complete the building could not be repaid: as was written at the time — early in 1883 —

> '*The Memorial Hall has come to grief. It was finished and opened but the Miners of the district did not seem to have any desire to be educated.*'

The mortgagees took possession, and the Institute ceased to exist; the mortgagees found no bidder for the Hall and the situation became legally complicated — so much so that Counsels' opinions had to be taken, and the story ends with the Hall and its site the subject of a Chancery suit.

10. A BACKWARD GLANCE: MEMORIES OF A BARNSLEY CHILDHOOD

by Edna Forrest

I HOWLED AS I ROLLED DOWN THE STONE STAIRS. It was Christmas morning 1934, and, at three years old, I was eager to see what delights the pillowcase held for me. I remember feeling a great sense of relief on seeing it bulging, almost bursting its seams with odd and fascinating shapes. My last sighting of it before I finally closed my eyes, had been of a flat, lifeless and uninteresting piece of crisply starched linen. My mother's last words before she tucked me in were, 'If you haven't been good enough, he won't come!' Familiar words, designed to strike terror into the hearts of all children as Christmas Eve approached.

As I trundled down the staircase, the gifts, so carefully saved for and hidden throughout the year, and now packed tightly into the pillowcase, must have been over heavy for my tiny frame and I landed at the bottom of the staircase surrounded by the contents. A couple of oranges, an apple, a small doll, a pair of hand knitted mittens, lots of picture books and a jigsaw. There must have been many more cheap and probably homemade items, but these are all I can remember.

Although I was unhurt, I sat crying on the cold floor awaiting parental collection, which I knew would come.

I was, at that age, the apple of my parent's eyes. They had lost a child through scarlet fever just before I was born which led to my being rather spoilt, and with a gap of eleven years, the bane of my elder sister's life. She had been warned that she must not upset me because when I cried, I 'kinked'. I don't know whether this was one of my mother's own innovative words or not. No one else seems to have heard it, but it meant that I would hold my breath until I lost consciousness. I was informed by my sister, rather bitterly, in later years, that all it was was sheer ill humour and attention seeking!

I was picked up, together with as many toys as my hands could hold, and carried through the kitchen and into the living room, staring with some dismay at the strange face of my carrier. I remember everyone laughing and saying, 'She doesn't know you without your teeth.'

That was the one and only time I ever saw my dad [Norman C. Birkinshaw] toothless, although to this day I cannot look at a set of dentures without seeing a glimpse of that strange face with its frighteningly sunken mouth.

He was, as were most of the men in Barnsley, a miner, and another one of my early recollections is of hearing the sound of the 'knocker up' hitting the window with his long wire. My father worked regular days [at Woolley Colliery], which meant an early start, around four o'clock in the morning. No breakfast — just time to light the fire and pick up his snap tin. This would be the only food he would have during the whole of his shift. No canteens in those days.

Most miners' snap was cheese sandwiches, but my father had bread and jam. No butter. Every day of his working life, butterless bread and

Wedding of Edna's grandparents, Ann Brown and Arthur Ernest Sacre, Barnsley, 1899, aged 18 and 19 years respectively. Arthur Ernest died aged 26 years. Ann remarried, becoming Ann Millett.

jam and a bottle of water! Cheese, he said, give him indigestion when working in low seams.

After the sound of the 'knocker up' within a very short time there would be the comforting clink of miners' clogs marching purposefully down the street to where the 'paddy' was waiting to take the men to the pit. I'm not sure why I use the word 'comforting', except that perhaps I knew that I could go back to sleep for several hours and that when I eventually went down stairs, there would be a welcoming, lively fire blazing in the black-leaded fireplace. My mother's boast was that she had never had to light a fire.

Whatever else we went short of, we were never short of coal, although this did not come, as some people smugly and mistakenly say, free. It was part of the miners' pay. It was delivered, a ton at a time, at regular intervals, and tipped on to the pavement as near as possible to the 'coil oile', leading down to the cellar. Even at my tender age, I would feel sadness when I saw my father, after finishing a shift down the mine, approaching the mountain of black, shiny fuel waiting for him, and seeming to say, malevolently, "Now — shovel ME." And he would push back his cap from a face almost as black as the coal itself and, in spite of his small stature, attack and diminish the black pile with astonishing speed.

We lived in a two up and two down — outside ducket closet, no bathroom — at the top end of Silver Street. I emphasise the top end, because, for some inexplicite reason, I was not allowed to venture to the bottom end. I never thought to ask why. My mother's word was LAW. And woe betide my sister and me if we questioned it.

In addition to not having a bathroom, we did not have any running hot water. This had to be boiled in pans and kettles on the fire, and as there were no pithead baths, the zinc bath, hanging on a nail in the backyard, was brought in daily before my father came home from work, ready for it to be filled, monotonously, from the containers. My mother would scrub his back, although some miners would not wash their backs, saying that it would be weakened by the water.

They were a superstitious bunch, one of their beliefs being that if a pig was spotted on the road, they should not go down the mine. I can't imagine where this originated. I reckon it was sometimes an excuse to turn around and come back home because, although I lived in Barnsley for over twenty years, I never once saw a pig on the road!

But who can blame them. My mother went down the mine to see the working conditions and swore that she would never again shout at my dad if he missed a shift.

Presumably because of the claustrophobic conditions of the mine, and the need for fresh air, the miners followed many outside pursuits.

Edna's grandmother, Ann Sacre and mother, Lillian Sacre in 1900.

Fishing, gardening, pigeon fancying, but for the men from my street, the favourite occupations were nipsy, rounders and pitch and toss, this last game being illegal, requiring lookouts. This necessitated playing on open ground and took place on waste land near the now Dillington greyhound track. Pitch and toss is played with a couple of coins and some miners gambled heavily, inflicting much hardship on their homes although fortunately, these were in a minority.

The majority concentrated on nipsy and rounders. Nipsy, although frowned upon by their wives because of the danger of broken windows was the most popular of the two. This was — or is it still? — played by fashioning a small piece of wood to a pointed end, placing it on a brick, pointed end protruding, hitting it with a stick so that it flew into the air, then hitting it hard, making it travel as far as possible.

This 'playtime' was a most enjoyable part of the day, with the women, in clean pinafores, leaning with arms akimbo, on the doorjaums, children sitting on the doorsteps and dogs leaping into the air in a fruitless attempt to catch the nipsy before it landed. Fruitless because the nipsy was uncatchable, being hit with a stick held by muscular arms well used to wielding shovels filled to the shafts with the heavy, precious mineral that was their life blood. How we children managed to grow up with eyes intact in their sockets remains a mystery to me. There was always ill disguised relief on the faces of anxious mothers when nipsy gave way to the more genteel game of rounders, when the men would allow the children to take part, using the corners of the houses as 'home'.

Holidays were taken by almost everyone during BARNSLEY FEAST WEEK. Note - week. One week only, when the men were released from the bowels of the earth. Released from the hard toil of the backbreaking battle of wresting the black gold from the formidable and unaccommodating jaws of the coal seam, to partake of, hopefully, a little sunshine, fresh air and seaside fish and chips.

The queues for the coaches to Cleethorpes, Blackpool and Scarbro' would have gladdened the hearts of the present day bus companies. They stretched from the Bus Station along to Eldon Street. There were much shorter queues for the coaches to Great Yarmouth. These were the Barnsley elite! These were the families who stayed in those elegant establishments whose tables were covered with crisp white tablecloths and where the waitress would inquire if you wanted more toast and not sniff when you said yes — the PRIVATE GUEST HOUSE. These were the families whose houses had gardens and a bathroom. Who had a toilet roll behind the bathroom door, not squares of newspaper hanging on a nail hammered in to the back door of the outside lavvy! However, my mother must have been one of the perpetuators of the class system,

Left: Amy Egley, of Silver St. Right: Lillian Burkinshaw, Edna's sister and twelve years her senior. Centre: Edna, aged six. (What a PEST she must have been to those two young girls!). The photograph was taken in Locke Park.

because we travelled neither by coach or by train. We travelled by CAR. We travelled in Mr Purdy's car. He was the shopkeeper at the end of Silver Street and every year, he piled all our family, which by this time had increased by twins, into his Morris 8, complete with buckets, spades, dad's white plimsolls — and food, because we were self-catering.

We boarded with a Mrs Spedding. My mother provided the food and Mrs Spedding cooked it. We children were weighed before we left home and weighed again at the end of the holiday. If we had gained a few pounds, the holiday had been a success!

Twins, in a household whose budget must have been stretched to the limit even before they arrived, must have tested my mother's innovative skills to the ultimate, and it was only in later years that I began to understand why my requests for a halfpenny were so often refused. How my parents must have despaired at the frequent refusals and what shame I have felt over the years at my resorting to throwing a 'paddy'.

An illustration of a 'cash flow' shortage was the use of 'cinder tea' when the babies suffered from wind. This was made by pulling cinders from the fire into a cup of water, draining the residue, which when cool, was given to the child on the end of a spoon. No resources in our household for Nurse Harvey's gripe water!

I went to Agnes Road School when I was four, half-penny — or was it a penny — clutched in hand for milk. I was sent back home again because I was not old enough! I did eventually make it to school — and there I fell in love with a blonde haired boy named Ralph Burkinshaw — same surname as myself. Where are you now, Ralph and do you remember me?

I was slapped because I wrote my initials the wrong way round. I was slapped again because I was sick after drinking milk. Milk which had been left outside from first thing in the morning till eleven o' clock, by which time it was warm and disgusting.

I hated milk and learned to spend my milk money on an apple and a packet of biscuits. Unfortunately, one day I wandered into the house eating a biscuit and had to explain to my mother where I had obtained the said biscuit. Sinking deeper into the abyss, I lied and said that my gran had given me the money. My gran did NOT support me and I think I will gloss over that unfortunate incident.

One of the joys of my young life was the purchase of cockle peas, a welcome alternative to a bag of chips! Well seasoned with salt and vinegar, the peas had a taste on a cold frosty evening that has remained unrivalled. I subsequently learned that the correct name for this delicacy is CARLINGS. These are dried brown peas, and were sold by a lady

Edna Burkinshaw, aged nine. Pupil at 'Madame Butler's Dancing Academy', Pitt Street, Barnsley.

who lived in Fleming Street. She cooked them in the setpot and served them in a bag. Not a proper bag, but a square of newspaper rolled deftily into a 'poke'. A health inspector's nightmare now, I should think.

Another one of life's unsolved mysteries, for me anyway, is Hokey Pokey. What IS Hokey Pokey? A man would drive his van into the street, stop, blow his horn and shout at the top of his voice, 'HOOOOKY POKEEEE'.

And we would pester our mothers until they gave us a coin to buy one. It LOOKED like a tube of ice cream — but I still do not know what it is!

One of the horrors of my school days was when one of the children slipped off a wall in which were fixed iron spikes. Across the road from the school was a sweet shop and at play time, the shop keeper would sell sweets to any child who had a few pennies. The little girl had been jumping up and down on the wall and slipped, one of the iron spikes entering her throat and coming out through her cheek. I never heard the outcome of that awful incident, but the memory of her hanging on the spike stayed with me.

My mother cried as she related to me the tragedy of the Public Hall disaster of 1908, when sixteen children suffocated on the staircase after the children at the top were told to turn back. She cried because she saw it happen. She was there, at the top of the stairs. [This tragedy was the subject of Ian Harley's article in *Aspects of Barnsley 2* — Editor.]

I remember the 'Black Shirts' coming to town and setting up a marquee on waste ground in Pall Mall. I was warned by my parents not to go near, but on this occasion I defied them, even though I had to brave the horrors of walking to the bottom end of the street to reach the area. I do not know to this day what was so terrible about 'the bottom end'.

I listened to what the 'Black Shirts' had to say, but I might as well not have risked my parent's wrath, because I had no idea what they were talking about!

I would love to be able to say here that I had a great political awareness, but I have to admit that, although I was encouraged by my father to join the rest of the children at election time in some childish political battle, I never quite understood what I was meant to be doing. The battle involved the wrapping of a bundle of newspapers tightly and tying it with string. All the children did this. The idea was to inquire what colour poster was displayed in their window and if it was different to your own, you belted each others' paper parcel until one disintegrated. Much more civilised than planting bombs and shooting each other, don't you think?

I left Barnsley forty years ago. I have remembered with great affection, the 'Bug Hut', The Cuban, The Georges, The Ritz, pie and peas in the old market, Danny Blanchflower, the 'Bunny Run', Locke Park and its keeper, who kept us in order as teenagers and I have, in turn, hated it, defended it, despaired for it, loved it and been proud of it.

I have watched its town centre progress, whilst mourning the loss of some of its buildings and old established businesses. I have seen its bus station turn from being 'the best in Britain' to being a bit of a mess! (But Barnsley now has a new passenger inter-change — Editor). And the Town Hall seems to have shrunk since I was a child! I have seen the demise of its coal industry with sadness and cried with the miners during the strike.

What I have never been able to do is to forget or deny my roots and whenever I return and hear that rich, warm, distinctive accent, I am transported back, as if in a time capsule, to the safety and insularity of childhood days.

11. GREAT HOUGHTON OLD HALL

by Brian Elliott

ON A COLD SUNDAY IN FEBRUARY 1960, at a time when John F. Kennedy was beginning his presidential campaign, the Old Hall Inn at Great Houghton (Figures 1-2) was gutted by fire and subsequently demolished. The loss of a familiar building that had served customers since about 1820 was bad enough but it also meant that substantial remains of an important Elizabethan mansion, with interesting historic associations, was lost forever.[1] A small engraving of the house survives (Figure 3).

The Old Hall, if contemporary reports are to be believed, had been 'on the decline' for many years and had survived a similar fire in 1930

Figure 1. Substantial Elizabethan features such as mullied and transomed windows, gabled central hall and cross-wings are still clearly visible in this early photograph of the hall taken from an Edwardian picture postcard *(Dearne Local History Group)*

Figure 2. Another Edwardian view showing the very substantial proportions of the Hall. What appears to be the Rodes' Coat of Arms is just visible over the entrance doorway of the west wing *(Brian Elliott Collection)*

Figure 3. This drawing, by G. Bailey, was used by Joseph Wilkinson as a frontispiece for his book *Worthies of Barnsley*, published in about 1880.

when a previously unknown fireplace was opened up during restoration work. Its dimensions (nine feet wide and six feet high) and composition (with a stone arch and mantle) was in keeping with an early enclosed hearth — one of the newest innovations of the Tudor period, and generally confined to grand houses.

The Leeds historian Ralph Thoresby was an occasional visitor to the Hall as he had relatives living in the house and locality. He described one of his visits in a diary entry of 1686:

> *This summer, accompanied by Father Sykes, went to visit relations. The first night we lodged at cousin Rodes's, at Great Houghton; was pleased with the pictures of some eminent statesmen in Queen Elizabeth's time, and family pieces, originals of the Earl of Strafford and Sir Edward Rodes;*[2]

Despite political differences, Thomas Wentworth, Earl of Strafford (Figure 4) of Wentworth Woodhouse, Charles I's ill-fated chief minister, must have been an occasional guest at the house since his third wife, Elizabeth, was the sister of Sir Edward Rodes. The portrait mentioned by Thoresby may have been a personal gift to Sir Edward from the Earl or his widow. After Wentworth's execution, in 1641, Elizabeth moved to Hooton Roberts where she lived until her death in 1688.

Figure 4.
A portrait of Thomas Wentworth, 1st Earl of Strafford of the first creation.

The property continued to be occupied by the Rodes family until the death of Mary Rodes in 1789. It came into the possession of Richard Slater Milnes of Wakefield and Fryston Hall (near Ferrybridge), M.P. for York, who had married Rachel Busk, granddaughter of Richard Rodes, at Darfield in 1781.[3] Joseph Wilkinson, in his study of the Rodes family, described the state of the house at the time of the Milnes' inheritance:

> *Mr Milnes had at one time intended to have made Houghton Hall his residence. Not only the walls, but much of the original furniture remained. Some of the rooms were hung with tapestry; and in others were portraits of Queen Elizabeth, and many of the distinguished persons of her court. Mr Richard Slater Milnes found the hall in a state of some decay, and he found also that the houses of Queen Elizabeth, however striking as picturesque objects, and however curious as illustrative of the manners of an age long passed away, are little adapted to afford those conveniences and comforts which, in the improved state of society, are become requisite. He expended a thousand pounds in alterations and repairs, but after a residence of ten weeks he abandoned it to tenants. The furniture and tapestry were removed. Many of the windows were blocked up.*[4]

Wilkinson also provides us with a description of the house as it existed in about 1880 but was clearly unhappy about its deteriorating condition and diminished status:

> *Much of the mansion at Great Houghton still remains, and, disfigured and dilapidated as it now is, there is still sufficient left to give a tolerably correct idea of its former extent and magnificence. The great hall, the easy winding staircase, and cheerless though healthy lodging rooms, with their plaster floors, are yet in being, together with the low*

Figure 5. A recent view of Great Houghton 'Chapel'. The East end on the right of the photograph. *(The Author)*

and wide windows and confined quadrangular court, the whole of
which have been degraded to the uses of a village alehouse.[5]

According to historian Joseph Hunter, who is usually a reliable authority, Great Houghton Hall was built as a manorial residence for Sir Godfrey Rodes by his father, Francis, of Staveley Woodthorpe in Derbyshire, one of the Judges of the Court of Common Pleas in the reign of Elizabeth.[6]

The Rodes family were noted nonconformists. Godfrey's older brother, Sir John Rodes, a well-to-do lawyer who lived at Barlborough Hall, became a Quaker. Under Godfrey's son, Sir Edward (b 1660) Great Houghton Hall became a noted shelter of Presbyterian dissent. In about 1650 he built a private chapel in the grounds of the Hall. Following the *Act of Uniformity* of 1662 many clerics were barred from practising their beliefs and the house and chapel became both a much needed place of refuge and a place for 'safe preaching'. Edward Bowles of York, one of the most eminent of the Presbyterian clergy, performed one of the first religious ceremonies in the chapel when he baptised one

Figure 6. In this view of the chapel (c1950) part of the Old Hall appears to be visible in the background. The West doorway. *(Brian Elliott Collection)*

Figure 7. This rare interior view of Great Houghton Chapel, taken from a picture postcard, posted at Great Houghton by one of the congregation, on 13 October 1913, shows the fine Jacobean pews. *(Brian Elliott Collection)*

of Edward's sons. The chapel's first minister was Richard Taylor who resided for a time with the Wordsworths at Swaith. He was succeeded in 1672 by Jeremiah Milner of St John's College, Cambridge who continued until his death, in 1681. The last of the 'ejected clergy' to be appointed at Houghton was Nathanial Denton of Bolton-upon-Dearne who lived until 1720.

Oliver Heywood was a frequent visiting preacher and his diary entries are an interesting source of information concerning the early years of the chapel. Heywood slept the Saturday night of 8 December 1665, (the year of the Great Plague), at the Hall and spent the Sunday there 'with much comfort'[7]. He was again at Houghton in November, 1668:

> *Having been two Lord's Days at home, I went to Houghton to my Lady Rodes', where we had a solemn fast on Wednesday; Mr Clayton of Rotherham, and I, preached and prayed, and Mr Kirby closed the work with prayer. The day after, being 5th of November, my Lady*

prevailed with us to stay and spend some time in thankfulness. Mr
Grant began, and I preached and prayed, and Mr Kirby concluded.

Heywood returned to Houghton in 1674, 1678 and in 1679 'preached
and prayed four or five hours to a full assembley', staying the night at
the Hall.

At Archbishop Herring's visitation of 1743 the chapel was said to
be 'united to the Church of England'. Now dedicated to *St Michael and
All Hallows*, it has unusual rounded crow-stepped gables and rounded
'battlements', a distinctive sight near modern housing (Figures 5-6).
The soft sandstone has worn by age and atmospheric pollution, the
Rodes' family crest above the east window having disintegrated. Inside,
the puritan pulpit and box pews have survived (Figure 7).

A Royalist force under Captain Grey attacked and plundered the
house during the Civil War, ill-treated Sir Edward's wife, killing one
servant and wounding another. Edward Rodes served under Cromwell
at the battle of Preston and later became High Sheriff of Yorkshire.
There are numerous references to the family in Darfield Parish Register.
Edward's wife, Margaret, who had invited Heywood to preach at
Houghton, was buried in Darfield church at midnight, in 1681.
Nocturnal funerals, by torchlight, were not uncommon for gentry
families, householders on the route of the funeral procession illuminating
their windows with candles as a mark of respect. Lady Rodes's son,
Godfrey, aged fifty, was interred only a few days later. A funeral elegy,
published in the same year, contained the lines:

Now Houghton Hall with double mourning's clad,
The noble lady and squire's dead.

She hath her crown and he his coronet.

Let Houghton Hall their memory revive,
Keep up religion you that do survive,
Let's meet and pray and preach till we be fit
As blistful peers with them in heaven to sit.[8]

Houghton Chapel survives and is still used as a place of worship. Given
more enlightened circumstances the Old Hall could have been saved
and rightly listed as a building of historic and architectural interest.
What a feature it would have made today. But then again the 1960s was
a period when many of our historic buildings were shamelessly
demolished; a 'burnt out' old inn stood little chance of survival in the
context of such official vandalism.

Figure 8. *The Old Hall Inn,* built about 1961, following the demolition of Great Houghton Hall *(The Author)*

Notes and References

1. See 'All Our Yesterdays' by June Walton, *Barnsley Chronicle* 8.7.94; also 24.6.94; Elliott, B 'Barnsley: The Anatomy of a Yorkshire Market Town and its Neighbourhood c.1660-c.1760', University of Sheffield M.Phil. Thesis pp 177-178 (copy in Barnsley Local Studies Library).
2. Wilkinson, Joseph *Worthies, Families and Celebrities of Barnsley and the District,* c.1880, p 151
3. Wilkinson, *op cit,* pp 160-162
4. Wilkinson, *op cit,* pp 162-163
5. Wilkinson, *op cit,* p 138
6. Hunter, Joseph *South Yorkshire* V.2, 1831, p 130
7. Wilkinson, *op cit,* p 150
8. Wilkinson, *op cit,* p 147

12. BARNSLEY IN THE ROCK 'N' ROLL ERA

by Annie Storey

One, two, three o'clock, four o'clock rock,
Five, six, seven o'clock, eight o'clock rock,
Nine, ten, eleven o'clock, twelve o' clock rock,
We're gonna rock around the clock tonight

WHO CAN FORGET THOSE IMMORTAL WORDS of Bill Haley and his Comets when they burst upon the horizon in the fifties? For those lucky enough to be teenagers throughout that period, it was an exciting time. A star exploding upon the British sound of music. The slow, slow, quick, quick, slow, of Victor Sylvester, merged with the birth of rock n' roll. Elvis Presley caught the imagination, later followed by our own Cliff Richard, Tommy Steele, Adam Faith, Marty Wilde, and many others.

The young population of Barnsley were swayed, along with the same fever that gripped the rest of Britain. I remember going to the 'George's' ballroom around this time, and the 'Bath's'. Remember the maple floorboards placed across the swimming baths in Race Street, Barnsley? There was always an extra spring in the floor because it wasn't completely solid underneath. Another favourite dance place was the 'Arcadian'. It had lovely long mirrors in the sumptuous cloakroom, where the polite staff took your coat upon entering. The 'Drill Hall' in Eastgate actually put a rope across the middle of their floor, so that you could either do a modern quickstep on one side, or rock n' roll on the other, depending upon which took your fancy.

In the winter time, when the dark nights were upon us, the dance hall was like a bright beacon beckoning the young after their day's work. For quite a few years, the standard dress of the young girls' was almost uniform.

'Mother, I have to have a black taffeta skirt, everyone else has got one'. These were circular round skirts, usually worn with a cap-sleeved white blouse. A 'waspie' belt was worn with them. This was a wide elastic belt, usually black, and snapped to, with a gilt adornment at the front. A must, to show off a small waist. Black court shoes would be worn, with cuban heels, stilletto's had not quite hit the market then. Sometimes, flat black pumps would be worn (not the sporty kind, I hasten to add,) these were used to dance in, they were known as 'ballerina slippers'.

Another popular skirt was the 'dirndl'. This was made from material

The Blackpool weather is so bracing. Hold onto your hats girls! Lily, Thelma, me and Pat. 1954.

that was gathered in at the waist, usually of the floral variety. I can remember my mother making me one for Whitsuntide, when I was fourteen. I had a white blouse, and a white skirt with bold flowers printed around the hem and halfway up the skirt. I went to New Lodge woods with my friends for a walk, dressed up in my finery. We decided to make our way along the stepping stones at the base of the waterfall. My friends were gingerly picking their way along, but I decided to jump onto the first stone (how stupid can you get?) but fell flat on my back into the water. Luckily, it was only about six inches deep. I lay there like a stranded fish, but my friends were helpless with laughter. I was covered in thick green slimy moss, and my mother went spare at me when I got home. So much for my first wearing of my treasured 'dirndl' skirt!

Later on these skirts were supported by a full starched underskirt, consisting of many layers of net, which made the top skirt stand out. They were of course, another version of the 'can-can'. These came out though more around the time of the late fifties and early sixties. As for the boys, well, what can you say? I should think that everyone knows about the Teddy Boys. Their dress consisted of draped loose fitting jackets, stovepipe trousers, and suede shoes with thick crepe soles and

'BEANIE' HAT WITH FEATHER.

HAIR CURLED AT FRONT. SMOOTH AT BACK.

BLEACHED

'BUBBLE CUT'

REMEMBER THE HOME PERMS? 'WHICH TWIN HAD THE TONI?' (TONI PERMS STILL GOING TODAY)

'TEDDY BOY' QUIFF AT THE FRONT.

D.A. AT THE BACK.

PONY TAIL HAIRSTYLE. ALSO POPULAR WAS BLACK VELVET CHOKER AND LOCKET. (HOME-MADE)

SHOELACE TIE.

VELVET COLLAR.

BLACK ELASTIC 'WASPIE' BELT WITH SNAP FASTENER.

JIGGER COAT. BACK VIEW.

FRONT VIEW WITH BELT THREADED THROUGH. SLACK AT BACK.

DOLMAN SLEEVES, FLARING FROM WAIST.

(Just a few of my scribbles, of fashion in the rock 'n' roll era. Annie.)

heels. The hair would be done in D.A. fashion, a style invented by the film star Tony Curtis. The front hair would be flicked forward, and the back would be combed so that both sides met simultaneously, giving the appearance of a duck's hindquarters. That's the polite version of a D.A. haircut. Neckties were very slim, or they resembled two shoelaces. Sometimes, the Teddy Boy would also sport a frilly shirt, instead of the conventional type.

There was one young man who used to go dancing at the 'Baths' in the fifties who had a variety of brightly coloured suits. They were very vivid, not unlike todays 'Showaddywaddy' group. He was similar to Tony Curtis with his black hair and good looks too. Very striking! Talking of clothes, three-quarter jigger coats were very fashionable for the young ladies. You could wear some of these in different ways. I used to have a red one. It was a flared jacket, but it was supplied with a belt which you could either wear all round the waist, gathering the coat in, or you could thread through holes in the sides and then tie it. This would enable the garment to be fitted at the front, but slack at the back. It had Dolman sleeves too. These were baggy, the underarm flared out from the waist.

Twin sets were often worn. These consisted of matching cardigans and jumpers. For underwear, you've only to look at todays' 'Madonna', the singer. Our pointed bra's were watered down versions of hers. Rows and rows of circular stitching gave this effect. They were the first 'uplifts'. I would say the forerunner to the modern underwire type.

Very often, the girls had their hair styled in the 'Bubble Cut'. This was a short, curly hairstyle which was usually done with a home perm kit. Another style was to curl the fringe at the front, and to have the rest cropped and cut to fit like a skull cap. Often, in the late fifties, the curly fringe would be bleached as well. A ponytail was a happy option too. This was in keeping with the rock n' roll image. Back-combing into the 'Beehive' came in the early sixties. The majority of girls would also possess a 'pencil' skirt with a slit up the back, about six inches from the hemline, which stretched to just below the knee. No tights then. Just seamed stockings. It was quite a ritual before walking onto the dance floor for all the girls to look at the back of each others legs to see if the seams were straight. My favourite shade was 'Gunmetal Grey'. This shade was introduced to me by an old friend of mine, Joan Keeton, who used to live at Kendray. We met each other when I worked at the handbag factory (Racecommon Road) for a short while.

We used to love going to the 'Georges'. It was in George Street, hence the name I suppose. The Robinson School of Dancing used to hold classes on Tuesdays and Fridays. They were beginners classes for all types of ballroom dancing. The admission fee was two shillings (10p).

They would have the ordinary dance on the Saturday night, when all the young bloods turned up, in hope of a conquest. We would queue for ages to get in, and if we wanted to come out in the interval, probably to nip to the Vine Tavern, just round the corner, then we would have our wrist stamped to show that we had paid. Lots of girls, me included, would queue in the cold night air with our hair in curlers, or tight little pin curls secured with hair grips, which would be hidden under a scarf or a beret. Upon reaching the cloakroom, we would take them all out and set the hair accordingly.

Max Factor panstick was a very popular make-up then. I used it for covering up my freckles. The mascara was the block type. We had to wet it, work a little lather up, and then brush our eyelashes with it. A dab of *Evening in Paris* perfume in the tiny blue bottles would add the finishing touch. Unfortunately, I was allergic to it, and I came out in a rash. Joan bought me a small bottle of another perfume out at that time. It was named *Red Fire*. Strangely enough, considering the name, it suited me very well! *L'aimant de Coty* was also well liked, and is around to this day. Hair lacquer was only just becoming popular, so if you had some, you would be everyone's friend. It was not in pressurised cans, like today, I suppose you could say they were environmentally friendly. Just plastic bottles with a spray attachment. The cloakroom would get so full that it was a job to find a place in front of the mirror. It was all good natured hustling though, with plenty of laughter.

I remember the very first time that anyone squirted lacquer onto my hair. I was about seventeen or eighteen, and I was a bridesmaid for another good friend of mine, Jean Thake from Gilroyd, who married Ken Wilson. It was pouring down on the great day, and I remember thinking that we would all have rat's tails on the photos, but one of Jean's aunties from London produced this lacquer and the day was saved! I never knew that such stuff existed. After the wedding, we all went to the 'Alma' pub at Gilroyd, (now pulled down). I smoked a cigarette, another first for me, but it has never really interested me, and I did not take it any further. Ronnie Evans played the piano with one finger, and everyone had a good time. This was the first time I had ever been a bridesmaid in the fifties, thanks to my old mate, Jean, and it was a very happy time in my life.

To go back to the dance halls again. At one stage, Barnsley's own Geoff Haigh, had three bands. In a radio broadcast that he made in recent years, he mentions introducing the Mayor at one of the Saturday night dances at the Baths in the rock 'n' roll era. One of his bands was playing that evening. The next stop for the Mayor was the Arcadian dance hall. To his great surprise, Geoff popped up again to introduce hims to the dancers. One of his bands was playing there too. The third

Fireman's Ball, mid-fifties Arcadian Hall. Sisters Janet and Pauline Beverley in the centre all having a cracking good time.

venue was at the Three Cranes Hotel. The self same thing happened again. Geoff introduced him along with his third band. Needless to say, the Mayor was flabbergasted, but it just goes to show how popular our own Geoff Haigh and his tunes were around that particular time in Barnsley. At this time also, Bert Clegg and his band were very much in demand.

The father of an old class-mate of mine, Julia Butterfield, (now Mrs Cooper) used to play the saxophone and the clarinet in the Ambassadors Band at the Baths. His name was Alec Butterfield. Harry Gibson played the piano. There was a lot of respect for the young women in those days. The girls would stand in groups around the edge of the dance floor and wait patiently for a young man to come across and ask them properly to dance. Not for them, a jerk of the head in the direction of the dance floor.

More often than not, when the last waltz had finished, along with the iridescent lights caused by the mirrored globe suspended from the ceiling, it would be time to go home. Usually, the girls would be safely escorted by the boys. Lots of Barnsley youngsters would congregate on the 'Bunny Run'. This applied also if you had been to the pictures on Sunday, the ritual would still be the same. Everyone would stand around in groups talking and laughing. It was a good way of meeting up with all your friends. I suspect that many a romance started off on the 'Bunny Run'. The area covered was mainly Back Regent Street, Gordon Pallisters' shop being a favourite place to congregate. The bobbies would move you on. 'Come on, no loitering.' No one took any notice though, we just moved to a different spot.

I was chatting with my friend, Pauline Beverley, the other day. I mentioned Pauline in *Aspects 1* and *Aspects 2*, but we do keep swapping snippets of information. We were talking about clothes in the fifties, and she told be about a brown hat that her mother made her wear. It was fastened under her chin with a net bow. Poor Pauline had to run the gauntlet of young lads playing football in the cricket field at Locke Park. They all 'wolf-whistled'. She said that her face was scarlet, and she vowed never to wear it again.

I said that I had had to go through a similar ordeal. I didn't realise at the time of course. I was about fifteen, and I was wearing my very first pair of silk stockings and high heels. I wore a turqoise two piece suit and a maroon coloured 'Beanie' hat. For the uninitiated, I will explain. It was sections of corded velvet joined together to fashion a skull cap. It had a broad roll around the edge, and a feather stuck in. I too felt like a million dollars until I passed a group of young footballers. All I heard was 'Hi, Ho, Silver, and here comes Tonto'. I was mortified, and needless to say, the hat was pushed to the back of the drawer, never to

CUBAN BALLROOM

ELDON STREET, BARNSLEY.   Tel. 3631.

Present

MODERN DANCES

every

WEDNESDAY and SATURDAY

7.30 — 11.0 (Adm. 2/-)   7.30 — 11.30 (Adm. 3/-)

Featuring

ERIC DRAKE and the Cubaneers

with Jimmy Russell and his Dixielands

STILL THE BEST I

BARNSLEY SWIMMING
CLUB

ANNUAL

DANCE

at the

BATHS HALL

Friday, 31st October

to the

AMBASSADORS
DANCE BAND

8-12 p.m.   Refreshments

nce

Hall

2/9

B

sley

SDAY, 6th NOV.

8 p.m. to 12 to music by the
Ambassadors Dance Band

BAR AND BUFFET

Admission - 1/6

Labour League of
Youth

(Barnsley Branch)

YOUTH

DO

PR
SEA

Co   ginners

MON   rd NOV. "TANGO" for
the Beginner and separate class for
Quickstep and **Waltz**

NEW COURSES

Having a good time dancing to the 'Ambassadors' at the baths during the fifties!

see daylight again. So much for fashion!

Sometimes, even in the present day, certain things happen that jog the memory of the years throughout the fifties. My mother sadly died last year. She was in her eighties, and amongst her belongings were old tins that she had put buttons, etc, inside. It was very nostalgic, looking through the little bits and pieces she had left behind. I was reminded of the first record that my former husband had bought for me in the fifties. It was *Forgotten Dreams* by Leroy Anderson. Also amongst my mother's things was an old fashioned pair of curling tongs. They are dropping apart now, but I can remember just before the early fifties, I sat my little brother down on the kitchen chair, when we lived at Kingstone, and told him that he had to sit still because I was going to curl his hair. My parents were out. He had lovely, silky blonde hair, cut in a fringe like most little lads. Even though he was small, I can remember him protesting about it, but I told him that he just had to trust me. Anyway I stuck these same curling tongs in the fire, and looked at Frank appraisingly, determined to do a good job. I curled one part of his fringe, and was immensely pleased with myself. I put the tongs in the fire again, (like I had seen my mother do), but this time, to my absolute horror, his hair came away. There was a row of sizzling yellow bubbles on his forehead, and the tongs were sticking together. I frantically tried to comb his hair over the burnt bit. It didn't work. My mother walked in, and all I can say is that those old-fashioned curling tongs certainly brought the memories back.

Thinking about records, if you wished to hear your chosen record played before you bought it, then you could take it into a soundproof cubicle and listen at your leisure. This was a good way of hearing your favourite record before buying, and listening for any faults.

There was a music shop near where I used to work. I worked at a private library up Sheffield Road, called the Strand. I didn't work there for long, but I loved being surrounded by all the books. It was my favourite job at that point in time. I remember that particular summer, the music shop was playing the tune *Limelight* from the film of the same name. The stars were Charlie Chaplin and Claire Bloome. The music flooded the street during the hot summer days. It was played for many weeks, being the current hit, and in the end I was groaning, 'Oh no, not again'. In those days, a song or tune would be in the Top Twenty for a long, long, time.

The early fifties were eventful for me because having done tap and ballet for many years, I went dancing with the Tiller Girls. I wasn't happy though, because basically, I am a home bird. One moment I was going to the Barnsley Girls' High School, and the next I was living on Greek Street in the middle of Soho, London. I was only fifteen, and

Preparing for the dance the year the 'Tillers' accepted me. 1952.

it was a big change. It was quite respectable though, the Theatre Girls Club really looked after you, and the girls were well chaperoned. But I gave everything up because I missed my Barnsley friends.

The only dancing I wanted to do was to the strains of Geoff Haigh playing *Zambesi* or *Cherry Pink and Apple Blossom White*. Two of the many popular tunes of that era. Records that were often played at the 'Georges' would be such as Dickie Valentine singing *Finger of Suspicion*, David Whitfield singing *Cara Mia Mine*, or Kay Starr with *Wheel of Fortune*. Also who could possibly forget Johnny Ray, *Walking My Baby Back Home* and *Cry*.

A different kind of music came from Lonnie Donegan and his group. Remember *Rock Island Line?* Skiffle became an instant hit. The groups dug out old washboards, and tea chests. A length of string was attached to a broom handle and in turn to the tea chest. This gave out a surprisingly good beating sound. A guitar completed the ensemble, and good melodies could be turned out in this fashion. A lot of groups sprang up also where the main instruments were guitar and drums. If memory serves me correctly, I believe that Barnsley had a group called 'The Moonshiners'.

Two more national singers around this time were Tommy Steele and Guy Mitchell. They both recorded *I Never Felt More Like Singing the Blues*. They were both competing in the market with each other, but in my opinion, both sounded great. By the end of the fifties, I think that most dance halls and clubs had reconciled themselves to the advent of rock 'n' roll and had introduced this form of dance along with the more conventional type. What did it matter? Teenagers had abundant energy to cope with both.

February 1959, brought a triple loss to the music industry with the death of three stars killed in a plane crash at Fargo, North Dakota in America. Buddy Holly (*Peggy Sue, That'll Be the Day*), Richie Valens (*Donna, La Bamba*), and the Big Bopper. His one and only hit was *Chantilly Lace* but what a song! This was a bad blow to the music industry. It was also followed by the death of Eddie Cochran, killed 17 April 1960, in a car crash on the A1. He was best known for *C'mon Everybody* and *Summertime Blues*.

A lot of our performers, even our own Cliff Richard, were influenced by the American stars. Elvis, who Cliff tried to copy, even to curling his top lip, made his debut when he was twenty-one in January, 1956. But he had been superseded by 'Little Richard' Penniman, born Christmas Day, 1935. He was twenty when he startled the world with *Tutti Frutti*. Also Chuck Berry in the same year with *Maybelline*.

In 1955 we were also dancing to Pat Boone's, *Ain't that a shame?* That was in the top ten for fourteen weeks, but I must admit my own personal favourite was *Friendly Persuasion.*

All the travelling fairgrounds would be belting out the pop tunes of the day, a tradition is still carried on. Before the new market sprang up in Barnsley, there would be a fair every holiday time where the stalls used to be. There would also be a huge one at Worsbrough Park every year, and one at Pogmoor. The biggest ones were held at Easter and Feast Week.

Speaking of Feast Week, this was usually the outlet for holiday fun. All the workers would take their holiday week, and more often than not go to Blackpool. You would think that it had just been invented for the youngsters in the fifties, and yet in actual fact Barnsley people had been going there for many years.

Blackpool Tower itself was opened 14 May, 1884. The admission was sixpence, two and a half pence in todays coinage. The Tower Ballroom was not completed untilo 1899 and until 1918 was used for variety shows as well as dancing.

The majority of Barnsley folk will think of Reginald Dixon, whenever the Tower is mentioned. He was playing the 'Wurlitzer', from 1929 until a spell in the R.A.F. in the forties. In actual fact his return was in the fifties. Dancing in the Tower was the high spot for a holiday in Blackpool. I wonder how many romances were forged on the dance floor. Too many to count I should think. I can remember Bonar Colleano, the film star, asking me to dance with him one night.

In 1956 there was a serious fire. Restoration work lasted for eighteen months, and a total of 6,750 books of gold leaf were used to bring the ballroom back to it's former glory. Also celebrating a century in 1994 were the Grand Theatre and Yates Wine Lodge. The latter, a very popular venue for Yorkshire folk.

I had a week's holiday in Blackpool with three friends when I was seventeen: Lily Howe, Pat Atkinson and Thelma Senior. It was a good week, I did notice though that trying to burn the candle at both ends left us more prone to stay in bed the morning after. On the first day, we were up with the lark, leapfrogging across each other's backs, on the sands before breakfast. The second morning we rose a bit later, and by the middle of the week, we just turned over and went back to sleep again. Breakfast was delayed, and looking back, I felt sorry for the landlady. She was a friend of Lily's mother and she kept everything warm for ages. We were issued with dire threats of telling Lily's mother, but we just ignored her. Upon reflection, we were typical teenagers and might have been a bit kinder.

One of the current hits that particular year, 1954, was a Dennis Lotis song, *Cuddle Me.* My friends and myself spent a lot of time on the pier playing it over and over again on the juke box. I have tried to

Blackpool here we come. Me and Thelma on our first day. 1954.

find this record in recent years for nostalgic reasons, but without success. I even thought that senility had set in early and my imagination was playing tricks with me, because a man at a 'flea market' assured me that no such record existed. He went through his thick file of records and it wasn't there. Undaunted, I wrote to the Ronnie Hilton Show on Radio Two. I received a very nice letter back advising me to write to a music firm down south. They in turn told Dennis Lotis, and one night I nearly dropped with shock because he rang me personally and assured me I was not going batty, and the record did exist. He mentioned also that he had not got the record himself and he was sorry that he did not know where I could get a copy. He said that all the girls had screamed for more when he had sang it in Blackpool, and it was nice to speak to someone who had remembered the old songs. Pauline, my friend, was one of those who saw him, and got his autograph. Happy memories!

What of the 'Golden Mile'? I don't think there is anywhere in England to compare. People would walk up and down eating ice cream or candy floss, with a hat displaying 'Kiss me quick' on it. In those naive and innocent days that's as far as things would go with the majority of the young lads and lasses.

We went in the Funhouse one afternoon, and my head was reeling by the time I had gone on everything in sight. If it moved, walked or whirled, I was on it. My face looked green by the time I came out and I tried desperately to come round for the evening's entertainment.

With regard to music of the fifties, I have only to hear that great song, *Oklahoma*, and another holiday venue is brought to mind, Butlins, Skegness. Holiday camps were becoming an alternative to staying in a guest house. With everything being self-contained, you need not travel from the camp if you did not want to. *Oklahoma* would blare out from the loudspeakers first thing in the morning, along with the strains of 'Hello campers, Hi-de-Hi.'

This was around the mid-fifties. I was on holiday with (yet again) Pat Atkinson, Sheila Wood, Valerie Mountain and Elsie Clapham, neighbours from New Lodge Estate. It was the kind of holiday that catered to everyone's needs, from children and teenagers, to young

Posing outside our chalet. Elsie, Sheila, Valerie, Pat, and Me, 1955. Skegness.

Mum and Dad among the Barnsley throng arriving at Butlins Skegness, 1955

Below: The old favourite every year: the knobbly knees contest!

Opposite Top: Lucky Barnsley lad (David Charlesworth) dancing with a Redcoat.

Opposite Top Right: My brother Frank (left) and a friend looking cool on a famed Butlin's four-wheeler.

Opposite Below: Having fun trying to keep upright. Barbara, Marie, Carol, Joyce and Janet, my future sister-in-law, 1962.

Brother Frank and his merry band. 1962

married couples and grandparents. There was always some kind of entertainment. This ranged from Holiday Princess, to Glamorous Granny, and the Knobbly Knees contest.

Water sports were very common. Lots of fun was to be had on the boat race days. The boats were so overcrowded that they would sink, but it was so shallow that they could be pushed to the finishing post. You could have a laugh just watching everything. Redcoats would organize the events. The men wore red blazers and white trousers, and the women, red blazers and white pleated skirts.

My dad would enter into everything he could. The men's Knobbly Knees was a must, also, the women's v men's football match. Men dressed as women, and women dressed as men. Standard wear for lots of young girls on holiday was three-quarter trousers and white socks, known as 'bobby-sox' in the U.S.A.

Another enjoyment at the camp were the four-wheeled bikes. You could sit in comfort with a friend and pedal all around the camp. They

Opposite: Roll call for Barnsley folk. Including Holiday Princess Joan Griffiths, Barnsley's Beauty Queen, Skegness, 1955.

Opposite Top Left: Pauline complete with three quarter jeans, socks and headscarf. Typical fifties holiday gear.

Opposite Top: Snaps of the boat race. "May the best man win and no ramming".

Opposite Centre: Enjoying dinner, Butlins style, 1955.

Opposite Below: Ready, Set, Go! Mum fourth from left.

Above: Girls just wanna have fun! Janet, Carol, Barbara, Marie & Joyce. But where's the guys?

Below: Here's the guys at their favourite pastime, but where's the dolls?

Fun and frolics. Men versus women's football match at Butlin's. Dad kneeling, second from right.

Hope he doesn't mind us hanging on to his legs.!

were stopped eventually, because I think that some youngsters fancied themselves as Stirling Moss! So much for holiday camps.

Another source of entertainment during the fifties was a trip to the pictures. Barnsley had lots of cinemas in those days. The Ritz, The Globe, The Princess, The Alhambra, the Star and the Empire, (now the Odeon) the only one left. The Ritz was the grandest of the lot. Upon entering, there was a huge foyer mirrored on either side. Also, on each side, magnificent, sweeping staircases leading up to the circle seats. Soft furnishings and opulent lighting completed the luxurious look.

The Ritz also boasted its own organ, and resident organist, Mr Trevor Willetts. During the interval, when people queued for ice-cream, the organ and organist would rise up from the basement and regale everyone with good music. He would be bathed in spotlight, with the organ itself constantly changing into glorious colours. This in itself was worth coming to the Ritz, for it was a bonus. More often than not, in those days, there would be two films showing besides the news. These were classed as A films, and B, the latter being more of a filler than the main event. Of course, the advent of television, and subsequently bingo halls, were the death knell of cinemas all over England.

Popular films around this period were musicals, and biblical epics. Coming out into the cold night air in Barnsley was a far cry from the lavish musicals and the sun-drenched desert stories, but it was a nice form of escapism. I must admit that 'Do yer want any chips?' or, 'What time's yer last bus?', does tend to bring you down to earth a bit!

James Dean appeared at the Ritz on November 26th, 1956. *Rebel Without A Cause*, with Natalie Wood. He stood for youth, and was a great favourite with all the girls of that era. For me, he symbolised the breakaway of teenagers. They wished to be recognised as a symbol of young maturity. Marlon Brando, was also thought of as a similar cult figure. The black leather jacket and the blue denims made a statement which carried into the sixties and beyond.

Jobs in the fifties were much easier to come by. This in itself made for a happy youth. There was a great deal of satisfaction to be gained for a youngster, when he or she drew their wage packet at the end of the week and then had the joy of dressing up and going out and having a good time. There was a stability about those days that has gone forever. The eventful moment for me was marrying in 1956. This was closely followed by the birth of three baby girls and a son. Sadly, my second daughter did not live. In retrospect, and perhaps pure imagination on my part, I like to think that there was a rebirth and an excitement about the fifties and early sixties. Everyone had gone through the conflict of World War Two, and people had been denied the simple pleasures of youthfulness. This was the first time that the young could have their say, and by golly, they certainly said it when rock n' roll bounced on the scene.

Holding my daughter, Debbie, at Pogmoor Fair, 1958.

Acknowledgements

To everyone who has helped me with memories and photographs of the rock 'n' roll years, the famous, and the not so famous, my very grateful thanks.

13. PIGOTTS — AN ENTREPRENEURIAL ESTATE AT DODWORTH

by Sam Sykes

In 1836 the devisees of William Elmhirst were selling an estate at Dodworth to the new coal speculators, J. and J.D. Charlesworth. The exact area was in dispute and local intelligence was sought to define the boundaries.[1] Thomas Wilson, an ageing labourer, testified that the estate in question was known as 'Pigotts' and had been for so long as he had lived. In fact, it had been so known for considerably longer. Like many local farm names, its name was derived from one of its owners. However, in this case, unlike in most others, the owner had never resided in the village. Richard Pigott purchased the estate by stealth in the early seventeenth century and his descendants continued to act as absentee landlords until 1797 when it was eventually sold to William Elmhirst of Worsbrough.

Pigott had not acquired a defined farm, but between 1618 and 1656 he and his family pieced together several disparate holdings which became united into the estate thereafter known as Pigotts. These fields were scattered throughout the northern fields of the village and serviced from a farmhouse on the north side of the Town Street. Tracing the lineage of these plots creates some of the most frustrating enigmas in Dodworth's history!

Most of the transactions involve a Hobson at some stage, primarily because Percival Hobson had been the dominant one of several Dodworth landowners who, in 1614, had acquired speculative land from the crown. But it seems also that there may have been a more intimate connection, possibly marriage, between the Pigotts and Hobsons which is probably what attracted this Cheshire family to their Dodworth investments. They were never resident in Dodworth and had no connections here before 1618, when Richard Pigott is described in a deed as the younger son of Thomas Pigott, gent., of Buttyshall, Cheshire.[2] A very similar address, 'Butley Hall, Cheshire', is given as John Hobson's residence in 1651 when he is conveying five closes in the Hugsetts to Ralph Pigott.[3] This same John, the eldest son of Percival, was back in Dodworth by 1653 to start his own family on the patrimonial estates.[4] He had presumably been apprenticed at the Pigotts, which suggests that they too may have been tanners like their friends the Tanners. A further disguised Hobson connection is evident in 1618/9 when Henry Westby is granted by Royal decree:

license to alienate all those three closes of land, meadow and pasture known as le Thornclif Rods or Hugsette containing by estimation twenty acres, with a messuage formerly in the tenure or occupation of Richard Kaye[5]

This is then conveyed immediately from Westby to Richard Pigott,. Westby, who appears to be acting here as agent for Pigott, was brother-in-law to Percival Hobson.

The last mentioned deed cited the enigmatic name of Richard Kaye. He appears to have inherited land from the de Dodsworth estate and it is a small portion of this that forms the core of Pigotts holding. Although there is no definitive evidence it does seem likely that there may have been a marriage connection between Pigotts and Joan, one of the daughters of Richard Kaye.[6] Richard had left 167 acres of which one-third was to be divided up between his children. Joan's portion then could have been no more than 50 acres, even if the younger children had not survived to inherit their share. Pigott's in 1764 was estimated at almost twice this size. Its 104 acres would accord reasonably with Joan's lot as a core, plus the subsequent known purchases of 44 acres from the Hobsons and another Dodworth family, Oxleys.[7]

This second series of purchases may indeed have been lands that were formerly Richard Kaye's but had been sold to defray the expenses of his will. Whatever their occupational heritage, it is clear from their dispersion that these were lands that had formerly been part of the common field, but had subsequently been enclosed and grouped together. There can be no doubt that they were already enclosed by 1618 for the conveyance between Pigott and William and Ralph Oxley[8] specifically refers to 'all the ground lying within the hedges of the said close'. It seems safe to assume therefore from the coincidence of acreage, field names, tenants and early enclosure, that the Pigotts so clearly defined in 1745, was the Pigotts that had been established by 1656.[10]

For the next century the farm was sub-divided into three lots, which possibly reflected the acquisition process. In 1745 an estate map (Figure 1) shows three tenants, Garnett (52 acres), Nathaniel Shirt (47 acres) and Widow Shaw (13 acres).[9] At this time Garnett was occupying the house on Town Street associated with the messuage, however the map was probably drawn up to facilitate a rationalisation of the estate, for only a year later in 1746 the three tenancies had become merged into a single unit of 104 acres in the occupation of Nathaniel Shirt.[10] Shirt is described as a 'Corn miller of Denby Dale', although this could be a slight geographical mis-interpretation, for in 1738/9, Nathaniel and Sarah Shirt are occupying, together with John Shirt, part of 'Oakinthorpe Mill alias Jowett House'[11] at Cawthorne. This is situated almost upon the borders of Cawthorne and Denby as there are numerous

Shirts buried in the Cawthorne churchyard and this seems likely to have been their home base.

It also appears from the leases that they shared the tenancy of Jowett House with the Lindley family. The seventeenth century buildings still stand today and one can clearly see the divisions into separate housing lots. Like Shirts, the Lindleys have a long history in Cawthorne, gravestones show them to have been dying at 'Jow't House' since 1634, but a branch moved to Champney House at Dodworth around this same time and the family remained resident here into at least the late eighteenth century.[12] It may be that Shirt's were enticed to Dodworth by the testimony of their neighbours.

The twenty-one year lease upon Pigotts which Nat Shirt took in 1746 gives us a fine view of contemporary agricultural practice in the locality. Whilst still insisting upon fallowing and placing a heavy premium upon grass leys, it also endorsed the practice of manuring and liming. The rental of £55 per annum (plus taxes) for 104 acres, equates closely to that in neighbouring Stainborough, where the Earl of Strafford was charging ten shillings per acre. Pigott retained the rights to any 'woods, coal, iron and quarries and to use wains, carts, carriages and horses to

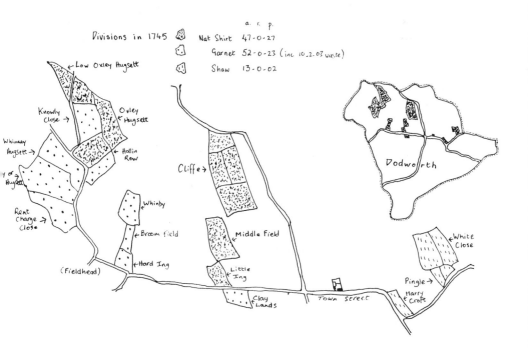

carry away same' and Shirt had to agree to what were then standard clauses:

> ...*lay or spread upon every days work with a plow...to be sown with corn or grain 20 sufficient horseloads of well burnt and unfallen lime or four sufficient wainloads of manure and shall not take above three crops together without fallowing and liming and manuring the same as aforesaid and shall also lay and spread upon the said premises for the better husbandry thereof all the hay, straw, fodder, compost, dung and ashes which yearly come, grow, begotten or raised on the said premises...[shall leave all dung etcetera for Pigott at end of the lease]...on the eighteenth year shall lay down in a husbandry manner 40 acres to be set out by Pigott to be sown with grass seed to lay in grass for the remainder of the term...and for every acre that Shirt shall plow and use in tillage or sow with grain or corn and for every acre of the said 40 which he has neglected to sow with grass Shirt shall pay Pigott 40 shillings over and above the rent...for his part Piggot will at his own expense with all convenient speed erect and build instead of the old house upon or near the same ground, a new dwelling house to consist of three rooms on the ground floor with chambers over the same and finish same in an orderly manner suitable to a farmers use and also a new stable to hold six horses with a corn chamber over same...he will repair all existing buildings and keep them in good order and allow Shirt timber as shall be necessary for the repair of buildings, gates, stiles and sewars.*

The old house had been described in the pre-amble as 'the messuage called Dodworth Hall', this epithet is not used on any other contemporary building and it raises the possibility therefore that this may have been the seat of Richard Kaye and prior to that, possibly the de Dodsworth family. Its position however is unimposing, being situated half-way along the Town Street with no particular prominence, the only significant feature being that it was close to the tithe barn. It seems that this is also the house (or part house) and associated appurtenances which Thomas Pigott bought for fifty pounds from George Hobson in 1632.

> *half a capital messuage in which he lives, two bays of a barn, cowhouse, half a fould, a garth, two gardens, one third of an orchard.*[13]

John Hobson, the diarist, records in 1730 that a previous Hobson had reputedly lived in the house then occupied by James Garner. The property shown on Pigott's 1745 estate map shows one house perpendicular to the roadside and one barn adjacent to it. This barn has been demolished in recent years but the replacement house still stands solidly upon the site of its predecessor and what must be the new barn now slumps in a dilapidated condition lower down the courtyard.

It is clear that when Nat Shirt took this lease he was occupying one of the larger farms in the village and with it would attract a certain status. He appears to have served the community in the way one would expect of a leading yeoman, in 1759, for example, he is one of five signatories to the village Poor Law accounts, which suggests he was by then one of the village elite. He appears to have been succeeded at first by his unmarried son, George, who is paying Land Tax in 1781, and then by his second son Nathaniel who is paying the tax in 1790. George Shirt died in 1786, leaving the residue of his property to 'brother Nathaniel of Denby Mill'[14]. He was relatively affluent and unmarried, but not apparently without children, for as well as leaving £100 to his brother Thomas 'now in London' and £20 each to the five children of his brother-in-law John Best, he also leaves:

> *To a certain child born of the body of Sarah Hawksworth when a single woman and is now living with Rebecca Battye in Peniston, widow, two shillings weekly until the child is aged seven years, then one shilling per week until the child is twenty-one years at which time a legacy of one hundred pounds shall by payable.*

It says much for the emotional attachments and social climate of the period that although the child was obviously alive ('born of' not 'to be born') neither its name nor even its sex are noted. This will also demonstrates the position that younger sons were placed in by the custom of primogeniture. Thomas, the youngest brother, could not rely on any property inheritance and was forced to move to London, presumably in search of a trade.

Nathaniel Shirt junior died in 1797 and at this point Pigotts decided to sell out. The purchaser was William Elmhirst of the wealthy Worsbrough family, who paid £3,035 for the estate. Elmhirst was an astute businessman who held the estate 'in hand' but seems to have been primarily interested in the mineral rights. In 1800 he leased:

> *veins of ironstone in Whinney Hugsett, the Pigott Spring, Oxley Hugsett and the Rent Charge Close (except that below water level in the Whinney Hugsett).*

to Robert Swallow for £87 10s per annum[15]. At the same time he was negotiating with his neighbouring landowners, the Brook-Langfords, to construct a road for leading ironstone.[16] The Brook-Langford correspondence includes the following:

Mr Elmhirst wants a road over the bottom headlands of Upper Hugsett Close about 120 yards in length...no objection if he allows a road from Higham Common to the three Hugsett Closes...by the way now made by Mr Swallow for leading Mr Elmhirst's ironstone.

Elmhirst was not the only one exploiting the Hugsett ironstone. William Parker had recently bought the adjacent Fieldhead estate and constructed a furnace in the Lower Hugsett which was in competition with the nearby Barnby Furnace. The whole area was now alive with industrial developments. As the canal pushed into Barnby Basin and the waggonway extended from this into Silkstone, the Hugsett must have been one of the most intensely exploited areas within the district and this is reflected in the pressure to create new roads. The Brook-Langford correspondence continues:

There is a bridge and gate at the bottom of the Nether Hugsett and a road to Higham Common. The ancient road is up the turnpike leading from Dodworth to Silkstone for about a mile, then down a lane called Cinder Lane to Fieldhead gates and from there down a lane that leads through Mr Elmhirst's land to the top of Upper Hugsett. The ancient road to the Elmhirst's close in which the road has been made by Mr Swallow is the same as yours from Dodworth. But he also has a road from that close to Higham Common. There is also a road to the common which Mr Parker has built for his new furnace, which is in the next close but one to Lower Hugsett. These roads to the common are now claimed by prescription as a right.

The road between Dodworth and Higham Common that dog legs down through the Hugsett is still known as Elmhirst Lane and the other road to Higham Common is still a public right of way. Elmhirst seems to have been more astute than his neighbours in respect of mineral exploitation. They were more reticent about the industrial future. He held the estate for less than forty years, selling to the Charlesworth's in 1836 for £9,250, more than three times the amount he had paid. This is both an indication of the inflationary prices in the early nineteenth century and a reflection of the new value now being attributed to coal, for by this time the ironstone was no longer a valued commodity, Charlesworth's were interested only in the coal rights and the area around Hugsett was to become the centre of their operations. By 1838[17] Pigotts was no longer an identifiable unit, its dispersed fields, those remnants of what had once been the primary holding within the village, had been absorbed into the Charlesworth empire, some tenanted out, others the site of coaling operations[17]. And the house, that which may formerly have been the Dodworth Hall was rented out ignominiously.

Notes and References

1. Sheffield City Archives (SCA): NB 96
2. SCA: EM 1155
3. SCA: EM 1162
4. SCA: EM 284-286
5. SCA: EM 1154
6. A note to the 'Abstract of Title' SCLA: EM 1165 suggests this. Rich Key's will is BIHR: 29.9.1563
7. SCA: EM 1153, 1156, 1157, 1158, 1159, 1160
8. SCA: EM 1153
9. SCA: NCB 121
10. SCA: NCB 113
11. SCA: S-SM 129.14
12. See Silkstone Parish Registers and John Hobson's Diary
13. SCA: EM 1160
14. Yorkshire Archaeological Society Record Society
15. SCA: EM 359
16. SCA: NCB 275
17. Barnsley Local Studies Library, 1838 Rating Survey

Gravestone of Nathaniel Shirt, Cawthorne Churchyard. *The Author*

14. PENISTONE MARKET

by Phyllis Crossland

ALMOST THREE CENTURIES HAVE PASSED since Penistone's old historic market was established. Yet, according to long-standing tradition, an even earlier market was held in the parish. This was not sited in Penistone itself, but in Langsett, one of the several townships which together formed the old parish of Penistone.

We are told that in 1290 Sir Elias de Midhope, lord of the manor at Langsett, was granted the right to hold a market and fair at Penisale. Though this place no longer exists as such, it is believed that Penisale was sited near Alderman's Head, which for centuries was a large farmhouse on the hillside overlooking Langsett village and used originally by the monks of Kirkstead Abbey as a grange for their farming activities. Only in recent years has Alderman's Head been transformed from an ancient farmstead into a reputable guest-house and restaurant, catering for tourists who are attracted to its rural surroundings.

The medieval market and fair of Penisale were said to have been held under and around a great yew tree near Alderman's Head. This ancient tree grew to an enormous size, its bole having a girth of twenty-five feet. Sadly, it was accidentally burnt down in 1758 when a fisherman, seeking warmth and shelter from the elements, lit a fire inside. The late Mr. J.N. Dransfield, celebrated Penistone historian, recorded a long poem *The Yew Tree of Penisale* which sheds light on the tree and the first known market ever to be held in the parish more than seven centuries ago. A few lines from the poem read as follows:-

> *De Midhope, of Langsett, as chroniclers sing,*
> *Was lord when our Edward the First ruled as King;*
> *For Penisal, whither his serfs might repair,*
> *He purchased the grant of a market and fair . . . .*
> *Where weekly came vendors with basket and beast,*
> *And clothiers each year at St. Barnabas feast . . . .*
> *Hither came with stout ellwand the Webster whose pack*
> *Of Linseys and Woolseys were strapped on his back,*
> *He on the wide yew, keen with tenter hooks made,*
> *From bough-end to bough-end his fabrics displayed.*
> *Hither too came the pedlar with glittering things,*
> *Sharp whittles, gay girdles, hooks, buckles and rings.*

We do not know for how long this market continued or when it ceased

Market Street pre 1910. Ernest Bramall's 'shop' is on the extreme right — it stood in front of the Old Crown Inn. *R N Brownhill*

to exist. It would seem, however, that with the burning of the yew tree, this last tangible connection with Penisale market disappeared.

The present market was established at Penistone in 1699, mainly through the efforts of Godfrey Bosville of Gunthwaite. A well-known figure in the area, he was an active magistrate as well as a country landowner. His original intention was to revive the ancient market under the old charter, but removing its site from Langsett to Penistone. However, when a market was actually opened according to this intention, it was strongly opposed, chiefly by the people of Barnsley and Huddersfield. Application was therefore made to the Crown for a new charter. Numerous petitions were presented in favour, including some from Sheffield and Rotherham. Penistone folk petitioned their need for a market on the grounds of the bad state of the country between them and Barnsley, their nearest market. People had lost their lives in winter time when returning home from Barnsley. Happily the petition was duly successful and Penistone received its market charter.

On its establishment in 1699 the Cattle Market was held in front of the church gates where the remains of an old market cross were still to be seen during the early years of this century. For more than two hundred years farmers, butchers and dealers milled together with their cattle in Market Street and St. Mary's Street for the purpose of buying and selling. When business was completed news would be exchanged and a drink or two enjoyed with one's acquaintances at one of the many inns which Penistone boasted at that time. For some farmers who lived in the outlying areas of the parish, market days were the only times when they got away from home. During the eighteenth and nineteenth centuries men had, of necessity, to walk their animals to and from the markets. This involved long journeys on foot in those days before motorised transport facilitated travel for men and animals alike.

Penistone Market continued to flourish so that, by the nineteenth century, it was attracting dealers from the other side of the Pennines. According to John Ness Dransfield: 'Wheeler, in his *History of Manchester*, dated 1836, says, "The cattle dealers who attend the town market with milk cows make their purchases in the West Riding of Yorkshire. They produce the very best stock."' Mr. Joseph Ogden, of Fairfield near Manchester, was one of the chief cattle dealers in his day. Before his death in 1891 he had been attending Penistone Market

The market in St Mary's Street with Penistone Church in the background.

for nearly half a century and was the largest purchaser there of milk cows for the dairymen of Manchester and other places. Milk cows were said to realise higher prices at Penistone than in most other markets of Yorkshire, Derbyshire and Lincolnshire. Several dealers who came from long distances arrived in Penistone on the previous night so as to be ready for market the following day. In addition to its milk, Penistone was noted for good butter, hams and bacon, good oats, and moss mutton from its moor sheep. In 1819 there were four annual fairs held chiefly for the sale of moor sheep.

The market received a setback in 1866-7 when it was forsaken by cattle dealers because of the plague. Rinderpest was the name given to cattle plague in those days, though it has since become known as foot-and-mouth disease. The rinderpest, supposed to have been brought from abroad in 1866, ravaged various parts of the country. Luckily, farmers in the immediate vicinity of Penistone, with few exceptions, had none of their cattle attacked. There was no cure for the disease. Only slaughter and restriction of moving animals from infected areas stopped its spread.

With the advent of rail travel, the market became more accessible to people from further afield. At the beginning of the twentieth century Penistone was described as having

> *a noted Market, especially for Milch Cows, which are sent from the district to all parts of the Kingdom. The Cattle and General Markets are held every Thursday and are frequented by Cattle Dealers, Dairymen, Farmers and others from long distances and a wide area. There are also Saturday afternoon and evening markets.*

With regard to Saturday evenings, I remember my father, the late Ernest Bramall, telling me that, when he was a boy in the early years of this century, he had to stand in a small hut on Saturday nights in Market Street to try and sell the 'scrag ends' of meat which his father had been unable to sell on his rounds. Dyson Bramall was an Oxspring butcher who hawked his meat with horse and cart in the Penistone area, but delegated the Saturday night duty to his son. My father remembered being cold and tired as he stood in the 'shop' waiting for customers. It usually paid off, however, because there were always some poor women looking for a sheep's head or a bit of other rough meat on the cheap. In the absence of refrigeration, it was better from the butcher's point of view to sell them cheaply rather than have them wasted.

After two hundred years of existence, the old familiar market scene was soon to change. The days when cattle thronged the streets were numbered. The growth of the town, increase in population and, not

Ernest Bramall, local farmer and butcher, whose association with both the old and the new Penistone markets was lifelong.

least, the invention of the motor car were all contributory factors in the need for a change. Yet, although change was imminent, it took seven years to accomplish from the outset.

As early as 1903 the Board of Agriculture issued an order prohibiting the use of public streets or highways for the purpose of selling livestock within eight days of a previous sale, unless such streets or highways were paved in such a manner as to allow their being properly cleansed and disinfected after the holding of each market or sale. The Urban Council considered this would be a difficult matter because of the market being held in various parts of the town. The best way out of the difficulty would be to provide an enclosed market away from the streets, but for some time it appeared the Council did nothing about it. They seemed at first reluctant to take responsibility for the market, until urged to do so from outside.

In 1904 the Penistone Agricultural Society pointed out the importance of retaining the ancient cattle market and urged the U.D.C. to do their utmost to preserve it. The tradesmen of the town, too, said that the market might be lost if no action was taken. They asked the Council to consider buying a site of about three acres below the Vicarage garden, which would have a long frontage to Shrewsbury Road. With this in mind, the Agricultural Society wrote direct to the Duke of Norfolk, one of the Trustees of Shrewsbury Hospital Estates, to try and further the matter, but still nothing was done. It was said at the time that, out of twelve members on the Council, only two could be considered agriculturists.

In May 1905 the Council received an offer from Mr. Tom Lawton for purchase of a site comprising a Croft, Back Field and farm buildings, being Numbers 370 and 372 on the Ordnance Map. Again, no decision was taken. Then, in August a public meeting was held to discuss the market's future. Although the market served a wide area around Penistone, only people living in the township itself were called to the meeting. Here the Council suggested that a small area at the back of the Old Crown Inn might possibly accommodate the new market place, but this idea was strongly rejected. The farmers and cattle dealers in particular had no wish to see their old, historic market pushed into a small, out-of-sight spot behind a public house. Doctor Wilson then moved and Mr. Johnson seconded for the possible purchase of the four-acre site at Backfields which had been offered earlier. All members, except one, voted for this.

Meanwhile, it was rumoured that Stocksbridge Urban District Council, seeing how dilatory the proceedings at Penistone appeared to be, were considering the question of providing a market for the district. Barnsley, Sheffield, Huddersfield and Holmfirth were also showing interest. At last, fearing that other districts might absorb the market, the Council took action to view suggested sites. These included the one at Shrewsbury Road, one on Wentworth Road running up to Bridge End, and the Backfield Site off Market Street. The viewing took place in November 1905, two years after the Board of Agriculture's Order had first been served.

Another year elapsed before a resolution was finally passed:

That the owners and ratepayers of the U.D.C. of Penistone do hereby consent to the purchase by the said U.D.C. of land consisting of

The small, roofed structure jutting out in front of the Old Crown Inn, is
Ernest's Saturday shop. To the right is the shop of Hudson and Birks which
made way for the present-day National Provincial Bank. *R N Brownhill*

*Backfield and Croft containing 4 acres 1 rood and 21 perches or
thereabouts, together with the farm buildings thereon situate near
Market Street for the purpose of providing a Market Place and
conveniences for the purposes of holding markets.*

For the following four years negotiations were in hand, firstly for the
purchase of the Backfields Site and afterwards for the building of the
cattle market. During this time buying and selling still went on in the
streets. Under a Market and Sales Order of 1904 the Board of Agriculture
was able to give licence for this to be done while plans for the new
market construction were being formulated. The licences were granted
for short periods and extended as became necessary.

The Trustees of Thos. Marsden Estates had put a figure of £2000
for the site but in January 1908 it was resolved that the estimate be
revised as:-

Farm buildings	£ 200
Land for market purpose	£1200
Top half of Back Field	£ 200
Expense and Valuation etc.	£ 100
	£1700

On 19 August 1909 a meeting was called to let tenders for the construction of the Cattle Market. After various trade tenders were read it was moved by Mr. Crawshaw, seconded by Mr. Stones, and resolved unanimously that the following tenders as recommended by the Market Committee be accepted:-

Excavator, Bricklayer, Mason & Concreter	Frank Eyre of Hillsbro, Sheffield	£	815
Slaterer & Plasterer	George Beard & Sons, Thurlstone	£	34-15s
Carpenter, Joiner, Ironmonger & Painting	J. Tinker & Sons Thurlstone	£	107-6s-5d
Plumber & Glazier	Frank Tinker, Penistone	£	67-3s-7d
Founder & Smith	Atkinson & Sons, Harrogate	£	95-6s-10d
			£1119-11s-10d

It was resolved that Mr. John Swift be the Clerk of Works during the construction of the market. He was instructed to prepare the Agreement with the contractors which stipulated that the works were to be completed by 30 November of the following year under penalty of £1 a day. Penalties for breach of contract were to be £200 for the excavator, bricklayer and mason, and £20 for each of the other contractors.

Whilst the work was in progress the Council received a letter from Frank Eyre regarding the type of cement he should use. He said the price of Portland Cement was 5s-4d (25p) more than any other firm's and asked the Council's permission to use the cheaper product. It was resolved to ask Portland Cement to reduce their price, otherwise the contractor would be authorised to use Earle's Cement of Hull.

So the construction work at last went ahead, and an enclosed market to meet the requirements of the Order of the Board of Agriculture issued in June 1903 was finally opened on 24 November 1910. A portion of the ground not required for market purposes was converted into a bowling green and the remainder used by children as a recreation ground.

Throughout the twentieth century Penistone Market has continued to function as a vital, integral part of the local scene, though inevitably more changes have taken place over the years.

Before 1939 there were two market days each week. Monday's was for the selling of fat-stock and Thursday's for dairy cattle. During World War II, however, all animals destined for human consumption had to be sold to the Ministry of Food instead of to individual butchers.

Beef cattle, sheep and pigs all went to the big abattoirs for slaughter. Butchers then fetched their allocation of meat from the abattoir, the quantities depending on the number of registered customers they had. This system continued throughout the war and afterwards until 1954 when meat rationing finally ended and farmers could again market their stock to private buyers.

With regard to dairy cattle, tuberculin testing was in operation by the 1950s. As Holmfirth was their nearest attested market, Penistone and district farmers with T.T. cows to sell sent them there. The selling of dairy cattle at Penistone stopped as tuberculin testing became compulsory. So, after being a market noted for its milk cows for more than a century, Penistone became essentially a fat-stock market held weekly on Thursdays.

Since 1994 the market site has been put to further use. In addition to the regular Thursday sales it accommodates on two other days a week animals from Barnsley, whose market in that town recently closed. On Mondays sheep, pigs and cattle are sold by Wilby's auctioneers from Barnsley. On Saturdays they sell mainly store cattle and pigs. Auctioneers at Penistone's own Thursday Market are currently Bagshaws from Bakewell and Sykes from Holmfirth, who sell all types of fatstock. The through-put of animals has increased tremendously since the market place was first in use. This is evident by the size of the enormous cattle trucks transporting the animals. Yet the men who frequent the markets have much in common with their forebears who thronged the streets in 1910.

Adjoining the present-day cattle market is a good general sales area where a wide variety of articles and produce can be bought. Clothing, household equipment, carpets, flowers, fish, fruit and vegetables are all on display. The various stalls are well patronised, not only by the local townsfolk, but also by people from neighbouring towns. Some of the vendors travel from as far away as Lincolnshire to set up stall at Penistone.

Largely because of its market Penistone is a vibrant little town, especially on Thursdays. Shopping in the general market allows the womenfolk to socialise with friends and acquaintances whom they might only see on that one particular day, just as the men make time to talk with their contemporaries. Despite the changes over the years Penistone has, until now, retained the traditional rural character for which it is so well known.

Now that Barnsley Metropolitan Borough Council are formulating plans to change the town centre, it appears these could involve resiting the market place yet again. The plans have been met with considerable opposition and as yet nothing has been decided.

Penistone Cattle Market, before 1910, held in the streets near the Church.

When John Ness Dransfield was writing his *History of Penistone* in 1906, plans for the present market site were only at the discussion stage. The choice of a site had not been definitely agreed upon by the Penistone U.D.C. Mr Dransfield wrote that he hoped the Council's decision would be on lines that would be of benefit and improvement to the market and town, and not to the injury or disfigurement of either. These sentiments are echoed today by the present community of

Penistone and district. Let us hope that whatever changes our Barnsley M.B.C see fit to make, they will not destroy the traditional character of this old country town and its historic market.

Notes and References

Dransfield, J.N. *History of Penistone*, 1906
Wood, J *Penistone Almanack*, 1911
Penistone U.D.C. Minutes of Meetings, 1906-10

Acknowledgements

I thank the staff of Penistone Library, Barnsley Local Studies Library, and Barnsley Archive for access to sources of early information. I am also pleased to acknowledge information given on the 20th century cattle market by Norman Bramall, Haydn Fox, and Charles Crossland. Thanks too to Dick Brownhill for his loan of the photographs showing Ernest's shop.

15. E.G. BAYFORD OF BARNSLEY: A MEMOIR AND TRIBUTE

by John Goodchild, M. Univ

MANY TOWNS IN THE WEST RIDING have been the lifelong homes of men and women who, while nationally and even internationally recognised as experts in some particular field, have received little in the way of recognition in their own communities. Such a man was Edwin Goldthorp Bayford, a man of marked scholarly ability, whose name was known widely as a major authority on coleoptera (beetles), but who was known better in Barnsley as one of the town's shopkeepers, and as a local historian and naturalist.

He was born in the summer of 1865, one of the large family of Edwin Bayford, then about twenty-eight and a draper's assistant, and his wife Martha. The son was educated at one of Barnsley's private schools — the Market Street Academy — until, just before his tenth birthday, he was one of the four successful applicants, from among twenty-six, for one of the Locke Scholarships at Barnsley Grammar School. He was there from 1875 to 1878, until just before his thirteenth birthday, and he has recorded his recollections of the school, published in Greenland's 1961 history. Edwin wished to follow his own 'bent' in mathematics, but in fact he was put apprentice to the drapery trade.

As a schoolboy, he had collected and reared butterflies, and some of his notes of this time survive among the Bayford Papers which the present writer bought for his own Collection in about 1960. However, he found an attractive specimen of the longhorn beetle in 1883 when in his later teens, and he turned to what became a lifelong study of coleoptera. In the same year, he joined the Barnsley Natural History Society, one of a number of cultural societies in the town springing from lower middle class enthusiasm for knowledge, but in 1884 he removed to work in Wakefield, and from there to Bootle, to Doncaster, and then on to Scarborough.

It was in 1892 that Bayford returned to Barnsley after eight or nine years' absence, and the trade directory shows him in his own business as a draper at 18 Shambles Street, which he called his 'Family Mourning Warehouse'. In 1893 he took over the business of John Wagstaff, who had owned a cloth warehouse business at 20 Eldon Street, and he was subsequently in partnership with his own brother, Cyril George Bayford, who was much younger than he.

Edwin Bayford married in 1893, when in his late twenties and established in his own business: Mrs Bayford lived until 1956, when they had been married for some sixty-three years. They had three sons, who married and had families; their only daughter died unmarried in 1944, a bitter blow to the then elderly Bayford and his wife.

The business in Eldon Street as drapers was run as Bayfords: there is a photograph of the shop in one of Mr Tasker's excellent volumes on Barnsley Streets. The business sold silks, stuffs and prints by wholesale and retail, while the brother partners also described it as a velveteen and fent warehouse, and also sold specifically underclothing, aprons, corsets and fancy hosiery. The business was run in Eldon Street from 1893 until in 1938 the property was sold to Smiths, the dyers and cleaners; the original shop at Shambles Street was also carried on for some years after taking over that in Eldon Street.

By 1897 Edwin Bayford and his wife were living at 2 Rockingham Street, off Honeywell Lane, a house which they purchased on mortgage: this was a new development, and there were then few houses built there. One of Bayford's own personal cash books, meticulously entered-up in the manner of that time, records personal and household expenditure between 1901 and 1911. After Mrs Bayford's death, he went to live with a son in Dodworth Road, then to live in Manchester, and finally to Worcestershire, where he died in Evesham Hospital after an illness of only two or three days, immediately before Christmas, 1958. He left an estate valued at £6168 net, and by his will he left £200 to the Barnsley Naturalist & Scientific Society (£100 of which was in memory of his daughter Annie), and another £100 to the Yorkshire Naturalists' Trust. His body he desired to be cremated, and his ashes scattered 'upon the summit of Ingleborough'.

Upon his death, the *Barnsley Chronicle* carried an obituary account of E.G. Bayford on its front page, but of necessity that could not do him complete justice, and the purpose of this essay is to point out some of his scholarly interests and concerns. Upon his return to Barnsley in the 1890s, Bayford took an interest in the Barnsley Natural History Society: he was its (active) librarian from 1895 until 1946, took a great interest in its splendid museum, was its President in 1901 and '02; he lectured frequently before it, and became its Grand Old Man and ultimately an Honorary Member. The present writer has a number of written recollections of Mr Bayford in that Society. But he was active far beyond Barnsley, and *The Naturalist*, the journal of the Yorkshire Naturalists' Union, was but one such learned journal which ultimately accorded him an obituary account.

Bayford was also active in the field of dialect study, an active member of the Yorkshire Dialect Society and a lecturer to it; he resigned upon leaving Barnsley and no obituary notice of him was published in its

Transactions, despite all that he had done. He took an especial interest in the work of Walter Hampson, the Normanton dialect poet and writer.

Mr Bayford seems to have been an informed but tedious lecturer, according to report, but he spoke often as he was the only local man in several scholarly fields. In 1899, for example, he gave a lecture at the Cawthorne Museum on A Naturalist at Spurn; in 1916 he gave a lecture on the Dialect Literature of SW Yorkshire in connection with the 25th anniversary celebrations of the Barnsley Public Library; in 1916 too, he lectured in aid of the Camps Library (for men at the Front), to celebrate the tercentenary of Cervantes and Shakespeare; in 1918 to the Naturalists' Society twice on their library; in 1938 he was giving lectures in Doncaster. These are but a few of the talks he gave — they are known because the manuscript or notes survive in the writer's Collection.

Bayford was active in a number of other local organisations: he was a member of the Corporation's Library Committee from 1915 to 1945, and he was the local expert on local history, giving his own collection of books to the library upon leaving Barnsley. He was on the board of the Barnsley & District Mutual Plate Glass Insurance Association; he was a member and Vice President of the Barnsley Traders' Association — the local chamber of trade; he took an active part in the concerns of Barnsley Grammar School Old Boys' Association, and frequently occupied the chair at the school's prize days.

The present writer's own concern with Mr Bayford is principally in relation to our mutual concern with regional historical studies. He collected manuscript material and ephemera, and as well as collecting, he studied, interpreted, wrote, published and lectured on matters historical. He collected old papers from solicitors' offices; he bought local material, and was given more. By about 1924 he owned the Dearman Papers, and those of other Barnsley linen manufacturers, which have latterly been used in my own published study of the beginnings of the Barnsley linen industry. He himself wrote (and saw published) essays on various matters: an excellent article of his on Barnsley Markets was published in the 1940s, another on the history of Barnsley in the Barnsley Shopping Carnival booklet of 1922, and he is acknowledged as a source of information in many others' books. He was no Hoyle or even Jackson in publishing on the history of Barnsley, but as a collector of the raw materials of history, and a helper of others, and a speaker on and populariser in the field of regional history, he was active, useful and well-informed. Bayford was called upon to speak in 1944 when a 'treasured document' relating to the manorial rights of Monk Bretton was handed to Barnsley Corporation.

He had too a considerable and wide literary interest and read the

Manchester Guardian — a sign of a man of liberal views. He had a particular interest in English literature from the eighteenth to the twentieth centuries, and was enthusiastic to the works of Hardy and Sterne, as surviving notes show; he was also a student of the (earlier) Cervantes.

Mr and Mrs Bayford lived to celebrate their diamond wedding anniversary in 1954, and in the same year he was presented to the queen when she visited Barnsley. At his own death in 1958, the *Barnsley Chronicle* described him as a 'Unique Figure', and indeed he was such — a Mr Barnsley. And he was not only outstanding as a scholar and a collector, but perhaps unique to Barnsley in his time in the inspiration which he is still remembered for in passing on to others.

After his death, Bayford's collections were offered, I am told, to the Barnsley Public Library, then presided over by Miss Guest. She apparently refused to buy, and they were purchased by Douglas Symington, then a secondhand bookseller with a stall on Market Hill. From him I bought the Bayford Collection for what now appears a modest sum but which was then enormous to me — £40 if I recollect correctly — and I will always remember standing on the then single platform of Barnsley Exchange Station, surrounded by a host of cardboard boxes containing the Bayford Collection, and wondering how I would get them all to — and into — my home in Wakefield. But it was better-than-Christmas for me!

The material on Mr Bayford's life and concerns is considerable, and this is but a brief account of both. Perhaps it might be useful to end it with an account of Mr Bayford penned by my friend Barry Sutton, who as a young man knew him well:

> '*Mr Bayford was small in stature but stockily built. He spoke quietly but with a cultivated voice. He chose his words carefully and delivered them deliberately and in rounded sentences devoid of jargon. He had polished manners and great charm, but could speak frankly if the occasion required it.*
>
> *. . . he himself was not a very effective lecturer: his lectures were rather drily delivered and he wasn't a photographer. My father told me that the Natural History Museum in London used to consult him about coleoptera. He knew French, German and Latin.*'

Mr Tasker said that in his later days Bayford was what he described as a moody man — one day anxious to talk, another remote. A number of stories are recounted of him. Mr Sutton reports that

> '*On the perhaps rather rare occasions when there was a rush of customers (in his shop) he used to call out "Forward, Miss Bayford!" She would*

then emerge from the back room. He adhered to the Victorian custom of going to the funerals of people he had known. A notice bearing the legend 'Closed. Gone to funeral' was not infrequently seen in the shop window.

Many people of in Barnsley knew of his knowledge of beetles. They often pulled his leg about it. One story I heard was of someone rushing into his shop one day and saying "Mr Bayford! Come immediately! There's a rare beetle on the top of the gasometer!" '

A good man, a man of liberal opinion, a scholar, a helper of others: what better could be said of him?

Notes & References

This essay is based upon a lecture by Mr Goodchild to the Barnsley Naturalist Society — Editor.

16. WATER-POWER SITES IN THE DEARNE CATCHMENT: TWO BARNSLEY AREA CORN MILL EXAMPLES

by Tom Umpleby

The Project

IN 1992 AN ANALYSIS OF THE South Yorkshire Sites and Monuments Record (SMR) showed that, of the 260 sites recorded as water-powered, only nine were in the Dearne Catchment. The Sheffield Trades Historical Society had records of seven more sites, and the West Yorkshire SMR contained four records. A project was therefore begun to identify such sites, including their locations, industrial uses, periods of operation and current condition.

The river Dearne flows from Dearne Head (west of Denby Dale) to the river Don near Mexborough. Its tributaries include Flockton Beck/Bentley Brook, Cawthorne Dike/Silkstone Beck; Sough Dike; Cudworth Dike; Rockley Dike/Stainborough Dike/River Dove; Thurnscoe/Carr Dike; Harley Dike/Knoll Beck; and Brook/Hound Hill Dikes.

During the project information has been obtained from twenty-seven archives and libraries; from site visits; and from over thirty-five individuals, including archaeologists, family historians, local historians and the owners/occupants of sites.

The total number of sites which has been identified is seventy-three, of which twenty-one are in West Yorkshire and fifty-two in South Yorkshire, including forty-six in the Barnsley MBC area. The different types of use have been classified under seventeen headings, including flour and animal feeding stuffs production; iron smelting and processing; textile production; wood sawing and shaping; paper making and bark crushing. The historic periods range from the Domesday Survey, when five mills were recorded, to the present day, with Worsbrough Mill operating as an on-site industrial museum.

Two examples of the forty-six sites in the Barnsley MBC area are Barugh Mill and Gunthwaite Mill.

(1) Barugh Mill (NGR/SE 3172 0899)

Location

Barugh water-powered corn-mill was situated about ninety metres downstream of the confluence of Cawthorne Dike and the river Dearne, and 270 metres west-south-west of Barugh Bridge is where the river is

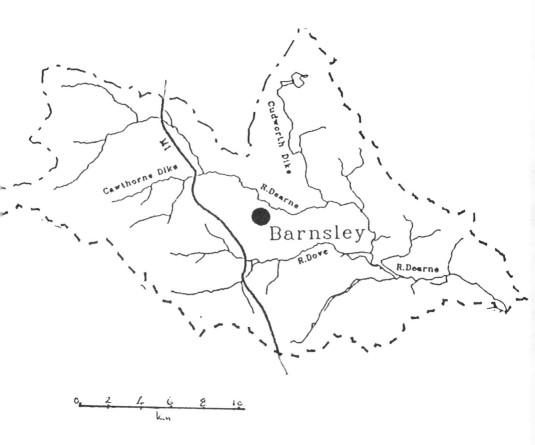

Map 1. The Dearne catchment. *National Rivers Authority*

crossed by the road from Barugh (c. 400 metres southwest) to Mapplewell (2.2 km north-east).

Documentary Evidence
Early in the thirteenth century 'John the Miller of Berch' (Barugh) was given a toft (a homestead with a plot of arable land) by 'Adam Clericus of Darton'. About two hundred years later the Prior of Monk Bretton granted to William Dodworth of Gawber Hall an assart (cleared woodland) called 'Elys Royde' and 'Newfal Myln washed by water from the Dyrn'.[1]

In 1610 a cottage and a water corn-mill in Barugh were leased by Thomas Wentworth to Anthony Roades;[2] and in 1697 the mill was

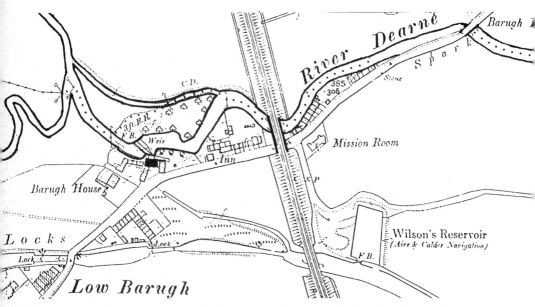

Map 2. Extract from O.S. 1/2500 1906 Edition showing site of Barugh Mill.

marked on a map of coal-pits.[3] Barugh Mill, a house and fields were occupied by Nathan Rhodes in 1718.[4]

John Stanley of Barugh was described as a miller in 1741 to 1749,[5] and was probably so in 1760 when the rent for Barugh Mill was paid on his behalf by David Dixon to the lords of the manor.[6] However, by 1766 Edward Crowther was the miller when a fire at the drying kiln was allegedly caused by an insane female vagrant.[7] The extent to which the mill was damaged is not recorded, but a 1767-70 survey map does not name the buildings shown on the site.[8] Barugh Mill was named on a plan which was part of a statement of opposition in 1792 to the proposed navigation canal from the Aire and Calder Canal Wakefield to Barnsley, Barnby Bridge and Haigh Bridge.[9] In 1796 Joseph Kay was recorded as a miller at Barugh.[10]

In the first half of the nineteenth century the mill was named or shown on Greenwood's map of 1818;[11] an Enclosure Award plan of 1821;[12] Teasdale's map of 1828;[13] and Ordnance Survey maps of 1824 and 1839.[14]

Edward Armitage was recorded as the owner of the mill in 1821;[15] paid £25 rent in 1828 to Gawber Hall Estate for the mill (which was described as having four pairs of millstones);[16] and was recorded as the miller in 1838.[17] However, when he died in 1860 he bequeathed to Edwin Armitage a corn mill, with only three pairs of stones and a drying kiln, and also a dwelling house known as 'The Miller's Inn'.[18]

Barugh Mill wheel, 1968. *John Goodchild Collection*

Barugh Mill interior, 1968. *John Goodchild Collection*

The corn miller recorded was not Edwin but Charles Armitage in 1861, followed by J Greenwood in 1867; Charles Armitage and George Shires in 1871; and Elijah Simpson from 1881 to 1904.[19][20]

There was a major change in the layout of the watercourses, following the acquisition by the Barnsley Canal Company of about two acres of land under the Barnsley Canal Transfer Act of 1871.[21] In order to supply water to the canal as well as to the mill, a large weir and a sluice to the canal were constructed. Instead of having a head race approximately 55 metres long, as shown on an O.S. map surveyed in 1850-1,[22] the mill was driven by water drawn immediately from the pond created by the new weir.

After 1904 no records of millers have been found. A map published in 1906 named only the weir, and showed the mill building, wheel pit, part of the tail race and part of the sluice to the canal.[23] In 1968 the buildings, machinery and wheel were photographed shortly before the mill was demolished.[24]

Topographical Evidence

The weir is apparently in good condition. A pair of cast iron toothed upright pillars indicate the position of the sluice-gate which controlled the water supply to the canal. The entrance to the wheel pit is closed by a concrete wall. The pit contains stone debris above which a small part of a cast iron frame is visible. On the external wall of the former wheel mill building (otherwise demolished) are the arcs of scars made by the wheel.

(2) Gunthwaite Mill (NOGR/SE 2494 0626)

Location

Gunthwaite water-powered corn mill was situated approximately 200 metres north-east of Gunthwaite Bridge and approximately 950 metres east-south-east of Gunthwaite Hall. Water from Gunthwaite Dam flowed along a short stretch of Clough Dike before being diverted by a weir and sluice-gate along a head race to a pond approximately 90m by 10m. The tail race was about 80 metres long and flowed into Bens Cliff Dike, a tributary via Daking Brook of Cawthorne Dike.

Documentary Evidence

In the thirteenth century the Gunthwaites became tenants of the Byrtons and later of the Darcys.[25] Henry Darcy in 1359 gave the Manor of Gunthwaite, including a water-mill and a suit of tenants, to John Gunthwaite and his wife Christina. Upon her death the manor was assigned to John Bosville of Ardsley and his wife Alice (possibly daughter and heir of the Gunthwaites).[26]

A breach of the dam and watercourses to the mill in 1563 resulted in

Barugh Mill, remains of the wheel and scarred stone wall, 1993. *Author*

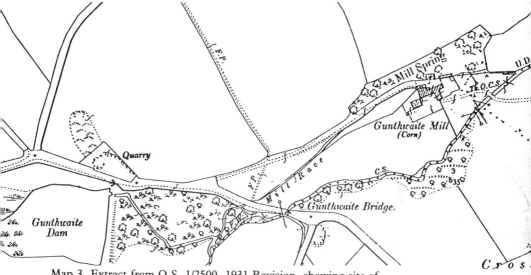

Map 3. Extract from O.S. 1/2500, 1931 Revision, showing site of Gunthwaite Mill.

an order that Godfrey Bosville of Gunthwaite was to have them without hindrance from Francis Wortley.

Half-yearly rents paid by Christopher Green in the seventeenth century included £25 for the mill and Downings Farm in 1657 and 1659, and £10 for the mill alone in 1676.[28] In the eighteenth century John Horn was the miller (1731-2),[29] when a new house was built for £15.7s. A watermill was shown on a map surveyed in 1767-70,[30] and Sam Langley, miller in 1776, was succeeded by his widow Rebekah until 1780.[31]

In 1807 over twenty-two acres of the estate of William Bosville in Gunthwaite were tenanted by Jonathan Wood and his son Joshua. These included the Mill (ie Gunthwaite) Dam, 3 acres 1 rood 8 perches; Paddock (ie north of head race and pond) 1 acre 16 perches; and Holme, House etc (ie including mill) 3 acres 1 rood 8 perches.[32] Maps published in 1818, 1828 and 1839 showed a mill on the site.[33] [34] One surveyed in 1850-51 named Gunthwaite Mill (Corn) and showed a narrow pond; (mill) building with an extension; and a separate (mill house) building.[35] Millers in the second half of the nineteenth century included John Burgin (1852-67); Robert Carr (1870); James Hargreaves (1881) and Thomas Smith (1889).[36] [37] [38] [39]

A map published in 1906, and revised in 1931 named Gunthwaite Mill (Corn), and showed areas similar to 1807 apart from the Dam which had been reduced by silting by approximately forty per cent.[40] The tenants were William Senior from 1906; Brook Charlesworth from 1925; and Mr A L Town (whose wife was Mr Charlesworth's daughter)

Gunthwaite Mill interior, 1993. *Author*

from 1949. The mill was then grinding oats and barley for local farmers, and continued to do so until 1956, when the wheel needed major repairs.[41] Finance for these was not provided by Messrs Lockwood and Elliott who had bought the estate in 1952 following the death of the seventh Godfrey Gunthwaite.[42] A member of the Macdonald Clan

Gunthwaite Mill wheel, 1993. *Author*

re-purchased the estate in 1963, but had to sell in 1982 (to tenants including Mr Town).[43] In 1986, when listed as a historic building, the mill was described as of seventeenth century origin, but predominantly eighteenth century. It had a cast iron pitchback wheel with forty-eight wooden buckets (mainly gone). Inside the building, the corn grinding machinery survived.[44]

Topographical Evidence

Gunthwaite Dam (now owned by an angling club) is in good condition. The line of the former head race is visible as a dry ditch, which is much wider where the pond was. A stone-lined wheel pit contains a pitchback iron wheel which is severely rusted and has only a few fragments of wooden buckets. A two-storey sandstone building, with a blue slate roof, contains a drying kiln floor; mill machinery; millstones; and a flour dresser. The drying kiln floor consists of thick vented tiles. Driving wheels, pinions and shafts include a crown wheel with a metal-toothed ring fitted to an earlier wooden wheel. Three pairs of millstones are French, gritstone and shelling, and a fourth pair is missing. The flour dresser can produce five grades. The adjacent building no longer contains evidence that it was a saw mill driven from the corn mill machinery.

Abbreviations

BCL LI Barnsley Central Library, Lancaster Inventories
BEA Lord Allendale, Bretton Estate Archives
DOE (LB) Department of the Environment (Listed Buildings)
HUDDBM University of Hull, Brymer-Jones Library, Deposited by Sir Ian McDonald of Sleat BF.
  JGC John Goodchild Collection, Wakefield
SCA Sheffield Archives
  EM Elmhirst Monuments
  NBC Newman and Bond Collection
  Sp-St Spencer-Stanhope Collection
  ScMus SC Science Museum, Simmons Collection
YAS AP Yorkshire Archaeological Society, Allendale Papers
YAS DD Yorkshire Archaeological Society, Deeds Deposited
Dir Directory

Notes & References

1. Hoyle E, *History of Barnsley and Surrounding District 1904-7, 60,90* (BCL)
2. YAS DD 709/3
3. YAS AP
4. BEA C3/B22/18
5. SCA Sp-St 60341
6. BEA C3/B2/19
7. JGC
8. SCA 98/Z1/1
9. SCA EM 1717
10. JGC
11. *ibid*
12. BEA C2/BK4
13. JGC
14. OS 1″ 1824 and 1839
15. JGC
16. *ibid*
17. White's Dir., 1838
18. BCL LI/XLVIII
19. Census: 1861, 1871, 1881
20. Sc Mus SC
21. BCL LI/XLVIII; SCA NBC 465
22. OS 6″ 1st Ed 274
23. OS 1/2500 2nd Ed 274/2
24. JGC
25. Nicholson V, 'Gunthwaite and the Bosvilles' in Elliott B (Ed) *Aspects of Barnsley* 1993
26. Penistone WEA History Group, *A Further History of Penistone, 1965*
27. HU DDBM/7/2
28. HU DDBM/28/14
29. Nicholson V, Letter, 8/1/95
30. SCA 98/Z1/1
31. Nicholson V, Letter, 8/1/95
32. HU DDBM/28/19
33. JGC Greenwood and Teasdale
34. OS 1″ 1839
35. OS 6″ 1st Ed 273
36. White's Dir., 1852, 1861, 1889
37. Post Office Dir., 1867
38. Barnsley Dir., 1870
39. Kelly's Dir, 1881
40. OS 1/2500 2nd Ed and 1931 Rev 273/7
41. Mr & Mrs A L Town, letter and orally
42. Nicholson V, 'Gunthwaite and the Bosvilles' in Elliott B (Ed) *Aspects of Barnsley* 1993
43. Mr & Mrs A L Town, letter and orally
44. DOE (LB, 21//7/86)

Acknowledgements

I acknowledge the considerable assistance from those who have provided information, suggestions and encouragement. In particular I thank Melanie Francis (South Yorkshire Archaeology Services) from whom I learned about the Sites and Monuments Record, and David Crossley (University of Sheffield) who has been my tutor throughout the project. I also thank John Goodchild for the loan of his photographs of Barugh Mill, and Jill Harrison for additional references; and Mr and Mrs Town, Vera Nicholson, and Harold Taylor for information about Gunthwaite Mill. Thanks are also due to Diane Thornton for typing my original manuscript.

17. WHEN BUFFALO BILL CAME TO BARNSLEY

by Brian Elliott

THOUSANDS OF PEOPLE FLOCKED to the Queen's Ground one
October afternoon back in 1904. Buffalo Bill's Wild West Show had
hit town. The event stirred up as much interest as any modern pop
concert or great sporting occasion. After all, one of America's living
legends was spending a few hours in Barnsley. The *Barnsley Chronicle*
was suitably impressed by the scale and importance of the visit:

> *This is no mere itinerant circus such as most people are more or less*
> *familiar with, but an unprecedented aggregation of horses and*
> *horse-men, numbering several hundreds, got together for the purpose*
> *of vividly representing, chiefly, scenes in the picturesque life of the*
> *Western American Plains in the days not long since past.*

The travelling show included 'genuine specimens' of Indian tribes,
'with appropriate costumes', performing 'equestrian feats' to the great
joy and amazement of the Barnsley crowd. The antics of roughriders

contrasted with the military precision of U.S. Army troopers. There was, in fact, two hours of non-stop entertainment with the star of the show, as befitting his status, occupying the latter part of the colourful programme — and receiving the loudest cheers. 'Splendidly mounted', Buffalo Bill introduced his Rough Riders of the World, followed by exhibitions of various methods of horsemanship, as demonstrated by cowboys, cossacks, Mexicans, Arabs and a North American Indian.

One of the highlights of the show was an attack on the Deadwood Mail Coach by Indians, almost as exciting as a mock assault on an emigrant wagon train crossing the plains; but perhaps the most dramatic spectacle was an 'authentic' reconstruction of Custer's Last Stand.

Surrounded by thousands of Sioux and Cheyenne warriors, Lt-Col. George Custer and 209 troopers of the Seventh Cavalry were massacred on the grassy ridges above the Little Big Horn river, south-eastern Montana, on 24 June, 1876, only twenty-seven years earlier. The traditional version is of whooping Indians racing their war ponies in ever tightening circles, until Custer, his pistols smoking in both hands,

Colourful posters announce Buffalo Bill's arrival in Edwardian Barnsley.

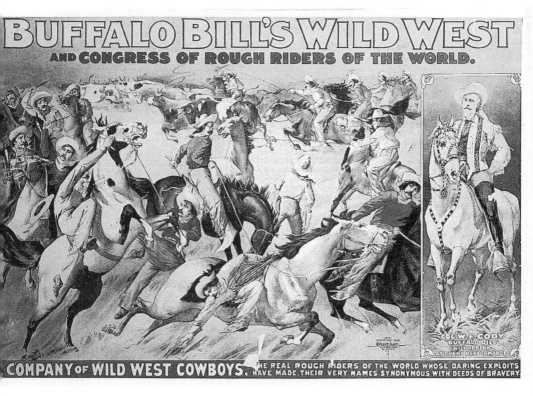

stood alone and was then mortally wounded. Since there were no survivors little was really known about what actually took place in those final hours. However, recent archaeological research, involving the unearthing of 2,000 artifacts and the skeletal remains of troopers buried where they fell, and historical investigations by a team of American academics, have helped piece together a more accurate picture of the battle.

We now know that there was no glorious 'last stand' and there was almost certainly no hand-to-hand fighting. The last troopers were shot in Deep Ravine, about half a mile from Custer's sixty-strong command post which had been wiped out high on the grassy hill that now bears his name. The facial bones of Michael 'Mitch' Boyer, Custer's scout, were found in 1986. Boyer was half-Sioux and could speak four languages. He is credited with warning his leader against entering the valley of the Little Big Horn to pursue women and children, who had fled from a large Indian village. Custer's 'heroic' stand was created by the U. S. press at a time when the nation was celebrating its centenary and nurtured by his widow who died in 1933.

Returning to Edwardian Barnsley, the crowd were entertained with a spectacular war dance of the kind that the Sioux might have performed prior to an attack on the U.S. cavalry: 'with grim visages, barbarous attire and piercing war-whoops'.

Light relief and considerable amusement was engendered by the antics of bucking broncos, handled by exuberant Mexicans, whilst cowboys showed off their skill with the lasso. There was even a kind of 'push-ball' match held between teams of mounted players which included 'genuine' Bedouin Arabs. Johnny Baker's skill with the rifle won enthusiastic applause but there was an even greater appreciation of 'Cowboy Carter' who performed a bicycle leap over a distance of forty-two feet. Buffalo Bill demonstrated that he had lost none of his abilities, gaining 'hearty applause by some feats of shooting while on horseback'.

Myth and reality became inseparable after a series of memorable cameo performances in Buffalo Bill's Wild West Show. The romantic and spectacular view of the American West was soon to enthrall millions on the silver screen, but to have 'real' cowboys and Indians, together with the legendary Buffalo Bill must have been something to tell one's children about.

'Buffalo Bill' or William Frederick Cody was born in Scott County, Iowa, on 26 February, 1846. After the death of his father eleven year old William found work in Kansas as a mounted messenger for the wagon-freight firm that became known as the Pony Express. By his late teens Cody was an accomplished horse wrangler, hunter and Indian fighter.

From 1861 to 1865 Cody served in the Civil War and, during 1866-67,

worked for the army as a civilian scout and dispatch rider out of Fort Ellsworth. For the next two years he earned a living by hunting buffalo to feed the construction workers on the Union Pacific Railroad. In an eight month spell he claimed to have slaughtered 4,280 buffalo and was hailed as 'Champion Buffalo Killer of the Plains'.

Cody soon gained a reputation for accurate shooting and had the much sought after ability of being able to recall the terrain he had surveyed with remarkable accuracy. His knowledge of Indian ways, his undoubted courage and endurance, meant that he was in demand as a scout and guide at a time when the government was trying to eradicate Indian resistance. In 1872 he was awarded the Medal of Honour in recognition of leading a cavalry charge against a Sioux raiding party. He killed two Indians and recovered several horses. The honour was revoked in February, 1917 (along with 910 other recipients), a month after his death, because officially he was never an army officer.

William Cody was reputed to have had sixteen Indian fights, perhaps the most famous being the scalping of Cheyanne warrior Yellow Hair in Sioux country, Nebraska, on 17 July, 1876, three weeks after Custer's death. In his own lifetime he had become a folk hero, perfect material for hungry newspapers and dime novels.

Cody's second career was as a superb showman, an impresario with tremendous flair. He used his fame to orchestrate a show that invariably pleased large crowds and brought in the money. When off-duty he offered his services as a guide to wealthy westerners. His first Wild West Exhibition was put together in 1883. It included fancy shooting, a mock buffalo hunt, a Pony Express demonstration, hard-riding cowboys, yelling Indians and was an immediate success. Early guest stars included Annie Oakley and Chief Sitting Bull.

Buffalo Bill's final public appearance took place in November, 1916. By then he was a sad shadow of his former self, having lost thousands of dollars earned from his famous shows, but his memory and legend lives on, as one of the giant characters of the American West. In 1989, after a long campaign by senators in his home state of Wyoming, the United States Army restored his Medal of Honour. The award was never in fact recalled and sits, under glass, in the Buffalo Bill Historical Centre at Cody, the Wyoming city named after him.

Notes and References

Barnsley Chronicle, 10.1904
The Guardian, 18.7.1984 (based on an article in the Los Angeles Times)
The Independent, 28.10.86 and 14.8.93
The Daily Telegraph, 11.7.1989
'Archaeology, History, and Custer's Last Battle', Richard Fox, University of Oklahoma Press, 1993.

THE CONTRIBUTORS

1. CURES AND CURIOSITIES: TALL TALES OF OLD BARNSLEY

James Walker was born in Rotherham, the youngest of four children. His father, a steelworks blast furnaceman, was from a mining background and his grandmother's family were of Penistone origin. He studied medicine at the University of Sheffield, graduating in 1983 and furthered his post-graduate training in Barnsley. Since 1990 he has been a full-time G.P. in Worsbrough. He gives talks on old remedies and related topics, and takes a keen interest in local history. He has written for medical journals and contributed a piece to *Aspects of Barnsley 2*, to which his current article forms a sequel. In 1994 he was appointed as a Trainer in General Practice by the University of Sheffield, and now combines his clinical work with teaching post-graduate doctors. He lives at Chapeltown, Sheffield with his wife Vicky and children Kate, Rebecca and Lucy.

2. TOWN END IN 1870

Ian Harley classes himself as a true native of Barnsley having been born at Monk Bretton, raised in Worsbrough and now living at Dodworth with his wife Pat, daughter Adele and son James. Educated at Ward Green Primary School, Barnsley Holgate Grammar School and Bradford College of Technology, he left the textile industry to join the reporting staff of the Barnsley Chronicle in 1969. He was appointed Chief Reporter in 1976 and News Editor in 1986. The author of *Black Barnsley*, he has previously contributed articles to *Aspects 1 & 2*. Ian is a member of Barnsley Crime Prevention Panel, Barnsley Canal Group, Barnsley Schwabisch-Gmund Society and a delegate to Barnsley Trades Union Council. When not chasing stories for the Chronicle, he enjoys chess, motorcycling and real ale.

3. TAYLOR ROW AND THE HANDLOOM WEAVERS OF BARNSLEY

Harold Taylor was born in Staincross. After attending Barnsley Grammar School, he studied Geography at Cambridge University before entering a career in schoolteaching. Since retiring he has followed his interest in local history. Tracing his own family history in Staincross-Mapplewell led him to make a study of the hand-made nail industry of the village and to research the influence of the nonconformist chapels on the musical, social and educational activities there in the 19th century. Membership of the South Yorkshire Industrial History Society, and especially of its Field Recording Group, led to a study of the former linen industry of Barnsley, in particular the bleachworks and the handloom weavers' cottages which feature in this book.

4. PAST FOWARD: TEACHING HISTORY IN BARNSLEY PRIMARY SCHOOLS

Andy Atkinson is a 'comer-inner'. he was born in the chemical and rugby town of Widnes. Educated on the terraces of Goodison Park, he completed his education at the University of Newcastle-upon-Tyne where he first met his Darfield born wife, Margaret. Andy has spent all his working life in Barnsley taking up his first teaching job at Priory School in 1978. Andy then joined the Advisory Service supporting and advising schools throughout the area. His particular field is in training teachers to get the best out of computers and not the other way round. His main hobby is walking with his wife and forcing his two children Katie and Christopher up mountains.

5. IRONSTONE MINING AT TANKERSLEY IN THE NINETEENTH CENTURY FOR ELSECAR AND MILTON IRONWORKS

Melvyn Jones was born in Smithies and educated at Burton Road Primary School, the Holgate Grammar School and the universities of Nottingham and Leeds. He taught for seven years at Myers Grove, Sheffield's first comprehensive school, and then for nine years at Sheffield City College of Education before its amalgamation into Sheffield City Polytechnic in 1976. He is now Head of Resources in the School of Leisure and Food Management at Sheffield Hallam University. He is a geographer by training, a countryside management specialist by profession and a landscape historian by inclination. He has written extensively on the economic and social history of South Yorkshire. Recent publications include *A Most Enterprising Thing* (an illustrated history of Newton Chambers) and a revised edition of the widely acclaimed *Sheffield's Woodland Heritage*. A new book on *Rotherham's Woodland Heritage* has just been published by Rotherham Libraries, Museum and Arts. He also contributed pieces on the riots at Newton Chambers' pits at Thorncliffe in *Aspects 1*, and on the history of the Welsh community in Carlton and Smithies in *Aspects 2*. He is the editor of *Aspects of Rotherham*, a companion to the *Aspects of Barnsley* series.

6. THE DEARNE AND DOVE CANAL

Roger Glister was born a stone's throw away from the Sheffield and South Yorkshire Navigation at Sprotborough. This close association with the 'cut' has resulted in a life-long interest in inland waterways about which he writes extensively. As a long standing member of the Waterway Recovery Group, the national body for the organisation of voluntary labour on the inland waterways. Lately his efforts have been concentrated on the two Barnsley Canals culminating in the on-going restoration scheme on the Elsecar Branch of the Dearne and Dove Canal.

Educated at Mexborough Grammar School and the Doncaster College of Technology, he is an engineer by profession and a specialist in church heating. Other interests include fell walking and vintage cars. A member of the Vintage Sports Car Club he has owned several examples of the genre.

7. THE NEWCOMEN-TYPE ENGINE AT ELSECAR

Arthur Clayton was born in the pit village of Hoyland Common in 1901. He started work at the age of thirteen, at Hoyland- Silkstone pit, and finished fifty-two years later at Rockingham Colliery, after more than half a century of work underground. Mr Clayton has been involved with researching and writing local history for very many years. At the age of sixty-four he started to teach local history to evening classes at Kirk Balk School and continued until he was eighty. His lectures were always meticulously prepared and well-attended. Arthur Clayton has published many articles, including an extensive series for the *South Yorkshire Times*. His work has also appeared in the *Sheffield Telegraph* and *Transactions of the Hunter Archaeological Society*. Studies of *Hoyland Nether* and *The Elsecar and Milton Ironworks*, based on many years of original research, have been much used by students of all ages and backgrounds. Mr Clayton considers his local study of *Parliamentary Enclosure* to be his best work. *A History of Earl Fitzwilliam's Elsecar Collieries* formed the subject of a very detailed work, recently completed. He was honoured with a B.E.M. in 1989.

8. A CENTURY OF PAWNBROKING IN BARNSLEY, c1840-c1940

Margaret Holderness was born in Stairfoot in 1925, the daughter of a miner. She has three daughters and four grandsons. Widowed in 1978, Margaret obtained her B.A. degree in Sociology at Leeds University in 1982. Her life since has been dominated by her commitment to the National Union of Mineworkers, the Labour Party and writing. Author of *The Changing Role of Women in South Yorkshire* (1983), *Marginal Women* (1987) — her autobiography — *Relationships* and a pamphlet, *Barnsley and Coal Mining: 150 Years of Benefit* (1993), Margaret's 'Childhood in Stairfoot' was a popular contribution in *Aspects of Barnsley 2*. She lives in Barnsley and is now working on her first novel.

9. THE JOSEPH MITCHELL MEMORIAL HALL: A SAD TALE

AND

15. E.G. BAYFORD OF BARNSLEY: A MEMOIR AND TRIBUTE

John Goodchild, M Univ, is a native of Wakefield and was educated at the Grammar School there. He has been active in local historical research since about the age of thirteen, and he is the author of some 130 books and published essays on aspects of the history of the West Riding. He was the founder-Curator of Cusworth Hall Museum near Doncaster, and subsequently Archivist to Wakefield M D C; in his retirement, he runs a Local History Study Centre at Wakefield which houses his immense collection of manuscripts and research materials, and which is open to all to use, free of charge by appointment. Mr Goodchild holds an honorary Master's degree from the Open University, awarded for academic and scholarly distinction and for public services. Outside historical research, his interests lie in Freemasonry and in Unitarianism — and in his dog.

12. BARNSLEY IN THE ROCK 'N' ROLL ERA

Annie Storey (neé Barrett) spent her childhood in Kingstone until the age of twelve, and then moved to New Lodge Estate. Educated at Longcar and Barnsley Girls' High School, she joined the John Tiller Girls, touring London, Leeds and Oldham. Her professional dancing career ended due to illness and a strong desire to return home. Annie has three children from her marriage (to Tony Wilson). She subsequently married Clive Storey and now has eleven grand children. Apart from her interest in writing, Annie enjoys art, with birds and flowers her favourite subjects, usually captured on wood. Her article *Barnsley in the Rock'n Roll Era* is the third in her series of stories about her memories of growing up in Barnsley; her first appeared in *Aspects 1* entitled *A Kingstone Childhood Remembered*, followed by *Agnes Road School in the 1940s* in *Aspects 2*.

10. A Backward Glance: Memories of a Barnsley Childhood

Edna Forrest, nee Burkinshaw, was born in Barnsley in 1931 and for many years, together with her twin sisters, was a child entertainer in clubs in and around Yorkshire. She attended Barnsley Girls' High School, leaving at fourteen and worked in Littlewoods and also in Slazengers. One of four sisters, all of whom were in the licensed trade, Edna and her husband, ex-policeman, Jock, were licensees of the *Devonshire Arms* in Sheffield before returning to Barnsley in 1958, to manage the *Staincross Hotel*, where their daughter, Gillian, was born. A long career as publicans and hoteliers followed in establishments all over the country, before 'retiring' into a village pub in North Yorkshire, and it was here that Edna turned her hobby of collectin antiques into a business by selling antiques in the pub. A second retirement enabled Edna to concentrate on her antiques, and she now lectures on cruise ships and at various organisations. She has cruised the world twice and will be sailing on the *Oriana's* maiden 'round the world' voyage in 1996. Edna began writing only two years ago and already has several stories being broadcast on Radio York, a poem published, an article in *Cat World*, and a story in *Woman's Own*. She is currently writing a crime novel, set in South Yorkshire.

13. Pigotts — An Entrepreneurial Estate at Dodworth

Sam Sykes is a native of Dodworth and began his working career as an apprentice at Dodworth Colliery. He left to take a B.A. (Hons) in Fine Art and Art History, followed by an M.A. in Local History at the University of Sheffield. He now lectures in the Adult Education Section of Sheffield College. Sam lives with his wife, Sue, on a Pennine smallholding where he practises his interest in agricultural history by keeping traditional breeds of livestock. 'Piggotts' is his third contribution to the *Aspects of Barnsley* series and a definitive study, 'Shepherds, Sheep and Gentlemen: Penistone Moorland Agriculture in the Early Nineteenth Century' will appear in *Aspects of Barnsley 4*.

14. PENISTONE MARKET

Phyllis Crossland was born at Oxspring. She received her early education in the village school and from there gained a County Minor Scholarship to Penistone Grammar School. Later on she successfully completed a two-year course at Darlington Training College and entered the teaching profession. Her last place of work prior to retirement was at Oxspring, the school she had attended as a five-year old. Coming from a farming background and married to a farmer, she has over the years,
helped with various kinds of farmwork. Mrs Crossland has always enjoyed reading, music and travels abroad. Her main interest in recent years has been research and study of family and local history. In this connection she has written articles for the national magazine *Farmers Weekly* and three books which are being widely read. Two of these were published by Penistone's 'Bridge Publications'. During her time as secretary of Penistone Local History Group she produced and contributed to *Times Remembered*, a book of short articles by members of the group, and she has previously contributed articles on Hunshelf and the Thurgoland Wiremills in *Aspects 1* and *2*. After living for more than thirty years at Hunshelf Hall, Mrs Crossland and her husband Charles are now at nearby Trunce Farm, Greenmoor. They have three married daughters, Angela, Julia, and Wendy, and four grandchildren.

16. WATER-POWER SITES IN THE DEARNE CATCHMENT AND TWO BARNSLEY AREA EXAMPLES

Tom Umpleby was born in Darfield, and spent his childhood in Brampton Brierlow. He was educated at Wath-upon-Dearne Grammar School and Barnsley School of Commerce, where he won a scholarship to London University. His studies there were interrupted by service in the Army, in which he was a Royal Signals officer. Subsequently he was a manager in the steel industry, including Stocksbridge Works. After his job became redundant, he became a part-time
management consultant and a student of archaeology. Since he retired he has worked as a volunteer with South Yorkshire Archaeology Services.

He lives in Dore, with his wife Eileen, who was born in Barnsley and became a teacher. They have three married children and four grandchildren.

INDEX OF PLACES

Brian Elliott was born in Royston but spent his childhood and youth in Carlton and Monk Bretton. He was educated at Carlton Primary School and Edward Sheerien Secondary Modern where he first became interested in local history. After an undistinguished spell as an apprentice professional footballer he obtained a proper job, working for Barnsley Corporation in a Dickensian office next to the Cleansing Department. He studied part-time at Barnsley College of Technology and gained a place at Matlock College of Education where he met his Barnsley-born wife, Angela. Brian was Head of Geography at Royston Comprehensive School for almost fourteen years before taking up a post in Further Education at Rother Valley College where he is Head of Division (General Education).